Hans-Dieter Evers, Rüdiger Korff

Southeast Asian Urbanism

Hans-Dieter Evers, Rüdiger Korff

Southeast Asian Urbanism

The Meaning and Power of Social Space

LIT VERLAG

Institute of Southeast Asian Studies, Singapore

First published in Germany 2000 by

LIT VERLAG

Grevener Str. 179 D-48159 Münster

ISBN: 3-8258-4021-2

First published in North America 2000 by

ST. MARTIN'S PRESS, INC.
Scholary and Reference Division,
175 Fifth Avenue,
New York, N. Y. 10010

ISBN: 0-312-23628-X

First published in Singapore 2000 by

Institute of Southeast Asian Studies
Heng Mui Keng Terrace
SINGAPORE 119614
http://www.iseas.edu.sg/pub.html
This soft cover edition is for distribution in the ASEAN countries, Korea, Taiwan,
Japan, Australia and New Zealand

ISBN: 981-230-101-1

Preface

This book contains an overview of our field research on urban areas in Thailand, Sri Lanka, Indonesia, Malaysia, the Philippines and Singapore for more than two decades. We have worked through our earlier published and unpublished papers, field notes and secondary data to provide an analysis of the dynamism of Southeast Asian towns and cities. Throughout our emphasis has been on the connections between micro and macro processes, between grassroots interactions and urban structures, between social theory and empirical data. We have not attempted to pressure the great variety of urban forms, the social creativity we observed in the slums of Bangkok, Manila or Jakarta, the variety of cultural symbolism and the religious structuration of urban space into an overly consistent theory. The reader will, however, observe that we are indebted to the German or European tradition of sociological research from Marx and Weber to Habermas and Bourdieu. Our theoretical arguments have been spelled out in the introductory chapter and throughout the text.

Our joint work on Southeast Asian urbanism was carried out within the research program of the Sociology of Development Research Centre of the University of Bielefeld in Germany, but also during teaching and research assignments at the Faculty of Political Science, Chulalongkorn University; the Department of Sociology, National University of Singapore; the Centre for Policy Research, Science University of Malaysia; the Department of Anthropology and Sociology, National University of Malaysia; the Faculty of Social Sciences, Andalas University, Padang; the Population Studies Centre, Gadjah Mada University; the Faculty of Political Science, University of Indonesia, Jakarta; the Department of Regional and City Planning, Technical Institute Bandung; the University of the Philippines; the Institute of Southeast Asian Studies, Singapore and various other institutions that have hosted or supported our research. We have to thank the Deutsche Forschungsgemeinschaft (German Research Council), the DAAD (German Academic Exchange Service) and the Volkswagen Foundation for financially supporting our field research. Sincere thanks are also due to our colleagues, students and friends in Europe, in Australia and in Southeast Asia, with whom we have worked together and who have supported us with ideas, criticism and many other forms of assistance. During our stays in the towns and cities of Southeast Asia we have seen poverty and violence, corruption and nepotism, illness and desperate struggle for survival but also to a much more significant degree generosity, caring, creativity and sincere friendship. For many years urban areas in Southeast Asia have been more than study objects. They have been fascinating places to experience history and religion, to live, to meet friends, to eat and drink and to bring up our children. We do hope that we have succeeded in transmitting our excitement and fascination despite a heavy dose of sociological theorizing. To our friends and readers we humbly apologise for any errors, omissions and misrepresentations in this book.

Table of Contents

1. Introduction

Modernisation and the Global City

It is common knowledge that Southeast Asia is currently passing through a period of rapid change. In terms of economic growth, Thailand, Malaysia and Indonesia have shown astonishing growth rates of the GDP and the countries of Southeast Asia are either on the threshold to becoming NICs (Newly Industrialized Countries) or can be defined as such. Despite occasional economic depressions and political disasters the region has shown great resilience in overcoming internal and external threats to their economies. Modernization is not limited to economic growth though. Especially in Thailand, Malaysia and the Philippines, and to a lesser degree in Singapore and Indonesia, strong pressures towards liberalization and democratization of the political system are being expressed. In terms of social change, the rise of middle classes and their specific life styles and cultures take up much of the attention of current sociological studies (Gerke 1999). This modernization does not affect all parts of the societies to the same degree though. Spatially, modernization is concentrated in the capital cities and the regional centres. Thus in Thailand most of the new industrial estates are located in the vicinity of Bangkok, and only recently have new industrial parks been set up around the regional centres. Democratization and the rise of the middle classes are also characterizers of political and social changes in the main cities.[1] One of the factors for the success of the modernization has been policies aiming at international integration (Evers and Gerke 1997). This led to a specific transformation of the large Southeast Asian cities. The primate cities have been transformed into metropolises, as much connected and related to the countries they are located in as to a "global society" of metropolises. Thus, just as "the rhythms of the giant cities dominate our globe" (Sutcliffe 1984:1), the rhythms of the globe in turn form part of the rhythms of the Southeast Asian metropolises.

---

[1] This was heatedly discussed in Thailand during the 1992 election, when it was feared that the "devil" parties, who voted for the coup d'état leader of 1991, would gain a majority due to vote buying in the provinces. In this election, the democratic parties had a clear victory in Bangkok and the larger cities. In the last few years of the millenium the call for reformation and democartization was heard throughout the cities of Southeast Asia.

The primate cities are the places of articulation of globalization, national integration and localization. These processes have their origin and reach beyond the metropolis but, and this gives a specific quality to the primate cities, coincide within the cities which gives rise to an ambivalence. The cities are neither global nor local or national. They are a combination of all these, and although they are regarded as foci of alienation and of corrupted ways of life, in contrast and even contradiction to genuine Thai, Indonesian and other cultures, they are equally much developing into showcases of global modernity and expressions of national self-consciousness.

The landscapes of the Southeast Asian cities bear a powerful imprint of globalization in the form of high-rise apartment and office towers, hotels and shopping centres with outlets of the world-wide fast food chains, following the latest post-modern fashions of architecture. Together with the flyovers and superhighways these buildings are constructed by transnational enterprises and rented out to multinational enterprises by real estate agents operating on a global scale. Although this leads towards a homogenization of the appearance of most large cities all over the globe, it is misleading to discuss globalization in terms of universalism, Westernization or Americanization, as globalization itself is not one process, but rather a bundle of very diverse processes. These have in common only that they imply global connections and form global networks. Thus we find global networks of finances and industrial production, but also of informal trade like for example the Sri Lankan and Ghanaian textile traders. Although the new information technologies allow an increased remote control, co-ordination and interaction, the global networks are not independent of space. "Indeed, the most fascinating paradox is the fact that in a world economy whose productive infrastructure is made up of information flows, cities and regions are increasingly becoming critical agents of economic development" (Castells and Hall 1994:7).

In the discussion of the globalization of culture and the economy the focus is on general issues like transnational corporations, world religions, etc. and in consequence the diversity and ambivalence of globalization is easily left out of consideration. Taking the cities as a starting point provides a different perspective. "When we focus on place and production, we can see that globalization is a process involving not only the corporate economy and the new transnational corporate culture but also, for example, the immigrant economies and work cultures evident in our large cities" (Sassen 1994:7). In conclusion, global networks are manifested primarily in the cities. This has two implications: Firstly, the diverse global networks, ranging from transnational corporations to networks of migrants and their respective cultures, media etc., provide linkages between the cities. This leads towards similarities, but similarities of diversity. Secondly, globalization concerns only parts of a city, not the city as a whole.

Within a real city like Bangkok, Manila or Jakarta, these particular parts stand side by side with other parts. Globalization is thereby changed into local specifics. Thus the diversity of the city is increased through globalization.

In the seminal study "Building States and Nations" edited by Eisenstadt and Rokkan (1973), Rokkan points at the "distinctiveness, the consolidation and the economic, political, and cultural strength of the territorial centre" (Rokkan 1973:18) as one dimension in the process of nation building. For the Southeast Asian states, whose population resided mainly in villages, after independence the capital cities formed the core on which control of a larger territory and its integration into a nation state was based. Nearly all states passed through a period of separatism and/or revolts and civil war on their way towards national integration. Parallel to the establishment of an administrative apparatus for the control of the territories, traditions were invented to accelerate cultural integration. These had their focus in the capital cities, which were developed into the "cult centres of nationalism" (McGee) with their national monuments, their national mosques, their national museums, parades etc.[2]

The position of the capital was further strengthened through the concentration of the economic, political and cultural élites in these cities. Ginsburg's (1976) argument that the primate city has a monopoly of the institutions most important for modernization is valid for the capitals of Southeast Asia. The concentration of these institutions in one city, and their strengthening in the process of social change, implies a strengthening of the position of the capital as the centre, and of the élites in the capital city. Thus the degree of primacy does not decrease through nation building but, on the contrary, increases.[3] This in turn prohibits the emergence of any competitive centre, or even of cities of larger size, as this would endanger the position of those élites associated with the capital. In consequence, urbanism itself becomes the precondition for gaining access to higher and more influential positions in the economy and the bureaucracy (Evers 1966; Korff 1988). Only during the last few years as an effect of globalization, have the regional centres gained in importance, although still subordinate to the capital.

The problem is that national integration is based on a centre which itself is increasingly integrated into global networks. This gives rise to a conflict among

---

[2]Nas (1992, 1993) provides an excellent analysis of the nationalism expressed in urban symbolism in Jakarta. For Bangkok see Korff 1993, for Malaysia Evers 1997.

[3]The change in the position of Jakarta and Surabaja can be taken as an indicator. Jakarta used to be the colonial centre, while Surabaya used to be the native commercial centre of Indonesia. After independence, the role of Surabaya decreased while Jakarta developed into a primate city.

those groups who can use globalization as strategic resource for strengthening their political position and accordingly try to push global integration, and those groups based on the nation state, namely the bureaucracy and the military, who point at the need for national identity. In consequence, the shopping centres or the concerts of musicians like Michael Jackson and Madonna are expressions of a self-consciousness of being part of the global world, and denounced as cultural pollution.

Since their founding different ethnic groups have resided in the Southeast Asian cities, usually in their own respective quarters. The cities display features of what has been described by Furnivall as plural society, where the different groups follow their own ways and culture and meet only at the market place. Besides these different ethnic groups, migration into the cities from rural areas has led to the emergence of segregated quarters.[4] During recent years, as an effect of rapid modernization, specific quarters, based on social differentiation, like the new estates of the middle classes, have emerged.

Localization is especially important for all those people who lack access to resources but are found in a strong competition with other groups. In this context an argument developed by Elias and Scotson (1965) is interesting. In their study of a small British town they found two groups: one group of the "established", monopolizing all positions of power in the community and a group of "outsiders'. They argue that the power-differentials between these two groups were based on the degree of social cohesion existing within them. Thus the degree of social cohesion implies power differentials between otherwise equal or similar groups. If we use this perspective for the analysis of processes in large cities, the degree of social cohesion of a group can be crucial in the competition for land and incomes. The creation of social cohesion can be based on the propagation of ethnicity, traditions etc. Although this might be purely fictive, it makes sense if an advantage is gained in competition. Informal sector activities are an important aspect in this context too. They are organized primarily on a local base, and thereby depend on local networks and social cohesion and because they form integrated local social relations, strengthen social cohesion.

Neither national integration nor globalization reduces localization (Castells 1997a). In contrast, a modernization process based on global integration, such as we are observing in Southeast Asia, accelerates localization. Modernization implies the re-location of urban populations due to possibilities for profitable

---

[4]This does not imply that these parts of the city are structured socially and culturally following patterns prior to migration. As Abu-Lughod (1961) pointed out in her study of rural-urban migrants to Cairo, adaptation to the urban culture is not an individual but a collective process. In this process subcultures are created.

land use. The setting-up of modern internationally oriented business centres in the cities implies an increased demand for land. It also provides new employment opportunities. On the one hand, these are higher-income jobs for professionals, financial managers and even clerks and industrial workers, who can be defined as the middle classes. On the other hand, the demand for low-income workers increases to satisfy the demands for services and goods by the new middle classes and the "high-income employees" (Sassen 1991). The attraction of the city centres for international investments is not least due to the availability of cheap services in the form of security guards, cleaners, servants etc. These have to reside close to their place of employment in the city centre on potentially expensive land, as travel from further away would be too expensive and time-consuming. The consequence is the coexistence of low- and high-income residences in the central areas, elsewhere discussed as the "metropolitan dilemma" (Berner and Korff 1995). Those living in the low-income areas are under the constant threat of eviction and have to be able to set up forms of resistance. As the inhabitants lack any power resources, their only possibility is to develop locally based social cohesion. This gives rise to integrated localities and reinforces localization.

Through globalization the cities of Southeast Asia become objects of similar processes and become integrated into one international city system. Thereby similarities between the cities emerge, expressed on the one hand in the building of high-rise office and apartment towers, shopping centres and consumption habits of the middle classes. On the other hand, national cultural values and symbols are enforced and dire warnings against western decadence expressed by national groups. Furthermore, local specifics differing from national symbols are pronounced as a form of resistance to state policies and urban development. The picture of the "modern" international city is contrasted with the city as a habitat for diverse social groups.

The Southeast Asian metropolis is integrated into global networks, nation states and urban localities.[5] This poses the question of what the Southeast Asian city actually is and what is Southeast Asian about it? Turning to official ideologies, the metropolises of Southeast Asia (including Singapore) are described as the symbiosis of tradition and modernity. They are both, indicators for the uniqueness of the respective societies and showcases of modernism.

In various publications of the Thai "Board of National Identity" for example, Bangkok is a symbol of pride in national history, expressed in the magnificence

---

[5]In this respect the processes described by Sassen (1991, 1998) for the "global city" apply as well for the metropolises in Southeast Asia.

of the old buildings, especially the major temples and the Grand Palace, so impressive to the visitor, and the city is also the symbol of Thailand's success in development towards a modern country - a country on the brink of becoming a Newly Industrialized Country - expressed in high-rises, super-highways, shopping centres etc. Bangkok is no longer the articulation of cosmos and world, as it used to be when the city was founded 200 years ago, but the articulation of modernity and tradition, the past of the Thai nation and its bright future.

The dissolution of a general meaning of the city, especially the Southeast Asian metropolis, implies that it can have several, often conflicting meanings. Thus at one and the same time it is in fact a modern metropolis, a national centre, a regional centre and full of localities. Globalization as well as state formation and localization are processes shaped by groups and giving rise to the emergence of new groups. Such an articulation is possible only because the city has lost its general meaning, is reduced to a form and can thereby become the point of articulation. The diverse groups are not necessarily urban. They are, however, articulated in the cities, if not socially and economically, then spatially and thereby through conflicts related to urban land use politically as well. "The structures of space cannot be explained by a vitality of an urban community. They are the result of history that has to be understood as a creation of social agencies or actors, generally of collective subjects. From their interactions, their strategies, success and failures, derive the qualities and characteristics of urban space" (Lefebvre 1976:137). The dynamic of Southeast Asian urbanism, accordingly, results from the struggles of different actors, who are trying to shape the city in a conscious effort, or who simply put their stamp on the city through their everyday life within it.

Approaches to the Analysis of the Southeast Asian City

Cities are a problem not only for urban sociology but for sociology in general. Obviously, cities exist and make their existence felt through revolts, conflicts, fashions, life-styles etc. but tend to resist attempts at sociological inquiry. What is valid for one city might be irrelevant for another. The characteristics of a city in one society differ from the characteristics of a city in another society or during a different historical period.

The present-day cities pose formidable problems as regards their analysis. On the one hand the cities are disappearing into an urbanized society. On the other hand there are the gigantic agglomerations and primate cities of Southeast Asia like Bangkok, Manila and Jakarta. Then there are city states like Singapore and cities in decline like Rangoon. A definition in which it is attempted to cover all these different patterns is impossible. Even variables generally valid for cities are hard to find. Jones (1975) argues that although urbanization is a universal phenomenon, it is based on numerous factors which differ in the respective countries, and even among cities within the same region the combination of variables is distinct. It is thus impossible to make generalizations (Jones 1975:19). Accordingly, the only way to approach the cities is to give up searching for generally valid definitions and start from a relativist perspective, giving the diversity of cities its due. This is especially required when discussing cities of the developing world. While the cities of Europe and North-America formed within more or less similar societies, based on similar cultural concepts and ideologies, the cities of Southeast Asia have their own distinct history of diversity stemming from their position as nodes in long-distance trading networks or of cultural flows from India and China. How can we analyze these cities without blinding ourselves in the attempt to find an "authentic" Southeast Asian urbanism or urban tradition[6] or with generalizations and reference to universal features of urbanization?

Research into the urbanization process in developing areas is heavily prejudiced by the notion derived from European experience and the relevant theories developed by social scientists - that the town or city is a centre of progress and development, a centre of social change. Max Weber did after all show in "Wirtschaft und Gesellschaft" (Economy and Society) how the specific way in which cities emerged in Europe was an essential factor in the development of the modern society based on rationality. It was in the cities, the centres of "non-legitimate power", that already in feudal times a bourgeois society had formed which finally enabled capitalism to prevail. For Karl Marx, too, the capitalist mode of production was basically an urban mode of production. In his scheme the rural petty commodity producers working individual plots of land were due to disappear, giving way to a thoroughly capitalist, i. e. urban, form of economy. By Lenin's time, this idea had already led to the development of "agrotowns" in the Soviet Union and to the hope that agriculture could be "urbanized" through electrification.

Social ecological approaches rooted in the Chicago School strengthened the bias of the European and American urban experience. Only the later works of Rednick (1964) on Rangoon, and Gist (1957) on Bangalore showed the cultural specificity of social ecological development of American cities. Rednick pointed out that while in Chicago a clear differentiation between a genuine commercial

---

[6]O'Connor's (1983) studies on Southeast Asian urbanism can be mentioned in this context. He tends to ignore the fact that urbanism in Southeast Asia is based on multiple influences and can hardly be described by reference to specific regional traditions. Furthermore, a general statement concerning Southeast Asian urbanism is difficult as Southeast Asia itself is extremely diverse.

centre, living areas and working areas existed, in Rangoon a combination was much more pronounced.

Although after World War II there were already doubts being expressed whether urbanism and urban culture can be defined from the western experience and whether cities necessarily were the centre of change and modernization, the usual image of the European-American city persisted in the sociology of development. One of the most influential thinkers on the subject, Daniel Lerner (1958), attempted to show in his work on the modernization of the Middle East how a broadening of an individual's imaginative horizons (empathy) is a prerequisite for modernization. For this to come about, heightened communication and access to mass media are essential and both can only fully be achieved in cities. In this way, urbanization came to be taken as a prerequisite for modernization and indeed development as such. The "correlation" school of comparative sociologists and political scientists also picked up the idea and showed by correlating social indicators that economic growth went statistically hand in hand with urbanization.

The criticisms which were leveled against modernization theories were also used to challenge the notion of the city as the centre of progress. Critical social scientists have come to accept that cities are not necessarily in themselves centres of modernization and do not necessarily embody the structures of modernity. Thus Castells speaks about the "dual city" in which rich and poor, first and Third World coexist (Castells 1989). Urban areas in general and the urban society of developing countries also are, to differing degrees though, an integral part of the world economy. With the partial integration of the cities into a global society, they undoubtedly play a crucial role in development processes. These do not have to follow the path expected in modernization theory. Cities are not mediators of change towards a particular objective, but transformers and points of articulation. In the cities, everything is concentrated and put together. Cities virtually negate distances, even in regard to time. They articulate tradition and modernity, local culture and global culture, the world economy, national and local economies. Thus the cities resemble neither authentic native society, nor an alienated modern or western society. Accordingly, although cities are integrated into similar processes, this does not imply that a universal urbanism is rising, but that diversity itself is one of the main features of urbanism. Furthermore, globalization as it is currently discussed is not leading towards global homogeneity but rather strengthening diversity.

As a matter of fact, the cities in Southeast Asia always have been the points of articulation between Southeast Asian societies and the wider world. Formerly the main influences inducing changes resulted from the combination of native developments, Indian (Indianization) and Chinese influences, which were articulated in the cities, either the sacred cities or the trading places. Later, the cities articulated colonial power and interests with the colonial hinterlands. At present, the large cities connect Southeast Asian society with a global society. The cities are still neither alien to Southeast Asia, nor can they be discussed purely in the frame of Southeast Asian traditions. Their tradition is heterogeneity, outside orientation and amalgamation. Thus, the cities face the main challenges of changes, and within the changes are integrated into society as a whole.

While in Europe, North America and Australia urbanization was accompanied by industrialization, an increase in agricultural productivity and economic development, the cities in the Third World were growing although industrialization remained limited and agricultural production did not increase. The productive capability of the developing countries was insufficient to feed the increased urban population. "The urban expansion of the Third World has been made possible, despite low agricultural productivity, by imports, particularly of grain" (Bairoch 1988:462). For Southeast Asia this remark of Bairoch's is only partially valid as urbanization still remained low and agricultural productivity was high. Most countries are net exporters of agricultural products. Bairoch's argument can be used though for the discussion of the role of the primate cities. Although urbanization as a whole remained within the frame given by Bairoch (10 - 15 % of the population resides in urban areas), the concentration of the urban population in one primate city, or a few very big cities (as in Indonesia), implies that the reproduction of these cities depends on the domination of an increasing territory, from which the urban population is supplied with agricultural products. Dominance and primacy are thereby self-perpetuating: The reproduction of the city depends on the domination of a territory, which in turn leads to the concentration of population in this city, which again requires the increase of territory under the dominance of the city. How to analyze these processes of urbanization?

There are five kinds of classical and neo-classical theory dealing with urbanization:

1. Demographic theories of urbanization and migration. These theories are dominated by the push-and-pull factors model, whereby the city is generally seen as a pull and rural areas as push factor. They tend, moreover, to be descriptive-analytical theories, limited to a demographic framework.

2. Theories about the urban system. This covers among others studies of the urban hierarchy and of central places.

3. Cultural theories of the city. This kind of theory is mainly concerned with aspects such as "peasants in cities" or the culture of poverty, for example, or else with social consciousness and the changing image of space in the city.

4. Theories about the spatial and social differentiation and segregation in cities, i. e. social ecology in this broad sense. The social area analysis introduced by Shevky and Bell and the factorial ecology which Brian Berry developed out of it have been applied to numerous studies since they enable dubious data to be effectively analyzed with relatively little effort by using the latest computer technology. The main problem with this approach is that it is difficult to interpret results or place them in a theoretical context. So far, at any rate, it has not proven possible to explain specific phenomena in urban underdevelopment or distinguish them from the spatial structure of developed cities by using the method of factorial ecology.

5. Neo-dualist theories: Taking works by the French school of urban political economy (Castells, Lojkine, English summary by Pickvance 1976) and older dualist theories as his starting point, Milton Santos attempted to develop a theory of the city in the Third World, a theory of dependent urbanization. Another author, Terry McGee, has been mainly concerned with the bazaar economy or what is now known as the "informal sector" and has presented the results of a large-scale research project on hawkers as the main component of this informal sector (McGee and Yeung 1978).

Santos (1979) divides the city into two sectors: an upper and a lower circuit, each of which functions according to a rationality of its own but which are linked to one another by middlemen, mainly wholesalers and transport company owners. In spite of disclaimers, Santos' theory strongly recalls Boeke's classical dualist theory which is, however, applied to the city itself and abstracts from Boeke's city-countryside dichotomy. Although Santos analyzes the inner dynamic structure of both "circuits", several essential aspects of urban underdevelopment remain unexplained, e. g. the fact that the two circuits do not necessarily lead to a spatial differentiation in the city, and that increasing income differentials often run right across both circuits and split them up into large segments, albeit unevenly. This renders it impossible to carry out an analysis of social classes and the consequent social conflicts.

To a certain extent Santos looks at the city in the Third World from the outside and tries to discern its basic structures. To us, however, it seems that in order to be able to assess the dynamics of the developing city and to trace processes of development it is better to adopt the position of a participant in the process. How does the inhabitant of a city himself perceive what is going on? How is he or she affected by the process of modernization or underdevelopment, how does he react?

As a matter of fact, in recent years a new direction has emerged under the label of a "new urban sociology". This school of thought started with the later writings of Manuel Castells (1983), especially his seminal work "The City and the Grass Roots". In this study on urban social movements, Castells' intention is to analyze the city as a creation by the citizen. "We have descriptions of people's lives, analyses of their culture, studies of their participation in the political conflicts that have characterized a particular city. But we know very little about people's efforts to alter the course of an urban evolution" (Castells 1983:3). In consequence the focus is not on urban ecology, but on the interpretation and perception of the city by the inhabitants, who socially construct the city through their actions based on these concepts and interpretations. This attempt has both a historical perspective, which was lacking in his earlier work (Castells 1979), and a focus on present-day urban social movements. To sum up, cities are made and experienced by the people. Not in a harmonious cooperative effort, but through conflicts between those dominating and imposing their understanding of the city on those dominated.

We take this last type of theory as the starting point for our present study. The social construction of the city by its inhabitants is not a smooth process without conflicts. It is a struggle for the access to land, as well as for the definition of the meaning of the city. Thus our focus is on cultural aspects, like rituals and religions through which cities are culturally constructed, but also on how people, especially the urban poor, arrange their living in the city and have an impact on the urban economy. Instead of theoretically de-constructing the city we would rather study the ideas, concepts and struggles underlying the social construction of the city by the urban inhabitants themselves. In this sense our endeavour could be called "emic constructionism".

Emic Construction of the Southeast Asian City

What are the processes structuring the present day urban agglomerations? Are the metropolises of Southeast Asia dissolving into a world economy and becoming "world cities"? Castells argues that the present-day city "is the space of collective alienation and individual violence, transformed by undifferentiated feedbacks into a flow that never stops and never starts. Life is transformed into abstraction, cities into shadows" (Castells 1983:314). The city is no longer necessary for communication and decision-making. A conference can be arranged via telecommunication. Access to information and communication is easily and rapidly provided through computer networks. Places and localities become obsolete. The flows of goods, information, capital and meanings which used to find nodes in the cities, and thereby gave rise to city systems, have lost their connection to locales. Through the flows without need of nodes and locales, space becomes abstract.

While capitalism transformed labour into a commodity and thereby into abstract labour and value, through globalization, based on flows of information, space is transformed into abstract space and places and localities into commodities

(Lefebvre 1976:164). The emergence of space as abstract space and the commodification of localities means more than exchange and the buying and selling of land. Land speculation is not an invention of capitalism but already existed in ancient Rome. In architecture, abstraction allows anything to be built anywhere in any style or combination of styles. The city which once represented an Arabesque (the Islamic city, Guidoni 1980), a Mandala (the Indian city, Wheatley 1972), a Gobelin (the medieval city, Mumford 1979), is now mass-produced, or displays monumental splendor and luxury. Abstraction thus allows differentiation and diversity by abstracting from the particular conditions of a certain place. The formation of abstract space allows an infinitesimal differentiation of space as abstract labour allowed a differentiation of the labour process. Abstract space permits the production of concrete space regardless of its history, its use and its meaning for those using it. A mixture between Greek temple, Gothic rose and Maurian house can be put on top of an apartment house in Bangkok as a penthouse. Speculation is not determined by the locality, it produces itself the locality used for speculation, be it industrial park, residence or market/shopping centre. The city becomes a department store of localities, open for those who can afford it.

Space as a commodity is produced for its exchange: the realization of profits. In everyday life, however, space is required as usable, i. e. in its use value. This gives rise to a particular contradiction. The process of creation of a locality is the development of interdependencies between those living within the locality, and thereby re-connecting (at least some) social, political, psychological aspects of everyday life. Produced space, however, fragments everyday life and disarticulates it from the locality. The functional differentiation of space and its specialized usability in the city is experienced as a fragmentation and potentially as a loss of identity. Instead of identification with a neighbourhood, the people have to be on the move from place to place (residence, department store, restaurant, bar, office, school, friends, etc.). The produced locality satisfies only a specific demand like work, residence, commerce etc. Only the localities produced for the affluent recombine the different aspects and needs of everyday life in the form of the "condominium", consisting of residential space, gymnasium, shopping area, swimming pool, tennis court and "putting green", providing secretarial services and linked to communication networks. Some are even directly connected to office towers so that there is no need to ever leave the produced locality. The perception of life in the city is limited to the view from a window on the thirtieth floor.

These processes can be understood as a substitution of interaction as means of the co-ordination of social action for the market and the administrative system. Through abstract space the symbolic meaning of a locality or a construction, deriving from communication, is replaced by the market or symbols defined by the administration. The rationale for the production of space is its exchangeability and the profitable usage of space, while the administration tries to develop the cities following the rationality of their plans.

The continuity of urban development is based on rules and regulations enforced and controlled by the administration. These rules and regulations are political decisions by the state and the municipalities. Their formulation and enforcement is based on a political struggle in which alliances, winners and losers often change. The urban planners and the architects are integrated into the relations of production of space and the struggle among strategic groups.[7] As long as a unified concept of space and the city existed (be it that the city was a replica of the cosmos, or that the city should express the central position of the absolutist king), urban development was more or less continuous and following a pattern, as centres and axes were clearly defined and a symbolic communicative meaning was attached to them. Abstract space and the commodification of locality dissolved the generalized concept and meaning of the city (Urry 1995). Under these circumstances (lack of a general concept and idea of the city), those dominating the city can try to put their stamp on it through buildings intended to dominate the cityscape, like city halls, office towers, shopping centres, apartment houses, highways running through the city, etc.

Because urban planning is based on a political process in which on the one hand the interests of those trying to use urban space profitably and on the other hand those negatively affected by development plans are involved, it is not astonishing that the implementation of the urban development plans faces severe obstacles and remains limited. The limitations of the administration allow the market to emerge as the dominant mechanism for the structuration of urban space.

The market has two faces: the face of anonymity, of "mechanism", of integration outside of intentions and of alienation, and the face of liberty, of making possible new forms of social relations. As regards the first face of the market, Habermas points at the role of the market as a systematic mechanism functionally linking unintended social action (Habermas 1981:226). The second face is referred to by Bahrdt (1971). The market is not a closed social system into which all those participating are completely integrated. Traders as well as consumers are integrated into social relations outside the market economy as well. Their behaviour is not determined by the order and rationality of the market, which allows a high degree of openness in regard to the intentionality of

---

[7]Rüland's (1997) study of urban management indicates that especially within the large primate cities urban politics and national politics are closely interwoven.

the subjects. This openness is a base for public life (Bahrdt 1971:63). The market is thus a semi-private, semi-public sphere facilitating social relations rather than restricting them.

Wuthnow (1987) speaks of the moral commitments to the market system. "The marketplace is fraught with moral connotations. This is true not only in the sense of economic behavior being surrounded by moral injunctions to act honestly, ethically, and with integrity. The marketplace is one of the arenas in modern society in which persons have an opportunity to participate directly in public life" (Wuthnow 1987:81). Due to this potential the market is an object of power relations. Those who have power (economic, symbolic and social) try to use their resources to dominate the market and in turn use their dominant position in the market for the domination of society. But as a moral aspect is associated to the market, it is not a purely "economic" affair but also structured by social relations. Through social relations the market is linked to the social creativity of the people.

Social creativity is the definition of a decent living and the effort to create the conditions for making such a decent living. It is a social creativity because being based on interaction, it implies social relations to others, in particular family members, friends, relatives.[8] Social creativity is the knowledge, usage and co-ordination of resources available on an individual, household or group base. Resources are broadly defined, ranging from finances, income, skills, social relations, to the understanding and usage of symbols and symbolic capital. Social creativity is, accordingly, closely connected to the differentiation of social groups, the value and goals of achievements, and the selection of resources. It is thus a process of reflection and conceptualization of the circumstances in which social action takes place.

Social creativity has several aspects. Firstly, it includes the creation of new demands and forms of political protest to express the demands; secondly, it is the creation of new economic relations and resources, which are often referred to as informal sector activities, coping strategies etc.; thirdly, it is the creation of new social relations, namely of cooperation and solidarity. Social creativity is accordingly a precondition for social movements. With "social creativity" it is stipulated that people not only react and adapt to changes in the city, but in their

---

[8]Understanding of what is a "decent" living differs between social groups. There is no uniform living standard. For a poor person in a slum area, a decent living means to have a hut, something to eat, and being able to live with his family in the slum area, while for a yuppie decent living means to own a car (preferably a BMW, Porsche or for those who are not yet in the upper echelon but trying hard to reach it: a Golf GTI), go to fancy restaurants and live in a thirty storey condominium.

reacting and adapting create something new as well. Social creativity emerges out of the totality of everyday life and influences in turn changes in everyday life. Accordingly it has an impact on politics, the economy and society.

The impact of social creativity on politics is in the creation of new forms of political protest and the creation of new forms of rationality by which the established political power holders can be challenged. The rise of strategic groups (Evers 1980a, 1982, 1983a; Evers and Schiel 1988) derives from their ability to establish their position, objectives and resources as important for political rule, which often implies challenging of other strategic groups. The impact of social creativity on the economy is the far-reaching differentiation of the market economy, and the challenge to big business through speculation and occupying those segments of the economy which under new circumstances might become profitable. The impact of social creativity on society is the change of norms and values and the establishment of new forms of social relations, communication and interaction. The impact of social creativity on the city is the creation of localities. Social creativity is the basis for the creation of localities through the creation of social relations and the emergence of interdependencies among people in a given area.

The change from the production of goods as the main basis for surplus and profits to the production of space (Lefebvre) and/or knowledge and information (Lyotard), involves the definition and identification of classes and social movements. The main conflict in capitalist society was defined as a conflict centred on production. Accordingly, the workers' class was identified as revolutionary subject based on its position in the production process, and the potential to dominate the production process. If, however, it is no longer the production process but reproduction and everyday life which is the main line of conflict in society, other social groups and other social and political conflicts become relevant.

Classes cannot be defined on the basis of their economic position. As Bergmann et al. (1969) noted, an analysis of classes based on economic criteria is incomplete, as in such a model it is impossible to point at the internal potential for the generation of historical change. This position is close to Feher and Heller (1983), who define classes as "human ensembles which essentially and consciously contribute to social change via purposeful action in keeping with their own interests and/or needs" (Feher and Heller 1983:212). Economic position and culture are the variables along which Bourdieu discusses classes. Bourdieu's analysis of classes based on different habiti focuses on the cultural, symbolic and economic differences and requirements within social groups. He calls for the construction of the objective class, defined as the ensemble of actors living in similar conditions following similar patterns of acting and perceptions and the analysis of incorporated characteristics like the specific forms of habitus.

These classes are not fixed but instead the individual is able to change from one class into another, and class factions can rise or decline in their relation to other classes.[9]

Taking culture into consideration for the analysis of classes and linking classes with the city requires the recognition of cultural features in the city. Urban culture in this framework, however, is different from urban culture as discussed by the Chicago School. Urban culture refers to the definition of the meaning of the city. The city enters into the habitus, as it is part of the living conditions of social groups and classes in the form of the spatial environment, and as such also the object of transformation based on the respective perception of the city and the different meanings of the city. In part these different understandings of the city and particular spaces are coordinated by the market through land prices, the prices for constructions, etc., in part they are the reason for conflicts and coordinated through political power.

In conclusion, two processes lead towards a new assessment of the cities. Abstraction from concrete space due to globalization allows new differentiations and a high degree of diversity, both in terms of architectural styles and of integration of urban space into global, national and local spheres. Through the new role of everyday life classes cannot be defined economically but at least three-dimensionally, taking into consideration economic abilities (income, purchasing power, profession), culture and symbolization of everyday life. Together these form diverse life-styles in which distinction, be it ethnic, religious, social etc., is of importance. Both processes find a connection in the creation of diverse spaces receiving a specific symbolic meaning through the association with distinct life-styles. Thus a generally valid meaning of the city disappears, as well as a general pattern of urban development. Instead of one meaning of the city or of a specific part of the city, diverse and conflicting meanings exist. Emic construction is in this sense the attempt to reconstruct the constructions of meanings of those living in the city. In the following we have our focus on two main aspects: the cultural and the economic construction of the Southeast Asian City.

The Cultural Construction of Southeast Asian Cities

Certainly, several "objective" conditions have to exist within a society to allow the emergence of cities and urbanization, conditions like exchange networks and trade, a political system, agricultural surplus and a class division of society.

---

[9]In his recent study "Beyond left and right" Giddens (1994) points into the same direction.

However, although these conditions explain why cities can emerge, they do not explain why cities were built as they were, why they differ and why they bear similarities. As the building of a city involves many resources, the shape of the city can neither be the result of pure chance nor of "objective" conditions. Most probably, the shape of the city, the main constructions forming the urban structure socially, spatially and symbolically, are results of some sort of planning and coordination. The planning of the city follows, we would argue, an image of what the city is and should be. In other words, the city itself is supposed to carry a message and act as a symbol for society in total. As the idea of the city is socially constructed, the symbolism associated with the city and formed by its socio-spatial structure is the result of struggles among social groups. Those groups dominating society, especially the urban society of the particular city, try to concretize their images and visions, so that the city fulfills functional as well as ideological requirements. In this direction Castells (1983) argues that "cities like all social reality, are historical products, not only in their physical materiality but in their cultural meaning. ... A city (and each type of city) is what a historical society decides the city (and each city) will be. Urban is the social meaning assigned to a particular spatial form by a historically defined society" (Castells 1983:302).

What makes Castells' argument particularly interesting is the linking of a socially defined urban meaning with the spatial form of the city. The process of defining the meaning of the city and concretizing this within the city depends on the ability of strategic groups to dominate society and to control access to the material and artistic resources required for concretizing the meaning of the city. The urban constructions are concretizations of an urban ideology of élites. Thus changes in the configuration of élites often imply re-definitions of the meaning of the city and urban "re-construction" so that the new social and symbolic demands are satisfied.

Here a differentiation is necessary between those societies in which the élites have an urban base, or the state is strongly dependent on the city, and those in which the élites are independent of or even opposing the city. As Braudel (1985) shows, there is a long historical tradition of competition between city and state in regard to domination of society. The city becomes a symbol of the state ideology when urbanism is one factor for access to positions of power and when the state's organization is based on the city. As a concretization of state ideology the city emerges as a "regalia" of domination and rule (Fox 1977).

Under these circumstances the city (and its constructions) emerge as a power resource of the élite for two reasons:

1. Spatial structures as a power resource:

Giddens points out that social structures are "virtual structures" and that "structure exists, as time - space presence, only in its instantiations in such practices and as memory traces orienting the conduct of knowledgeable human agents" (Giddens 1984:17). Spatial structures are not virtual but concrete. While language, culture, society as a whole only exist if based on subjects able to act according to them, spatial structures exist even after the subjects have vanished. While social relations can be negotiated, and rules can be ignored, spatial structures can only be blown up or "reconstructed".

Due to the relative persistence and immobility of spatial structures, they play an important role as "facts" for the invention of tradition. The tradition is easily and convincingly verified by reference to remains from history. Through the historical buildings, squares, streets etc. which are retained in the urban structure, the city becomes a container of history and of meanings, which can be selectively activated.

As relations between concrete objects, spatial structures require a behavior which is not negotiable. The acting of the individual has to adjust to the possibilities selected by the existing spatial structures and the spatial structures induce specific acting. From the perspective that spatial structures are "concrete" structures and thus not negotiable, the concern with space is less directed to social geography as a tool for the analysis of spatial relations, than to architecture. It is through architecture that objects are created in space.

In conclusion we will follow Lefebvre: "Space is not a scientific object removed from ideology and politics; it has always been political and strategic. If space has an air of neutrality and indifference with regard to its contents and thus seems to be 'purely' formal, the epitome of rational abstraction, it is precisely because it has been occupied and used, and has already been the focus of past processes whose traces are not always evident on the landscape. Space has been shaped and molded from historical and natural elements, but this has been a political process. Space is political and ideological. It is a product literally filled with ideologies" (Lefebvre 1976:31).

2. Constructions as symbols propagating an ideology:

Architecture is a manifestation of social, economic, technical and artistic developments in a society at a given time. The conflicts within society have an influence on the realization of a building which reflects these contradictions, and/or is leaning towards one main trend in social change. Through architecture, that is the construction of buildings, places and infrastructures, an image of the city is created which fulfills two requirements: Firstly constructions are created to provide necessary functions, secondly, the relation between the constructions and their design is based on a particular associative and communicative meaning. Following Eco, architecture has no code for itself, but the architectural code depends on social codes. Accordingly architecture is socially determined as a service satisfying socially defined demands in a socially acceptable form (the architectural design) (Eco 1988:330).

Eco differentiates between a functionality of architecture, and a communicative, symbolic value of a construction. In a similar vein, Benjamin (1976) differentiates between a reception of buildings through usage and through perception. He points out that in contrast to art, the perceptive reception of constructions emanates from custom, not from contemplation, but from casual usage (Benjamin 1976:40f). For those who have to use the construction, it is not perceived as an object of art, but from a utilitarian perspective. However, through usage the symbolic and associative function of the building is internalized.[10]

This brief discussion indicates that the construction and erection of a building is a social and artistic process in which meaning is connected to a spatial form. Because constructions cannot be reduced to their functionality (primary function), but their communicative and associative value has to be taken into consideration as well, the relation between constructions and the structure of the construction itself, are means of control and guidance.

The construction of the city and the main buildings within it follow social demands in regard to the functionality of the construction, which is not pre-given but defined through struggles, and the meaning of the city in relation to the design and arrangement of the objects, which in their communicative and associative function are similarly socially defined by struggles. The spatial structure of the city becomes a resource for power and control through non-negotiable spatial structures and through symbolic markers. Through its usage the meaning of the city is internalized as a "map" for orientation. Only those who have internalized the "socio-spatial image of the city" are able to orient themselves socially and spatially within it. Those with diverging views and images of the city 'get lost' socially as well as spatially.

The terrain of conflicts and struggles linked to the process of defining the urban meaning is not limited to the social and political sphere, but concretized in attempts to re-define and "re-construct" the urban architecture. "The conflict over the assignment of certain goals to certain spatial forms will be one of the fundamental mechanisms of domination and counter-domination in the social

---

[10]Zukin (1991) makes the interesting argument that "architecture is the capital of symbolism" (Zukin 1991:260) as it is closely linked to the rise of the post modern service economy and as calls it "strategies of cultural consumption" (Zukin 1991:259).

structure" (Castells 1983:302). But it is not only a conflict over the assignment of goals to spatial forms, or in other words a conflict concerning the utilitarian function of the city and a construction. It is at the same time a conflict over the assignment of a communicative and associative meaning and symbolism to a spatial form. Thus if no strategic group is able to dominate the cultural construction of the city, coexisting structures emerge and the city becomes pluralist. This pluralism can develop into fragmentation, where each social group occupies its own spaces and parts more or less clearly demarcated from others. Similarly to the plural society (Furnivall 1980), the city is held together only by the market and the frame of the administration. A different form of development of this pluralism is the overlapping meanings occurring when social groups attach a different symbolic value to the same space. In this case conflicts arise. The outcome of such a conflict is unpredictable, as it depends on the ability of the conflicting groups to define and use strategic resources. A third possibility is ignorance. The overlapping meanings simply coexist and are respectively ignored by the different social groups. Thus for the sweeper or the doorman the high-rise may have one meaning, while for the speculator or the manager working in the building it has a different one. Problems arise though when the meanings imply an exclusive usage, like the demolition of a kampung to build a hotel or office tower.

The Economic Construction of the Southeast Asian City

The money income of lower income groups, which has risen only slightly or has even sunk in real terms for some specific groups in the past decades, generates little demand for consumer goods produced by the formal sector. A large part of the income probably circulates in the relatively small closed markets of the informal sectors. The results of our 1979 survey of 1,201 households in Jakarta also showed that on average approximately 65 % of expenditure goes on food and 14 % on housing (rent, repairs). Little is left for industrial or other mass consumer goods. The basic needs of lower income groups are not sufficiently satisfied. Nevertheless, the need cannot be adequately expressed due to the low level of money income and for the same reason production cannot be directed to the satisfaction of basic needs.

When urban masses are unable to express how inadequately their basic needs are satisfied by means of demand in the market place, their only way out is to articulate their situation through strikes, political pressure and rioting. Illegal strikes and disturbances have indeed occurred at different times in Southeast Asian cities, in extreme cases taking on the appearance of racial disturbances directed against the Chinese commercial community. At other times they may take the form of an alliance with students against the government or parts of the ruling élite. The government's reactions tend to vary between cracking the whip and sugaring the pill, i. e. greater controls and repression or else rice subsidies and development projects. What does emerge, however, is that some truly successful low cost housing projects and urban renovation schemes do get financed by loans from the World Bank, thereby adding to the countries' foreign debts.

Observing the urban economy from "the outside", it is certainly possible to show a formal and an informal sector. Each sector has a distinct form of economic organization and is "socially-spatially" separate, if one selects small enough units for the purpose of analysis (for instance, there could be a skyscraper serving the needs of some public authority, surrounded by hawkers serving food and drink to the state employees who work there. From "the inside", i. e. seen from the angle of the smallest economic unit in the private households of the poor, both sectors are interwoven in terms of the family budget. Different members of the family may draw on various sources of income in both the formal and informal sector, or they may change from one sector to the other, or again even single individuals usually have several jobs and two or more sources of income in the different sectors.

It is precisely this constantly shifting pattern, as well as the heterogeneity of the income structure and of the resources drawn upon in individual households, that is characteristic of the city. In addition, there are frequent change in the composition of a household which means that the domestic development cycle often goes quickly through a number of wage-earners available at any one time. Families frequently move house or are forcibly re-settled. Our study of internal migration in Jakarta shows that approximately half the households questioned had moved more than three times (Resnahadi 1980:71). Visitors from country regions may strengthen or place an additional burden upon the family budget and there may also be changes of jobs within the same sector. The customary concepts used for classification proved to be inadequate. What is, on the contrary, typical, is change, the continual alternations of living standards and opportunities. The only truly permanent element is crisis and the need for continuous adaptation to a changing environment. It is therefore quite fitting to talk of a "floating mass" (Evers 1980b) upon which a thin middle stratum of the population and an affluent upper class have built a city like a pack of cards propped up by foreign capitalism, full of false glamor and sophisticated consumption patterns.

For the bottom of the urban population, money income is not enough to survive. Our findings from studies in Jakarta and Bangkok show that an important part of domestic consumption derives from a third sector which we should like to call urban subsistence production. The concept of subsistence economy or subsistence production is normally associated with the agrarian sector and it denotes a form of economy in which a major part of production is for domestic consumption. This connection between production for the market and production for domestic consumption has been more clearly defined and dealt with in a series of Bielefeld studies (see in particular Bielefelder Entwicklungssoziologen 1978, and other works by the Bielefeld Sociology of Development Research Centre). But subsistence production for consumption by the producer or his household clearly also exists in cities, and not only as a remnant in semi-agrarian areas on the fringe of the city which may for administrative reasons figure in the statistics as part of the city outskirts. For one thing, there exists a strong link to rural subsistence production via the transfer of food and other goods into urban households by members of the family or "circular" migrants. Rice and vegetables from the city dwellers' original home villages, especially prepared foods and those that keep like krupuk, dried fish and spices, are brought into the city in small quantities which nevertheless add up to a significant total. But in the city itself and in relatively densely populated slum areas, foodstuffs like bananas, cassava, spices, vegetables and others are grown on even the smallest patches, animals are kept, and fish are caught in canals or on the coast.

But urban subsistence production is by no means limited to food. Houses and shacks are often put together or improved from waste materials, roads are built, clothing is produced in the home, wells are sunk and water fetched, firewood is collected from garbage and household tools are also produced domestically. So the areas where urban masses live are really vast workshops which hardly ever figure in statistics and which, together with the informal sector with its petty commodity production, make a quite considerable contribution to the Gross Domestic Product. This urban subsistence production is by no means just a leftover from rural ways of life: it is a specific form of production in the city. This result is similar to the famous "law" discovered by the Prussian statistician Engel, that the share of food in total consumption declines with rising income.

An important question remains whether or not these links between money income and subsistence production and between different sectors of production which we have detected by comparing individual households are also traceable as processes in time within an overall process of development or underdevelopment. A survey of the family budgets of urban workers carried out by the Batavia city authority in 1937 suggests that subsistence production existed at the time, too, following the world economic crisis, because one key finding was that urban workers' expenditure exceeded their income and that this could not be fully explained by higher levels of debt. We conclude that already in those days the gap must have been filled by subsistence production (Wertheim 1958:85-224).

Modernization theorists have defined underdevelopment as "backwardness", as being not yet developed. In contrast, we point out that the development of the urban economy includes a limited capacity for reproduction caused by specific social structures. This limited capacity for reproduction can be seen at two levels. At the individual household level, adequate supplies and satisfaction of basic needs are not continuously achieved. At the level of the whole - in this case urban - society it has been shown that this can only be accomplished with the help of inputs from outside. So resources from the raw materials sector (oil revenue, export taxes on zinc, timber and other goods), as well as development aid and loans, are used in the city to maintain the urban infrastructure and the urban economy. At the same time rural-urban migration results in a constant transfer of labour power. This labour power is first reproduced in rural areas. Then when it has reached its highest level of productive capacity it typically migrates into the city to employ this productive labour power in the urban economy in return for low wages. These wages are normally so low that they are just about to ensure reproduction or survival in the city but they are not enough to finance the whole reproductive cycle of a family. Only through the meshing of the three productive sectors subsistence economy in its agrarian and urban form and the formal and informal sectors - as sources of income, is it possible to maintain the majority of the urban population. This means that the formal sector, especially wage labour, is being subsidized by the surplus labour performed in the subsistence production area.

The reproduction of lower income groups, of "the poor", of the urban marginal masses, as well as the reproduction of the city as a social and economic system is ensured only so long as urban subsistence production exists. The latter is therefore an essential and indispensable characteristic of the urban economy.

Facets of Modernity

The coexistence of economic forms like subsistence production, based primarily on local social relations like the family, neighbours and friends with informal sector activities and a big business in the cities finds a counterpart in the coexistence of different spaces in the city, like the slums, the kampung, the middle-class housing estates, the factories, office towers and hotels and the monuments. The construction of economic relations and the cultural construction are closely linked. The kampung is the sphere of a locally organized informal sector and of subsistence production, while the commercial districts are global spheres in their architecture as well as the economic activities which take place within them. The modernity of the Southeast Asian city is thus not economic growth, industrialization and the emergence of modern high-rise quarters and housing estates, and underdevelopment is not subsistence production, the slums and kampung. The modernity consists of both, the slum and the high-rise, subsistence production and global finances. In conclusion, the large cities of Southeast Asia like Bangkok, Singapore, Manila, Jakarta and

Kuala Lumpur are characterized by the parallelism of global spaces (the international banks, hotels and shopping centres in which international commerce is conducted and a cosmopolitan life-style followed), national spaces (namely the monuments, government buildings, palaces and temples) and local spaces. For all these spaces and the city as a whole certain ideologies and traditions are created, like the capital as the showcase of modernity and development, or as the symbiosis of tradition and modernization, or the condemnation of the capital city as the centre of Westernization and alienation. These ideologies are neither right nor wrong. They are the expressions of the pluralism found in these cities.

2. Urbanism in Southeast Asia

The discussion of cities in Southeast Asia faces several puzzling facts. As a whole the region is only slowly urbanizing and the overall degree of urbanization is comparatively low. In most countries the major proportion of the labour force is still employed in agricultural production. The societies appear as predominantly rurally oriented ones in which life in an urban environment is rather an exception. In contrast to the impression of Southeast Asian societies as rurally based or oriented are the big cities with several million inhabitants like Jakarta, Manila and Bangkok.[11]

The impression that these big cities are alien to genuine Southeast Asian society is strengthened by the multi-ethnic composition of the population, and the fact that all are recently-founded cities, with the exception of Bangkok, founded by a colonial power as a centre for administration and exploitation.[12] Jakarta, with Manila the oldest of the present capital cities, was founded under the name Batavia by the Dutch. Rangoon, although founded in 1750 by Alaungpaya after a war against the Mon empire of southern Burma under the name "End of Strife", remained a small town until it became the centre of British colonialism in Burma following the second Anglo-Burmese war in 1852. Singapore was founded in 1819 by Raffles, and Manila in 1571 by the Spanish. Bangkok,

---

[11]The official number of inhabitants given for these cities is usually misleading. Bangkok for example has officially some 6 million inhabitants. This number includes only those who are officially registered in Bangkok and who reside in the area defined as Bangkok Metropolis. In real terms (including the suburbs which officially belong to other provinces and including those living in Bangkok without official registration) the population is estimated to be at least some 8 to 9 million people.

[12]Other cities already existed prior to colonial penetration. Batavia was founded by the Dutch at a former, unimportant Kratong (Palace), and Rangoon was founded in the seventeenth century by Alaungpaya, following the conquest of the Mon Kingdom, below the sacred Swedagon Pagoda with the name "End of Strife". Singapore had already existed for a long time as a settlement of Chinese traders and fishermen. Even Bangkok and Thonburi are not newly founded cities but already had a long history as minor places in the Ayudhya kingdom. The predecessors of the colonial capitals and the current primate cities had, however, only a very limited significance.

formerly a village at a bend of the Chao Phraya river opposite the harbour town of Thonburi, was founded in 1782 by Rama I as the new capital of Siam.

The overall low degree of urbanization combined with the concentration of the urban population in one heterogeneous, metropolitan and international rather than national primate city, together with the fact that these primate cities are young (hardly older than 200 years) and with the exception of Bangkok, founded by colonial powers, reinforces the impression that urbanism is alien to Southeast Asian culture and society. In this regard McGee (1967) argues that "The Southeast Asian city is a mosaic of cultural and racial worlds each invoking the memory of other lands and people" (McGee 1967:24f). Similarly, Ginsburg (1976) describes the big cities of Southeast Asia as "essentially alien to the Southeast Asian landscape" (Ginsburg 1976:3). Due to their early development and founding as "head-links" or "bridgeheads" of the colonial powers, the big cities are multiethnic, multicultural and metropolitan rather than national, with commercial rather than cultural ties between city and hinterland (Ginsburg 1976:3ff). Comparing Malay and Chinese urbanism, the existing cities in Malaysia and partly Indonesia are based on Indian or Islamic concepts of the city as a centre, while in the Malay context the centre is the palace (Kraton) or the central mosque, but not a city.

All big cities in Southeast Asia strongly display the features of "primate cities". As Chong (1976) shows, all capital cities in Southeast Asia are by far the biggest city in the country[13], with a population of several times the population of the second biggest city, they are all the capital city, the major port, location for the headquarters of business and administration, cultural and social centres and prime location for industrial production (Chong 1976:166ff). The urbanization process is concentrated in these primate cities, in which already up to half of the overall urban population resides, and which still have growth rates exceeding the overall growth rate of the urban population.

Rapid urbanization centred in one primate city leads to several problems like congestion, pollution, slums etc. So far all attempts of the states and municipal administrations to control and reduce the pressure on the primate city has failed (Kasadra, J., Parnell, A. M. 1993). "It can be argued also that the overwhelming dominance of the primate city inhibits the growth of lesser cities and that the larger cities will expand more rapidly than the lesser ones. There are in effect only a limited number of services to be performed by cities within a predominantly village and folk society, although it may be industrializing

---

[13]Of course, these ideas are developed predominantly by urban intellectuals, and the concept of village society tends to be imaginary and does not reflect reality in the rural areas.

slowly, and the great cities continue to posses a virtual monopoly of these services. Thus, even as a society changes, new and increasingly complex functions tend to be performed by institutions already established in the primate cities" (Ginsburg 1976:3). But even in these big primate cities, a dualism between modern, westernized institutions and seemingly rural life-styles seems to exist. In the economy, Armstrong and McGee (1980) speak of an urban involution, and the coexistence of a firm-type modern economy with a bazaar-type economy. Laquian (1972) discusses the slums in the big primate cities (in which between 20 to 50 percent of the urban population lives), as continuation of a folk culture within the city, or as linkages between rural folk culture and the urban culture.

From these points of view urbanism appears as alien, as an effect of colonialism and Westernization. This impression is contradicted by the fact that cities have already existed in Southeast Asia for the last twothousand years, and that some of these were of quite a considerable size, larger even than European cities during that time (Wheatley 1983). Thus we certainly find a tradition of "Urbanism in Southeast Asia". This urban tradition did not, however, lead towards independent "bourgeois" cities, but was closely linked with state formation and systems of domination. In this regard colonialism was both a continuation of this urban tradition and a break in that the élite shifted from natives to an alien élite.

Following Wertheim (1980) two main patterns of state formation can be differentiated: the inland states and the harbour principalities. The forms of urbanization are closely related to these patterns of state formation.

1. The city as a centre for territorial control in the context of the inland states:[14]

In this pattern, the capital city is the centre, surrounded by provincial capitals as way stations of the central authority. The élite is defined through its position within the capital city and legitimated by a cosmology in which the capital city, and the main temple, and/or the palace of the king, articulates the secular with the sacred world. This articulation was essential because the religious institutions were one base for territorial control and administration. The main danger was that the provincial cities utilized their power over smaller territories to gain independence in relation to the system of overall control into which they were integrated. This is indicated by the attempts at secessions which happened regularly in Southeast Asia when the centres showed weakness. This type of city

---

[14]Territorial control does not mean the control of land. Territory is used here in the sense of Sack, as control over everything (land, people, resources etc.) within a given area.

emerged in connection with the formation of the "inland states", states based on peasant production.

2. The city as a centre in trade networks:

In this pattern the city, often as independent commercial city or as entrepôt city, was a node of trading routes. Control of trade (regional and long distance trade) through the control of nodes of trading routes, i. e. commercial cities, was the main function of these cities. The weakness derived from either threats from the territorial states or from changes in trading relations.

These two patterns did not exist in isolation from each other, but were interrelated and connected. Goods for trade and for consumption in the commercial cities were supplied by the territorial states, and the élite of the territorial states needed luxury goods, acquired through long-distance trade, for the expression of their status. An overlapping of both systems existed when the capital of a territorial state was also a node in trading relations, thus providing a resource for power and territorial control, as it was the case of Ayudhya, the former Siamese capital city. If, however, a provincial city was integrated into the trading system, while the centre was not, it gained a resource which allowed an increased independence from the centre, usually leading to a conflict with the centre. Examples of this are the conflicts between Nakorn Sri Thammarat and Ayudhya in Siam, or the conflicts between Pegu and Syriam with the capitals of the Burmese state.

These two patterns imply a different focus of development. Territorial control put the main emphasis on the integration of the provinces into one framework, dominated by the élite in the capital city. Interest in trade is limited, as trade could potentially allow the emergence of commercial centres or groups independent of the state and its ruling élite. The history of Burma up to the present is characterized by such an inward orientation, and a continuous conflict with the commercially oriented cities along the Indian Ocean. Only for a short period during the sixteenth century was the centre of a Burmese state located in the predominantly commercial city of Pegu in southern Burma, which, however, led to severe problems, as territorial control was challenged from upper Burma. For territorial integration the location of the centre in upper Burma was more appropriate. The rise of Rangoon is due to British colonialism. Following independence, again a policy of inward orientation and territorial control was instituted, leading to serious problems with the so-called "ethnic minorities".

The states on the peninsula, like Malaysia and Singapore, in contrast, have a history of integration into trading networks rather than the establishment of territorial states. Malaysia was established as a territorial state by colonialism, which makes the creation of a "national" ideology at present complicated. The "nation" has its "traditional" base in colonialism.

Initially, the first cities emerged in connection with state formation based on diffusion from the existing empires and states in China and India, a process referred to as "Indianization". From India the concepts of government and administration of larger regions was adopted, together with the ideas of how a city can be constructed and what has to be built where in the capital cities. It would be misleading though to interpret the rise of the cities and their continuity purely as an effect of intrusion from alien groups. The Indian concepts were not just applied but modified in a specific way. Obviously, the potential for both state formation and urbanization existed in Southeast Asia prior to Indianization. Indianization provided only the concepts and ideas which could be applied to the material conditions existing already.

The Development of Urbanism in Southeast Asia

Urbanism and State Formation

In Southeast Asia two main patterns of urbanism connected to state formation can be distinguished: the commercial cities, predominantly alongside the coastal areas, of which Melaka was the most prosperous and the most central within the international trading network, and the inland sacred cities of the rulers like Angor. Both were integrated into a division of labour in which the commercial cities provided goods from foreign trade for the élites, and the inland states provided rice and other goods for the commercial cities. While the inland states had as centres of power strong capital cities which were integrated into sacred rituals through which kingship was legitimated, and expressed their centrality through the articulation of heaven, world and underworld by magnificent tectonic marks (namely the chedis and prangs of the main temples and palaces), the centrality of the commercial cities did not need an outer expression, it expressed itself in the success of business.

The inland states of mainland Southeast Asia were based on strong capitals, following in their construction Indian and, to a lesser degree, Chinese urban concepts. The capitals of Burma fall into this category. There, similarly to the situation on Java, a conflicting interdependence between coastal principalities and commercial centres (Pegu, Syriam), and the upper Burman political centre (Ava) existed. A special case is Ayudhya, the former Siamese capital. It was both a trading city and the capital of a powerful inland state. On the one hand, this gave the strength to Ayudhya and reenforced its position as the indisputable centre, but on the other hand, the conflicts between inland states and harbour principalities, a conflict between distinct states in Java, was a conflict within the élite itself in Ayudhya's history is characterized by shifts between élite factions and policies related to foreign trade.[15]

The cities can roughly be differentiated into three main categories:

1. The commercial cities as nodes in trading relations

Melaka was for a long time the undisputed centre of international and regional trade in Southeast Asia. First of all, Melaka was a place where traders met and made their deals, and where ships could anchor and be repaired. In these cities cosmology, religion and ideology were less important than commerce. As the population was multiethnic, the cities were necessarily heterogenetic. The stability of trading routes and of commerce was most important for the success of these cities.

2. The sacred cities as centres of inland empires

The empires of mainland Southeast Asia depended on definable centres of power. Centrality was defined through kingship, and accordingly, "centre" implied the location of the palace and the king as articulator between heaven and earth. In this concept only one centre could exist. Additional nuclei in the form of provincial capitals were subordinate to the capital, and were defined as way stations of the central power. Ideally, the provincial capitals were to be like planets surrounding the sun. In the cities, cosmology, ideology and religion were closely interwoven with the legitimization of rule.

3. The smaller intermediate cities

Besides the nodes of international trade and the sacred centres, there were numerous small cities of local importance. On the one hand, these were nodes of regional and local trading networks, on the other hand the smaller cities were provincial capitals of the inland empires. In both cases these cities were way stations of a central authority, be it as a commercial centre, or the centre of an empire. The main function of these cities was to serve the centre. Particularly in these smaller cities a combination between trade and provincial control could lead to a challenge of the respective centre. Pegu and Syriam in Burma were a potential and often a real challenge to centralized rule in Burma. In Java, we find an interdependency between the many port cities along the northern coast and the inland states centreed around a Kratong. The relation was uneasy most of the

---

[15]After regaining independence, following the first fall of Ayudhya the integration into the trading networks was strongly sponsored. Ayudhya dominated the western and eastern part of the peninsula. Ayudhya's position in the long distance trade is indicated as well by the quarters of the different ethnic groups in the south of the city. A shift took place following the reign of King Narai. In the subsequent period Ayudhya lost its control of the western part of the peninsula and trade meant primarily the junk trade with China.

time as the inland states were not strong enough to subjugate the port cities, nor were the port cities able to subjugate the inland states. Pattani, Nakorn Sri Thammarat, Korat and Phitsanulok can be cited as examples of provincial cities challenging the central authority in Siam.

Accordingly in Southeast Asia we find firstly a figuration of sacred cities as exemplary centres of empires (Ava, Mandalay, Ayudhya later Bangkok). These centres coexisted for most of the time, and shifts were due to military conquest. Secondly, a system of commercial cities in which centrality derived from nodality in trading relations, and thirdly, a system of provincial capitals politically and ideologically defined by the sacred centre or their position in the trading network.

With the involvement of the Europeans in the Southeast Asian world economy, the commercial cities were the easiest prey. The reasons are that the main intention of the Europeans was to control and dominate trade. Thus the control and dominance of the commercial cities, either through conquest or through establishing competitive new centres like Batavia was more important than territorial control. Another advantage of the Europeans were their ships, namely the fortified trading ships. The security of the commercial cities depended on having a navy, exactly the sphere where the Europeans had most advantages. They could switch between being trader or pirate.

The inland states were less important for the dominance of trade, and thus less relevant for the Europeans. Only in those regions where goods which the Europeans found interesting were produced did they try to gain influence, as in the "Spice islands". But as the inland states and particularly the empires had strong military power, conquest was an adventure and if possible avoided. Instead of expensive warfare, treaties were agreed upon. Until colonial policy changed from the control of trade towards the production for trade in controlled territories, the inland states remained independent.

The Colonial Cities

Initially, colonial cities emerged as commercial cities to either facilitate the trade with an adjacent region, as in the case of Amboon on the Moluccas, or as a competing commercial centre like Batavia. Colonization of the interior remained limited for the sake of protection, or, as in the case of the Moluccas, to monopolize the production of spices. "The first intrusion into the world of Southeast Asia was not accompanied by profound structural changes within the fabric of the affected societies. Most of the Western activities and interests were in the realms of overseas trade and naval war. ... It was not until the introduction of large scale cultivation of commercial crops that the structure of Southeast Asian societies underwent a basic change" (Wertheim 1980:13).

In the eighteenth century market-oriented production was enforced in Java by the Dutch through the cultivation of coffee, tobacco and spices under the so-called method of contingencies and forced deliveries. A plantation economy developed in the middle of the nineteenth century, initially under the management of the colonial governments and the companies, later under the management of private "planters". With the colonial administration turning towards territorial administration a dualism between the traditional rule of indigenous local élites and a colonial administration emerged. In Indonesia, intentionally, a dual pattern of administration was established with the western bureaucratic apparatus superimposed on the traditional structure. In Burma, which was under British rule after the third Anglo-Burmese war in 1885, the regions directly under British control were administered by a bureaucracy centralized in Rangoon, while other regions were left under so-called indirect rule.[16] This dual pattern prevailed in the economy and society as well, and is discussed as "dual society" (Boeke 1980) or "plural society" (Furnivall 1980). With regard to urbanization, duality or plurality is indicated by the coexistence of the colonial capital (Batavia, Rangoon) and the indigenous centres (Yogyakarta, Mandalay), and within the cities by the coexistence of the European quarter, the centre of administration and international commerce, and the "native" quarters.

The changes in the pattern of colonialism affected the rural areas, but also the cities, which is often overlooked. Besides their role as commercial cities, they became centres of territorial administration. In territorial administration, the colonial powers very soon proved more efficient than their indigenous predecessors. The colonial headquarters turned into real centres of commerce and administration.

The changes in the pattern of urbanism in the course of colonialism differs from one country to another. In Indonesia, where multiple nuclei and nodes existed, Batavia was the centre of colonial administration and colonial commerce while Surabaya remained as a centre in the commerce among the Indonesian islands. The change from a centre of trade, and city defined as a commercial city, towards a centre of territorial administration, i. e. a colonial capital city, took place in Batavia with the introduction of the culture system, and especially the plantation economy in the middle of the nineteenth century. In Burma the transformation took longer. Initially, the main interest of the British were the resources of timber in Burma; later, with the conquering of the whole of lower

---

[16]One particular problem in Burma was that it became part of the Indian empire, and accordingly, a semi-autonomous self government of villages based on the Indian pattern was introduced, neglecting the differences between Indian and Burmese social structure.

Burma, the delta region was developed into a major rice producing region in Southeast Asia centred around Rangoon. However, it took until the end of the nineteenth century that the last independent Burmese state was conquered, mainly in the interest of finding an overland trade route to China.[17] With the fall of the Mandalay kingdom of Burma in 1885, Rangoon became the commercial and administrative centre, but Mandalay still remained the second biggest city, as the traditional capital of all Burmese, just as Yogyakarta remained the centre of Javanese culture. In Malaya, Singapore took over the position formerly held by Melaka as the node of international trade, with smaller cities like Kuala Lumpur developing as administrative seats when Malaya became a major producer of latex and tin at the early twentieth century.

The main impact of colonialism was the forced integration of bigger territories into an economy dominated by the European colonial governments. As the colonial administration proved more efficient and able to integrate the regions under control into one territory administered from a centre, the former separation between commercial and peasant production regions was dissolved. The colonial "bridgeheads" and "enclaves" became economic and administrative centres. This development is portrayed in quite some detail for Indonesia, the Philippines and Burma. Siam, as it escaped direct colonization, is not usually discussed in this context. This is in so far astonishing as the development of Bangkok bears several similarities to the development of Batavia as a centre of administration and the economy, but in contrast to the other colonial cities, developed in the framework of a "sacred city". In Siam it was not a foreign élite introducing those changes in the economy and administration which are the characteristics of colonialism, but an indigenous élite. The reason for embarking on this course was not colonial intervention, but the conditions when the new Siamese state was forming some twohundred years ago, which enforced the development of an outwardly oriented state, integrated into trading relations and instituting the production of goods for use in trade. The interesting point is that the development of Siam was in some regard a forerunner of colonial policies. A form of plantation economy was introduced already in the early nineteenth century, and a functional provincial administration of the whole kingdom was developed at the end of the nineteenth century and beginning of the twentieth. As these socio-economic and political changes were induced by an indigenous élite, from an indigenous centre, Bangkok was not defined as a "colonial city", but as a sacred city in which traditions were conserved, which had important

---

[17]Quite similarly, the conquest of Vientiane and Luang Prabang by the French at the end of the nineteenth century aimed at establishing a trade route to China.

impacts on the emergence of nationalism in Siam and the ideology of Bangkok up to the present.

The commercial cities, where colonial domination found its starting point, were governed by the market, and those who dominated the market were the élite of the city. When the Europeans were able to dominate the market, either through military conquest of the city, or through founding competing centres, they emerged as the élite. They could, however, not become the ruling élite of the inland states by this method as they clearly lacked sacrality. The relationship between the European colonial power and the inland states became uneasy with the establishment of a plantation economy as this necessitated territorial control and administration. In the course of military conflicts the colonial centres became dominant, and on the basis of an efficient, western bureaucratic administration were able to turn the colonial capitals into the real centres of the colonies. The lack of sacrality, however, prohibited the integration of the Europeans into the traditional élites, and the colonial capitals, which also lacked sacrality were unable to replace the former exemplary centres. These later became a base in the struggle for independence.

The conflict between "traditional" élites and "colonial" élites already took place in Siam during the early Bangkok period, and was settled when the administration turned into a real centralized administration, integrating regions outside of the core territory like Lanna Thai, Laos, the northeastern and southern regions at the end of the nineteenth and the early twentieth century. Thus no competing centre of indigenous culture could emerge in Siam. Neither was any other centre of power allowed to emerge, as this would have been a threat to the dominant position of the élite in Bangkok. Economic and political developments initiated by the élite to keep or enhance their position of power strengthened Bangkok's position as centre, thus giving rise to an extreme case of primacy.

Jakarta: From Commercial City to Colonial City and National Capital

Looking at the development of Batavia the changes in the pattern of colonialism can be recognized. At the beginning of the seventeenth century, at the mouth of the Tjiiliwong river, a factory with the name Nassau was founded following a treaty with the local ruler in the village of Jakarta. Initially, the place was used as intermediate anchorage for repairs of ships on their way to the Moluccas and as a warehouse.[18]

---

[18]The representative of the V.O.C. resided in Banten, the commercial centre of the island region.

As this proved successful, the directors of the "V.O.C." thought to extend the station and transform it into a place where the sailors could rest after the long journey from Holland, making it the main wharf in the region, and a location where the goods to be sent to Europe could be stracked before being dispatched to Amsterdam (Cobban 1976:47). The existing warehouse and factory became too small for these tasks. After more land was granted to the Dutch, in 1618, the emerging city was named Batavia.

The main commercial competition for the new Dutch city was Banten, further in the west of Java. After Bantam was suppressed, Batavia was further extended in size and developed as a fortified city. The layout of Batavia followed the pattern of a Dutch city in Europe with several canals crossing through the area. To gain protection from fire, it was decreed in 1633 that all houses in the enwalled city had to be built of bricks. The success of Batavia as a centre for trade led to a rapid influx of people from other countries and regions who resided in specific quarters of Batavia, transforming Batavia into a real trading centre, quite similar to the former commercial cities.

In the middle of the seventieth century, Schmalkalden describes Batavia as follows: "Die Stadt ist mit einer hohen Mauer und tiefen Wassergräben umgeben, und stehen in der Mauer gegen alle Gassen große viereckige Türme, welche mit vielen Stücken versehen und mit Soldaten besetzt sind. Durch die Gassen, so alle nach der Schnur gleich angelegt, gehen Wassergräben, so mit wachsendem Wasser voll - und mit fallendem ablaufen. In dem Castell wohnet der General in einem schönen, steinern Hause, ..., desgleichen alle Ordinar- und Extraordinar-Räte von India, item etliche Kaufleute und Assistenten. ... Die Bürger oder Inwohner der Stadt Batavia, exklusive die Soldateska, welche auf den Punten liegen, sind entweder Indianer oder Holländer. ... Unter den Sinesen sind ihrer viel großen Vermögens. Haben ihre eigenen Junken auf der See und treiben starken Kaufhandel. Etliche treiben Krämerei oder nähren sich mit Garkochen, Brandewein, Tobak und Bierzapfen. Diese letzteren haben mehrenteils keine eigenen Häuser, sondern wohnen zur Miet und geben monatlich dem Eigentumsherrn großen Zins davon" (Joost 1983:103f).

As Cobban points out, the ruling élite of Batavia was outward-looking, and not keen to engage itself in territorial control of inner Java. For the supply of the inhabitants the vicinity where rice and vegetables were grown was sufficient. "For most of its early existence, Djakarta was isolated from the life of other parts of Java, particularly the interior. During the first part of the seventeenth century, the city was largely outward-looking in its interests and heterogenetic with regard to cultural change, though during the first two centuries it was perhaps more heterogenetic than the traditional city of Southeast Asia" (Cobban 1976:55).

Primarily due to security reasons the territory surrounding Batavia was extended in the course of several wars with inland Javanese powers, until the island was under the political domination of the governor general residing in Batavia. When with the rise of British colonialism the centre of commerce in Asia shifted from Southeast Asia to India, Batavia's position was weakened in favour of Calcutta. Initially as addition to profits from trade, later increasingly as the base of the V.O.C.'s profits, the production of goods for trade was enforced by the colonial government. Batavia changed from a primarily commercial city towards an administrative centre of Indonesia.

When the military threat from the interior was removed, people could move out of the direct environs of Batavia, which proved to be rather unhealthy, into the suburb of Weltevreden. Obviously, to build a city in the tropics following Dutch patterns and urban concepts was not appropriate. The canals, which were useful in the Netherlands, proved to be excellent breeding grounds for anopheles mosquitoes, making Batavia the graveyard of the "white men" in Asia. In Weltevreden "the stuffy Dutch canal houses were replaced by country villas - roomy, airy and cool - surrounded by extensive gardens. The new houses of the Dutch certainly gained some inspiration from the Javanese Priyayi home (aristocratic home), just as the suburb plan of the streets, with a large square and wide roads radiating out from it, was imitative of the Javanese kratong-based cities" (McGee 1967:51).

With the move of the colonial élite into the suburbs, the old city area became the main residential area of the Chinese and the less well-to-do Europeans. Surrounding the old city were several kampung of different ethnic groups. Until the end of the nineteenth century, the population was hardly in excess of 100,000. Karsten describes the living conditions in Batavia as follows: "As regards housing, the Europeans lived in large, spacious 'old Indies' houses with enormous yards, ... The kampung were extensive, but the buildings in them were primitive and scattered, hence a certain amount of crops were still usually grown in the large compounds. Hence also, the character of the kampung in the town was, with only a few exceptions, still completely rural. The Chinese were required to live in the 'Chinese camp', which, with the old Dutch quarters dating from the seventeen and eighteenth centuries, was the only section of the town fully built up. The intermediary group of lesser Europeans did not live 'in the kampung', or practically not so, but rather for a part in the older sections of the town and for the rest here and there along the highways" (Dutch Scholars 1958:VI).

The urban growth of Batavia remained limited. Most of the population increase resulted from immigration from Europe, China etc., less from rural urban migration in Java itself. Urbanization was not centred on Batavia alone, as Batavia did not emerge as the undisputed administrative and even less so, economic centre of Java. Besides Batavia, Yokyakarta, Semarang, Surabaya, Bandung played a role. A survey in 1930 indicated in general that urban growth remained limited, but it was concentrated in the larger and biggest towns, namely Batavia, Bandung, Semarang and Surabaya. In fact, in comparison to other Southeast Asian capital cities, Jakarta, as Batavia was later called, did not reach a high degree of primacy. While the change of the relation between biggest and second biggest city during the period from 1911 to 1958 changed in Burma from 1:2 to 1:4, and in Thailand from 1:15 in 1947 to 1:26 in 1960, in Indonesia the shift was small with a change from 1:1 to 1:3 (McGee 1967:54).

Batavia was founded as a commercial city, as a competitor of Melaka and Banten's. The élite of the city were the representatives of the Dutch V.O.C. Any challenge to Batavia and the élite of Batavia implied a challenge to the V.O.C. However, as a commercial city, there was only limited involvement in internal conflicts on Java itself. Batavia was a place for entrepôt trade at a location selected due to its value for navigation. Only in order to secure Batavia was the territory under control extended. In this regard, Batavia fitted into the pattern of Indonesian states as differentiations between inland states dominated by landed élites, and commercial cities dominated by traders.

With the rise of British colonialism and the increasing dominance of the British in trade, the policy shifted towards the production of goods used for trade, and Batavia was transformed into a centre of colonial administration and the colonial economy. Batavia was the link between colony and mother country. Batavia as administrative centre of the whole of Indonesia implied the integration of two indigenous élites, namely the landed aristocracy and the commercial élites of the harbour cities (Schiel 1985:428ff). The integration of these groups was based on Dutch overrule, that is, the domination of territorial control and the economy by the Dutch.

With independence Batavia (the capital of the Dutch East Indies) was renamed Jakarta (the capital of Indonesia). Just as Dutch colonial rule integrated the two main groups, nationalism provided a common framework for these groups after independence (Schiel 1985:429). The conflicts between the main groups did not lead to the emergence of a new, competitive centre, or secessions within the nation, as happened in Burma, but to a conflictual situation of the élite within Jakarta itself. As such, Jakarta was the national capital, but not necessarily the undisputed economic or cultural and political centre. Under Sukarno Jakarta was developed as undisputed administrative centre while Surabaya, partly because the city was located away from the administrative centre and thus less controlled, remained the centre of trade in Indonesia. Under Suharto, who again sponsored the policy of integration into the world market, Jakarta was developed as the economic centre, at the expense of Surabaya. Thus, the primacy of Jakarta is comparatively small and quite a recent phenomenon.

Singapore: From Commercial Entrepôt to City State

Singapore was founded by Raffles after Java, which he regarded as a better location, had to be returned to the Dutch following the Napoleonic Wars. From the very beginning Singapore was to be a centre of trade in Southeast Asia, and the east-west trade between British India and China. The British Colonial government was the administration of the city, in which, however, the settlement of Chinese, Indians, Arabians and Malays was sponsored. Singapore was multiethnic just as Melaka had been before. As long as the different groups obeyed law and order that is, did not involve themselves in fights with each other, put obstacles in the way of commerce in Singapore, etc. they were more or less left under the government of the local leaders. The élite consisted of different, loosely connected groups, namely the British colonial administrators and the businessmen of the different ethnic groups.

Singapore's role as commercial centre remained even after Malaya was under British colonial dominance. The administrative capital was at Kuala Lumpur, not in Singapore. After independence, initially it was planned that Singapore should become part of the Malay Federation. This, however, was problematic for the Malay government as with Singapore the Chinese would have been the biggest ethnic group of Malaysia. It was also problematic for Singapore as it was expected that the different ethnic groups within Singapore would lose their status. Obviously, Singapore could not be integrated into the Malay territorial state, as it might have implied that Singapore would become the economic and potentially the administrative centre of Malaysia.

The continuity of Singapore as a commercial city implied its development as an independent city state. As such, however, Singapore was a foreign body within Southeast Asia: the population consisted predominantly of non-Southeast Asians.[19] While elsewhere the territorial nation states emerged, Singapore developed as a city state. In the nation-states nationalism was propagated as ideology, in Singapore it was difficult to construct nationalism as the different groups came from different nations. The meaning to be connected to the new city state was the meaning of Singapore as an entrepôt in which the different groups were connected by the market, integrated primarily into the world economy, and only secondarily into the region. The city government had as its task keepking law and order so that commerce was not endangered, and sponsoring commerce in the city. A nationalism of a commercial city developed, not based on former glory or sacrality, but on current economic success. Any

---

[19]The autobiography of Lee Kuan Yew (1998) provides excellent information about the political struggle between Singapore and Malaysia, after independence when Singapore was merged with Malaysia.

challenge to the ruling élite was defined as a challenge to the economic success of Singapore.

Rangoon: From Colonial City to Capital City without a Nation

Rangoon's rise as a centre of territorial administration was based on the development of the Irrawaddy delta region into the main rice-producing area of the world. Prior to colonialism the centre of Burma was in upper Burma, as this was the main region for agricultural production, and more densely populated than lower Burma. The development of the delta region led to an overall shift towards lower Burma as population centre and as main agricultural region. Thus Rangoon in fact became the centre of Burma while Mandalay was the subordinate centre of upper Burma. The meaning of the city was defined by the British and Indian immigrants as the centre of colonial administration based on the Indian pattern, because Burma was part of the Indian empire. As Hall argues, this was "Britain's greatest mistake in dealing with Burma" (Hall 1977:730). For the Burmese, Rangoon was a place of residence only, as it was not a "legitimate" centre.

The legitimacy of a centre was defined by a ruler through his support of Buddhism, but as Hall shows, "the Queen's proclamation of 1858 following the Indian Mutiny ordered all British authorities in India to abstain from all interference with the religious belief or worship" (Hall 1977:733), and furthermore the governors of Burma saw this post only as an intermediate station in their career which was focused on India, and were not interested in Burmese society and customs and followed the Indian pattern of colonial administration. This had three effects:

1. Buddhism provided one major base for nationalism and the challenge to colonial rule;

2. the lack of support of the Sangha by the authorities led to its decline and internal factionalism, thereby destroying the Sangha as an organization into which the different regions of Burma were integrated;

3. the colonial administration did not provide a base for national unity. Thus, the tendencies of factionalism, segmentation and secessions could not be controlled after independence.

While in Indonesia colonial government led to national unity, and nationalism could be used as common framework for diverging factions, in Burma "British rule did nothing to foster national unity. On the contrary, both directly and indirectly, it stimulated sectional particularism. It separated Burma proper from the frontier peoples ... Also by opening the armed forces to the minor peoples and barring them to the Burmese, it fostered racial antagonism and subverted the internal balance of power, rendering it unstable. ... The object of British policy was to develop the material resources of Burma by throwing it open for free enterprise to all the world on equal terms. This multiplied sectional diversity by attracting a host of inassimilable alien elements" (Furnivall 1960:22). For Furnivall, nationalism could provide a framework for the integration of the different groups and ethnicities of Burma. As Taylor notes, following Furnivall, nationalism hardly ever emerged as a unifying force, but the nationalist movement was factionalized and several groups within Burmese society were excluded or alienated (Taylor and Turton 1988).

Taylor describes Burmese culture and society as an amalgam of cultural adaptations, borrowing, enrichments and convolutions. Crucial here is the varying relationship and evolving synthesis between a central culture and ecological system and a variety of different, but internally rather homogeneous peripheries, from whence the central culture had received varied inputs (Taylor and Turton 1988:44). After independence this synthesis was destroyed and Burma was unmade through factionalism and secessions. Rangoon was the capital city of a country, the centre of an administration, but far from a "national" capital. The nation was limited to the vicinity of Rangoon and some bigger cities. After the coup d'état by General Ne Win in 1962, the separatist and opposition movements were suppressed, the world beyond the borders shut out, and all enterprises, industries etc. put under state ownership in the course of the "Burmese way to Socialism". Except as centre of administration, Rangoon lost all of its former meaning and function as a link between the world economy and national economy. Due to Rangoon's position as administrative centre, any conflict in Rangoon is a conflict with the governing élite, Than, Rajah (1996) and is crushed accordingly. Nationalism is ruined through its exercise by the government, and national unity exists only on the basis of the gun barrels of the military. Rangoon is the base of an élite exploiting the people of a divided country.

Present Patterns of Urbanization

Cities are definitely not alien to Southeast Asian society. Since the emergence of the first empires and integration into long-distance trade, cities have been a feature of Southeast Asia. They emerged as sacred centres of the empires and as independent commercial cities at the nodes of long distance trading systems. The heterogeneity of the cities is not generated through colonialism. Even the sacred cities had large proportions of non-indigenous populations, namely the traders from all over the region, the Brahmins, Arabs etc. Primacy is not a recent phenomenon either. The capitals of the different states had to be primate cities to reflect their position as the centre, and the commercial city states depended in their rise and development on their ability to create and control a node of long-distance trading routes. Colonialism in this regard realized the implicit ideology of Southeast Asian urbanism. The capital as exemplary centre became the real centre of the economy and administration.

The focus of discussions of protest and revolt in terms of peasant revolts or peasant movements is in line with the perspective of Southeast Asian society as primarily a peasant society. Only recently workers have been mentioned as a potential for revolt. While quite a lot is known about peasant revolts, knowledge about urban social movements is extremely limited, especially for periods prior to colonialism or independence. Does this imply that revolts did not happen in the Southeast Asian cities?

During the last decades, revolts and protest movements (with the exception of separatist movements) usually took place in the capital city. In Burma, the revolts initiated by students and intellectuals were centred on Rangoon and spread from there to other cities. In Thailand, the abolition of absolutism in 1932 and the dissolution of the military dictatorship in 1973 were results of revolts in Bangkok, not of peasant movements. In Malaysia, the riots of 1969 happened in the cities.[20] The fall of the Marcos regime in the Philippines was not brought about by the National Liberation Army of the Philippines, but by protests in Manila (more precisely, the financial quarter of Manila). The case of South Vietnam and the Lon Nol government of Cambodia indicate, from a different perspective, that only after the capital city is taken can lasting changes be implemented. After the coup d'état in 1970, the Lon Nol government of Cambodia hardly had any control over the country apart from the direct vicinity of Phnom Phen; it remained in power, however, until 1975. In Burma, during the civil war (1948 - 52), the central government at times hardly controlled more than central Rangoon. Obviously, cities, and particularly the capital primate cities, are crucial for stabilizing or destabilizing governments and élites in Southeast Asia. There is undoubtedly a need for an analysis of social movements, revolts and political change from the perspective of the cities, i. e. the nodes of political, economic, and cultural relations.

The concentration of political power in the capital city and the heterogeneity of social groups make an analysis of urban social movements in Southeast Asian cities both important and difficult. Conflicts in the cities might be struggles between factions of an élite, popular uprising might be supported and functionalized by a social group to enhance its own position either within the élite, or in relation to the élite. Small demonstrations might short-circuit and

---

[20]As these revolts had an ethnic dimension, it is logical that they took place in the cities, as most Chinese resided in urban areas.

progress into all-out revolt, thus losing there character as movements focusing on urban issues. While movements of peasants can be defined as "peasant movements", in the cities there are several political and social movements, which cannot unequivocally be regarded as "urban movements", namely the workers' movements, ethnic movements etc. Was the fight against the Ne Win government in Burma in 1988 or the revolt of 1973 in Bangkok an urban movement? The revolution of the Khmer Rouge had far-reaching implications for the cities in Cambodia, but it was definitely not an urban movement. In the same way, the demonstrations in 1998 on the streets of Jakarta were doubtlessly crucial for the removal of Suharto, but they were not part of an urban social movement.

In Southeast Asia it is difficult to point at genuine urban social movements, understood as movements based on specific urban issues, because movements aiming at general political change and urban movements can hardly be separated. The concentration of power in the major cities implies that urban issues are simultaneously issues touching the basis of state power. As the political élite was and still is based in the capital city, and depends on the capital city, any modification of the meaning of the city implies a modification of the élite and the organization of the state. We find a congruence between capital city, élite and state formation.

The development of the cities as "national capitals" implied an increase of the bureaucracy, particularly the substitution of the colonial administrators with native people. As Evers shows, the number of civil servants increased rapidly following independence. This bureaucracy was necessary for the domination of the territory. Agricultural production was sufficient to feed the urban population, but economic growth was insufficient to create employment opportunities. Only a small percentage of the inhabitants of the primate cities found employment in the industries newly established at the periphery. "The result was a proliferation of people in low-income service sectors" (Armstrong and McGee 1985:89), "cities grow, despite their failure to industrialize, not because of industrialization" (McGee 1967:18).

The bureaucracy and particularly the bureaucratic élite was centred in the capital city. McGee points to the importance of nationalism as the ideology, propagated by the western-educated new bureaucratic élites, in building up loyalty and as a powerful and believable rationale for change. This nationalism was essentially an urban phenomenon and had its base in the cities, because within the cities the educational and political institutions were located. This nationalism was connected with authoritarian rule, or personal leadership, most strongly shown by Sukarno in Indonesia, Phibulsongkhram and later Sarit in Thailand. Personal leadership and nationalism found its expression in the cities in the form of monuments, most important of course "national monuments", spacious boulevards used for parades, central squares etc. The style of these constructions was characterized by monumentality, somewhat reminiscent of Italian fascist style. The national capitals assumed the "character of the 'cult centres' associated with the pre-industrial era, only now the rites of nationalism replace the rites of the 'god-king'" (McGee 1967:19). This led, to what Ginsburg refers to as the "pseudo-investment into the costly trappings of nationalism".

Until World War II urban growth remained limited, hardly exceeding population growth. Bairoch calculates that under the condition of a traditional agriculture the maximum possible of urbanization is between 10 and 15 % (Bairoch 1988:495). Following data of McGee's (1967), with the exception of Malaysia and the Philippines the degree of urbanization in Southeast Asia during 1960 was around 15 %. Nevertheless, due to the concentration of urban growth on the biggest city - the primate cities - in the late fifties, urbanization was not regarded as a blessing any more. The pattern of urban growth discernible in some Southeast Asian societies was defined as "over-urbanization", "hyper-urbanization", "urban hypertrophy" (Bairoch 1988:457), to indicate that urbanization was not based on industrialization and modernization.[21]

While in Europe, North America and Australia, urbanization was accompanied by industrialization, increase of agricultural productivity and general economic development, the cities in the Third World were growing although industrialization remained limited, and agricultural production did not increase. The productive capability of the developing countries was insufficient to feed the increased urban population. "The urban expansion of the Third World has been made possible, despite low agricultural productivity, by imports, particularly of grain" (Bairoch 1988:462). For Southeast Asia this remark of Bairoch's is only partially valid as urbanization still remained low and agricultural productivity was high. Most countries are net exporters of agricultural products. Bairoch's argument can be used, however, for the discussion of the role of the primate cities. Although urbanization in total remained within the frame given by Bairoch (10 - 15 % of the population resides in urban areas), the concentration of the urban population in one primate city, or a few very big cities (as in Indonesia), implies that the reproduction of these cities depends on the domination of an increasing territory, from which the urban population is supplied with agricultural products. Dominance and primacy are thereby self-perpetuating. Reproduction of the city depends on the domination of

---

[21]This is certainly changing at present. Economic development, leading to the discussion of Thailand and Indonesia as the "little tigers" and new NIC, is strongly concentrated in the large cities. Clearly, urbanization is at present closely linked with industrialization.

a territory, which in turn leads to the concentration of population in this city, which again requires the increase of territory under the dominance of the city.

For the sixties and early seventies, McGee (1976) differentiates between the following patterns of urbanization:

1. Singapore as a city state deliberately sponsoring urbanization. Up to the late fifties, Singapore was rather similar to all other big cities in the region, characterized by the dominance of low productivity tertiary occupations. During the sixties, Lee Kuan Yew sponsored the integration into the world economy, through the establishment of export zones etc., and urban renewal, or the destruction of the old Chinese-type houses in the inner city area, and the building of new high-rise flats as residential areas. With political stability, foreign capital investment increased. The policy of establishing educational institutions and bringing them up to European and American standard led to the growth of a qualified labour force in Singapore. Evidently, Singapore proves that urbanization and economic development coincide.

2. In Malaysia, urbanization and economic development are closely interwoven as well. There is, however, a problem in that the cities are primarily inhabited by Indians and Chinese, while the Malay reside mainly in their Kampung. This imbalance between ethnicity and rural or urban residence is a potential for conflict, which in fact took place in 1969, and is still smouldering below the surface (Abraham 1997).

3. Indonesia is cited as a case of urban involution. Java is very densely populated, but shows only a low level of urbanization. People are pushed from the countryside into the cities, but economic development is not proceeding fast enough to provide employment for the urban population. "Thus the majority of population in the cities moves into a labour-intensive traditional economic sector characterized by underemployment, low productivity, and very low incomes" (McGee 1976:70).

Thailand was not taken into consideration by McGee in his typology. Following Goldstein's (1976) discussion of the pattern of urbanization in Thailand from 1947 to 1967, economic growth was based on the export of agricultural products, mainly rice. Industrialization was limited. Most of the newly established industries (1,127 of 2,177) were located in metropolitan Bangkok. At the end of the sixties, the situation was modified through American military spending and development aid. Based on these, infrastructure was built in the provinces, thereby connecting these regions more strongly with Bangkok. The use of Bangkok as a Rest and Recreation station increased the demand for service and petty occupations. Altogether, economic growth took place in Thailand, but it is difficult to estimate in how far urbanization was a catalyst for development or not.

While the capital cities in Southeast Asia had fewer than 1 million inhabitants after World War II, now they are among the world's biggest cities, with several million inhabitants. Urban growth implies on the one hand in-migration into the cities, the search for employment and urban "involution", shanty towns etc. On the other hand, urban growth implies the extension of the territory of the city. While in the case of migration, the peasant becomes integrated into the city due to his decision to migrate the transformation of villages at the urban periphery into suburbs does not leave any chance for decision-making among those affected. Urban growth is accompanied by readjustments of the urban ecology, and shifts of the central areas of the city.

While in the period following independence nationalism was the major ideology, after the sixties, development and modernization were taken as the main ideologies. In Indonesia the policy of dissociation installed by Sukarno was dissolved in favour of a policy of integration into the world market. In Malaysia, an ideology of modernization was propagated as the new state ideology under the name of the "look east" policy. In Singapore, modernization and development was the main issue after Lee Kuan Yew became prime minister. Development was installed as the major ideology in Thailand during the Sarit regime. Whether or not these policies led to an overall improvement of the living circumstances of the people in Southeast Asia can be disputed; it cannot be ignored though that economic growth took place, and that at least for some, namely the new élites, their living conditions were significantly improved.

Since the seventies, the pattern of urbanization has changed again. Altogether, Southeast Asia is one of the fastest developing regions of the Third World. Armstrong and McGee differentiated four main patterns:

1. Slow urbanization, slow economic development and industrialization. Population growth is predominantly absorbed in the countryside, as in Indonesia;

2. high degree of urbanization, rapid economic growth and industrialization, as in Singapore;

3. quite rapid urbanization accompanied by economic growth and successful sponsorship of industrialization, as in Malaysia;

4. slow urbanization with large rural populations and a policy aiming at rural development and industrialization, as in Thailand (Armstrong and McGee 1985:89ff).

The capital cities shift from being national centres, or the "cult centres of nationalism" to being the centres of modernization in a globalizing world. Just as the "rites" of nationalism needed national monuments as regalia in the national capitals, the regalia for the rites of modernization are the skyscrapers used as office towers, apartment houses or hotels, and the shopping centres and yuppie bars, often built following latest architectural fashions. The Brahmins conducting the state ceremonies in the sacred cities, and the military using the open spaces for their rites of nationalism are more and more replaced by the technocrats. Institutions of higher learning, private and public, are erected, tutorial classes in English and MBA courses are offered in private homes or shophouses. The march towards a global knowledge society is under way.

Circuits of Urbanization on the Malay Peninsula

Urbanization in Malaysia, as indeed in any country, is not an isolated phenomenon but represents a process intricately connected with the overall economic, social and political development of the nation.[22] But in addition, Malaysia's urban past has been shaped by outside forces as much as by local ones. In fact, urbanization in Malaysia can be seen as a process of increasing local involvement, from entrepôt cities lacking hinterlands, through the period of colonial urbanization, to the post-colonial system in which the dynamics of urbanization are increasingly shaped by internal economic and social forces, before this is supplemented and eventually overtaken by the forces of globalization.

Two Circuits of Colonial Urbanization

The geographical position of West Malaysia has been one of the major factors in its development. It is at one and the same time a barrier and a connecting link between Indian and Chinese civilization, between the Asian land mass and the Southeast Asian island world and the Pacific. The historical importance of the Malay Peninsula is derived from this geographical position rather than from the size and development of its population. Indeed, Malaya seems to have been sparsely populated right up to the twentieth century and even now has reached a population density that is relatively low compared to those of other Asian areas. In line with the sparse population, productive capacity was low in pre-colonial times and the surplus for trade from agriculture, handicraft or mining must have been modest by all accounts. The first traces of urban life apparently developed under Indian influence with the establishment of small polities patterned on an Indian state ideology from the ninth century onwards. Unlike the large Southeast Asian empires of the Khmer, Thais, and Javanese - who could establish cities and strong central authorities based on surpluses accumulated from irrigation-fed agriculture, the Malay principalities flourished by means of entrepôt trade. These embryonic urban centres developed on the east coast as well as the west coast from the fourteenth century onwards. Kota Bahru, Kuala Terengganu, and

---

[22]This section is based on Evers 1983b.

Melaka are among the early centres that eventually developed into modern cities playing an important role in present-day Malaysia.

Melaka, founded in the fifteenth century, developed as a trading centre in competition with other ports on the Straits between Sumatra and Malaya, but it differed in one important aspect from its competitors elsewhere: "Whereas the other ports on both the Sumatra and Peninsular coasts existed for the export of the products of their hinterlands, Melaka was, by reason of history and geography, an entrepôt dependent for its prosperity on the volume of trade passing through the Strait. The fundamental basis of Melaka trade was an exchange of the staple products of the Archipelago for the staple manufactures of India" (Wheatley 1959:2). The early urbanization of the Malay Peninsula was thus the result of overseas entrepôt trade. Urban centres based on hydraulic peasant production never developed to any extent. It was only with the rise of mercantile capitalism that full-scale urbanization started on the Malay Peninsula. Melaka under the Portuguese and Dutch and later Penang and Singapore under the British became part of the urban colonial network that eventually extended from Bombay to Hong Kong. But even then, up to the middle of the nineteenth century, the Malay Peninsula itself produced little for international trade in comparison with neighbouring countries. It was only with the growing demand for industrial raw materials, particularly tin, that both urbanization and colonialism spread to the Malay peninsula proper.

In about the middle of the eighteenth century Melaka was still the primate city of the Malay Peninsula. Neither the small harbour settlements such as Batu Pahat or Alur Setar on the west coast or Kuala Terengganu or Kota Bahru on the east coast could rival Melaka's population of about 10,000 or its volume of trade. With the foundation of Georgetown, P. Penang, in 1786, and Singapore in 1819, Melaka's fame as the emporium of the East was lost once and for all. But already at this time a basic pattern had become visible which we would like to call hypothetically the "two circuits of urbanization in Malaysia". As an "urban circuit" we understand a system of exchange in which capital in its various forms, including labour, commodities, and money, is circulated and a consonant system of social interaction takes place[23]. The centres of the two circuits under discussion were Melaka and P. Penang respectively. Other types of urban

---

[23] An elabouration of a theory of urban circuits is found in Santos (1975). His emphasis is, however, on the interrelation between two sub-systems of an urban economy or, in his words, between two modes of production (Santos 1975:533f.). One is designated to reproduce labour power, the other to reproduce and accumulate capital. I am using the term in quite a different way to indicate a complex system of exchange between urban centres.

systems are represented by the primarily Malay "pekan or kota towns" (Nagata 1979).

Though both P. Penang and Singapore attracted a great many migrants from all over Asia during the first years of their urban life, their recruitment patterns were, nevertheless, quite distinct. A sizable proportion of the early P. Penang population appears to have come from the neighbouring state of Kedah and even from the southern provinces of Thailand. This applied both to Chinese and Indian migrants (Sandhu 1969:177-178). The Perak Chinese must have had a leading role in the establishment of early urban society in P. Penang, while the first Kapitan Cina, Koh Lay Huan, had moved from Thailand to the colony of P. Penang shortly after its foundation.

Singapore, however, drew heavily on Chinese merchants and craftsmen from Melaka. Despite a penalty for out-migration imposed by the Dutch, many Chinese left Melaka to settle in Singapore. The first acting Kapitan Cina in Singapore, Tan Tock Seng, was born in Melaka in 1798 (Wong 1963). Other leading Chinese businessmen in early nineteenth century Singapore also sailed from Melaka. Although this out-migration must have been a considerable drain on both manpower and capital in Melaka, on the other hand, the business and family connections between Melaka Chinese and Singapore must have provided the resources for the emerging southern circuit of Malaysian urbanization, and with it a certain rehabilitation of Melaka during the second half of the nineteenth century.

Until the 1830s the Straits Settlement had to share the title originally reserved for Melaka. They were "cities made for merchandise", to quote Tome Pires. Although plantation crops grown close to the city were certainly traded and gold and tin were brought in small quantities from the Malay Peninsula, it was primarily the entrepôt trade which provided employment and wealth. With industrialization in Europe, the demand for industrial raw materials rose and promoted the establishment of a colonial mode of production and colonial urbanization even before colonial rule was formally established in Malaya. This process activated the two circuits of urbanization centred on Georgetown and Melaka. The development of tin mining has been relatively well researched, but the foundation of towns and the urbanization process are somewhat less clear. Developments in the northern mining centres of Perak and in the southern ones of Selangor and Negeri Sembilan are separate but similar. Mining operations were largely financed by Chinese capitalists from the Straits Settlement. The mining camps of Taiping in the north and of Kuala Lumpur in the south quickly developed into towns that were administered by the headmen of secret societies who ruthlessly exploited Chinese immigrant labour, amassed considerable wealth which they protected in prolonged gang warfare, and were eventually graced by the title of Kapitan China and various government honors. "The mine owners received as royalty in kind of a large percentage of the tin mined by the coolies, bought the rest of the tin at rates below the market price, supplied the coolies with the necessaries of life at a very high figure and owned the opium saloons and gambling dens in which the coolies' surplus gains were dissipated. The coolies perished but the mine owners became wealthy men and soon left the hard life of Larut for the amenities of Chinese society in Penang" (Winstedt and Wilkinson 1974:82). The two outstanding figures were Chung Ah Kwee, who founded and administered Taiping, and Yap Ah Loy, who governed Kuala Lumpur until a British officer took over in 1879. They came from Georgetown and Melaka respectively and in a way represented the northern and southern circuits of urbanization.

The urban circuits also functioned for the indigenous Malay population. Thus, Provencher (1971:20) notes that many of the early settlers on the Malay Reservation of Kampung Bahru in Kuala Lumpur were Melaka Malays. According to McGee (1967), Melaka Malays were coming to Kuala Lumpur as early as the 1850s. In fact, there is some oral evidence which suggests they acted as carpenters and bullock cart drivers.

The British colonial government did not, of course, recognize these two distinct circuits of Chinese capital and labour, but stationed its officers, with the expansion of British colonial rule, throughout the Straits Settlements and the Malay States. When it tried to intervene in the two circuits, however, conflict arose, as for instance in Kuala Lumpur in the 1880s when the state government allotted the tax farms to Hokkiens from P. Penang (Gullick 1955:75).

In the 1880s the urban system thus consisted of a northern circuit, including Georgetown as the centre and Taiping and Ipoh as the major mining towns, and a southern circuit with Melaka as its centre backed by Singapore, and with Seremban and Kuala Lumpur as its major towns. Little is known about the state of affairs in the pre-colonial pekan- and kota-type towns. Further research is, indeed, needed to test this hypothesis of early urbanization and to establish how far it was influenced by the two urban circuits in which capital and labour circulated freely.

The impetus given to urbanization by tin mining was further increased by the introduction of estate agriculture, at first coffee, then rubber and coconut. European, Chinese and Indian planters organized immigrant labour to open up plantations and at the same time stimulated the growth of a host of small towns that served as supply centres for the estate population. Again, this urbanization process is not very well researched, but studies by Leinbach (1974, 1972) suggest that the continuation of the early urbanization process on the Malay Peninsula maintained the northern and southern circuits as described above.

One of the characteristics of the southern urban circuit, namely, the transfer of human capital or workers from Melaka to Kuala Lumpur, is indeed maintained nowadays by the rise of the latter city to primacy in the urban hierarchy. Significant migration streams still connect Melaka, Seremban, and Kuala Lumpur but the "disequilibrium in diadic pairs of streams causes a significant population shift" to the Federal Territory (Pryor 1975:19). In a study of Kampung Pandan, a low-cost housing area in Kuala Lumpur, for instance, it was shown that, of the 40 per cent of the sample who had migrated from outside the state of Selangor, the largest group, about 28 per cent of the interstate migrants, came from Melaka (McTaggart and McEachern 1972:130).

The next stage in the development of the two circuits of early urbanization in Malaysia is even more hypothetical than the part discussed so far. The following remarks are based on the examination of land records, family histories, and monographs such as Gullick's study of Kuala Lumpur (1955) and Goh Ban Lee's study of P. Penang (1975). At any rate from the 1880s onwards, but increasingly towards the turn of the century, the ecological structure of the towns appears to have changed. Whereas earlier they were fairly undifferentiated boom towns, later - as described by Gullick in the case of Kuala Lumpur - the urban centres of western Malaya began to be more differentiated. Gullick observed a "notable change between 1880 and 1890) in the style of living of the Chinese citizens of K. L. In 1886 the (British) Resident noted that some of the wealthier traders had begun to build what he called villa residences for themselves on the outskirts of K. L. ... in departure from the tradition of Yap Ah Loy's generation who had lived in the middle of K. L." (Gullick 1955:108). A similar movement out of the city to wealthy suburbs and, therefore, an increasing differentiation of urban areas by social class appears to have happened in Melaka and Georgetown as well.

This movement into the suburbs of the larger towns was strengthened by what we would like to call "a return of the pioneers". Probably a good many Chinese and Indian capitalists who had lived in smaller towns near their plantations or tin mines now moved back into the old and new centres of the urban circuit. The stately family mansions in mixed Victorian and Chinese style are even now a striking feature of Georgetown, Melaka, and Singapore. This indicates the change of pioneering, rough secret-society leaders into colonial business-tycoons who now leave the exploitation of tin-mining and estate labourers to their managers while they develop into a leisure class hosting sumptuous dinners for British colonial officials, giving speeches at philanthropic institutions, and adorning themselves with British colonial titles. On the other hand, the rapidly increasing flow of migrants from the poverty-stricken areas of southern India and southern China, which reached its peak in the late 1920s, increased the urban population of Malaya and resulted in the development of the first squatter settlements and high-density slum area. The work of Purcell, Sandhu, McGee, and others on migrants will have to be continued in order to provide a complete picture of early urbanization in Malaya. In any case, it can be assumed that the rate of urbanization during the nineteenth century may possibly have exceeded present ones. The same probably applies to migration rates.[24]

The development of urban society of the "kota and pekan types" on the east coast is much less known than the rapid urbanization process on the west coast of Malaya, though Kota Bahru can boast a history that goes back perhaps to the fourteenth century and Kuala Terengganu was certainly in existence in the fifteenth century. Their nineteenth-century urban history under Siamese sovereignty is hardly known at all. This decline in economic importance and population during the early years of British colonial rule needs as much explanation as the rapid rise of urban centres in west-coast states. Thus, Kota Bahru and Kuala Terengganu were the only major urban areas that declined in population between the two census years of 1911 and 1921 (Kuala Terengganu had an estimated population of 12,000 in 1895 [Clifford 1897:26], the same as in 1921). They only assumed a place of importance again after the 1960s, a development to be discussed below.

In the preceding paragraphs we have tried to indicate that the present urban system of Malaysia has its roots in a northern and a southern urban circuit through which capital and population flowed. There was no unidirectional flow of capital or migrants, and "oscillation", a term used by Nagata (1974b:310), was the rule.

The old colonial port cities of Melaka and Georgetown served as the centres of these two circuits. The impact of tin and rubber, of migrants and bumiputera, of pioneers and speculators, on the emerging urban society still needs to be studied in detail. Although Melaka had lost its place in the urban hierarchy to Kuala Lumpur before the turn of the century, and although Ipoh's population had almost reached that of Georgetown in 1970, the two urban circuits still had an important impact on urban development in Malaysia before basically novel factors emerged during the 1960s that will probably shape the urban future of Malaysia in the same way as tin and rubber and the two urban circuits have done previously.

As the overall urbanization process between 1911 and 1970 has been well researched, we shall now turn to an analysis of the factors that have shaped the urban system of Peninsular Malaysia during the early post-colonial phase.

---

[24]This, again, points to the lack of research and of data on urbanization in nineteenth and early twentieth-century Malaya.

Post-colonial Malaysian Urbanization 1950-1980

The urbanization of Melaka, P. Penang, and Singapore up to the middle of the nineteenth century was primarily based on international trade. It was urbanization without an urban hinterland. During the nineteenth century the urbanization process followed the two urban circuits of Georgetown and Melaka as described in the previous section. Urbanization as a demographic process between 1911 and 1970, particularly the last decade, has been well analyzed by writers such as Ooi (1975), Hirschman (1976), Saw (1972), Narayanan (1975), and in a book-length study by Kuhne (1976). Most of these studies agree that "the pace of urbanization in Peninsular Malaysia was slower in the most recent intercensus interval 1957 - 70 than in the previous period 1947-57. Most of the small change in the rural-urban balance from 1957 to 1970 appears due to the growth of towns into the urban classification rather than to a redistribution of population into the previous urban settlements" (Hirschman 1976:445). In fact, of the thirty-six cities with a population of 10,000 and over in 1970, only ten exceeded the average annual growth rate of the population of West Malaysia during that period. In many towns the growth rate was below average: in Melaka, for instance, only 1.7 per cent per annum, in Georgetown 1 per cent. These figures indicate that in most cases rural-urban migration must have been low, a fact confirmed in studies on this subject (Fernandez 1975). It is even likely that there has been an out-migration, though it appears that this has been either a movement between towns (step-migration) or a movement out of city centres to the outskirts beyond the administrative town boundaries. Thus a study of urban conurbations shows that the total population of Melaka, including built-up areas outside the gazetted town, had reached 100,000 in 1970 (Chander 1971:14), in comparison to the 86,000 persons living in Melaka Town itself.

An explanation of why the urbanization process in Malaysia is quite different from that in most neighbouring countries has not been offered so far. To do that a much more comprehensive analysis, taking into account overall economic and social factors, will have to be provided instead of the type of studies based primarily on census statistics. At least some tentative suggestions in this direction will be made in the following paragraphs.

As indicated above, a first stage of urbanization was urbanization without a hinterland. The second stage in the two circuits was determined by the development of an export-oriented economy, based primarily on tin and rubber. Urban capital and labour were supplied throughout the area of production and the produce was taken to the nearest ports for export. The third stage was connected with three processes of autocentric development which were influenced, but not completely regulated, by outside economic forces. These three processes were: the commercialization of peasant agriculture, industrialization and bureaucratization.

The first results of these processes can be glimpsed by considering those towns that have grown rapidly either in terms of population or in economic importance. Whereas population growth is easily measured by census data, no decisive figures on gross urban product (GUP) are available. We therefore have to rely on general observations and on socio-economic indicators until more detailed studies have been carried out.

It is generally agreed that there are a number of "boom towns" in Malaysia. The first is the greater Kuala Lumpur area, including the satellite town of Petaling Jaya. The growth of this primate city appears to change the urban hierarchy and is a clear outcome of the bureaucratization process combined with industrialization. The latter is more relevant to the boom towns of Butterworth, Kelang, and Johor Bahru.

A third category of active towns, namely, Alor Setar, Sungai Petani, Mentakab, Kuantan, and possibly Kota Bahru and Melaka, were clearly influenced by the change in peasant production. Osborn (1974:162-3) classifies all these towns as still below the threshold of dynamism in 1970. His definition of "dynamism" is, however, biased in favour of modern production and modernizing investments by the central government. An urban area can, of course, be dynamic on account of its service functions to a surrounding agricultural area, expressed, for example, in the volume of trade.[25]

We shall now briefly outline this hypothesis and the importance of the factors that have led to the decline of the northern and southern circuits of urban development.

Bureaucratization

Bureaucratization and the rise of civil servants and government employees through the expansion of government services and the establishment of a host of agencies (Majlis Amanah Rakyat, Petroliam Nasional Berhad, Rubber Industry Smallholders' Development Authority, Malaysia, etc.) staffed by civil servants is quite phenomenal. In 1961 the combined federal and state bureaucracy had 82,132 officers, and only about 0.9 per cent of the total population was employed by the government (Tilman 1964:86). Today this figure has risen considerably. Bureaucratic employment is heavily concentrated in Kuala Lumpur, but civil servants, teachers, and other government employees have become a significant section, concentrated in new housing estates and even in smaller towns that were formerly dominated by Chinese businessmen. Thus a

---

[25]Thus Melaka ranked second after Kuala Lumpur in the value of wholesale sales per capita in 1970 (Urban Profile Study conducted by Kamal Salih, Centre for Policy Research, Universiti Sains Malaysia).

sample survey of small towns with populations between 1,000 and 10,000 shows that in 1964 about 15 per cent of the employed male population was in government service (Jones 1965:69-70). In addition to their official functions, which quite often include administration of and services to the rural hinterland, civil servants appear to extend their activities into rural areas in another sense, too. Our study on urban land-ownership has revealed that many have bought land outside the city as an investment.

Industrialization

The growth of industrial production during the 1960s and 1970s is well shown in the increasing percentage that the manufacturing sector contributes to the gross domestic product. This share rose from 12.2 per cent in 1970 to 14.4 per cent in 1975. Particularly the industrial and electrical machinery industry, including the manufacture of electronic components and sub-assemblies for export, registered a steady yearly growth of 15.6 per cent during 1971 - 5 (Third Malaysia Plan 1976:311). Part of this growth is due to "dependent industrialization" in industrial enclaves maintained by multinational corporations, especially in P. Penang and Selangor. This trend is strengthened by government development expenditure. "Manufacturing towns received relatively more expenditure than they otherwise should (Butterworth, Petaling Jaya, Kelang); those commanding primary and agricultural hinterlands drew less" (Osborn 1974:160).

Equally important appears to be the expansion of the small-scale industries that have added considerably to urban employment in medium sized towns. Whether this industrialization would be strong enough to provide adequate employment for the possibly increasing stream of rural-urban migrants and the rapidly growing, indigenous urban population remained a matter of doubt in the light of the experiences of other Third World countries until the 1990s, when full employment was generated by increased industrialization. Nevertheless a "protoproletariate" of hawkers, occasional workers, and those engaged in service occupations remained an important section of the urban labour force (McGee 1976).

Changes in the Peasant Economy

Malaysia's economy in the 1970s was still characterized by the extremely high contribution of exports of primary products towards its GNP. The production of tin, rubber and, increasingly, oil-palm products and timber, and the transportation of these products to the export harbours still add to the growth of urban service-centres. But another process that started perhaps as far back as the 1930s has gained momentum during the 1980s and shapes the process of urbanization and the structure of urban society. This is the commercialization of peasant agriculture and the decline in subsistence production. First of all, changes taking place in Malay padi production have transformed the urbanization process, the urban economy, and urban politics and society, particularly in the large padi-producing areas in Kelantan and Terengganu on the east coast, in Perlis, Kedah, and northern Perak in the northwest, and in Melaka and Negeri Sembilan in the "midwest" of Malaysia. Though a number of studies on changes in Malay padi agriculture are available, the link with urbanization has not yet been established. The following hypothesis might serve as a tentative guideline to expand research on Malaysian urbanization by establishing the link with the peasant sector of the economy and society.

Whereas production increased considerably during the 1960s and 1970s, namely, from round about 900 million tons in 1960 to about 1,500 million tons of padi in 1970, this increase is not due to the extension of the area under cultivation but to the extension of irrigation facilities, double cropping, and higher inputs of fertilizers and insecticides. There is some doubt as to whether this increase in production has also increased the net income of padi farmers, but it has definitely increased market activities, which tend to be centred in urban areas, as fertilizer and agricultural implements have to be bought, padi has to be sold, and applications for government assistance have to be filed. The level of economic activities in the urban centres of irrigation projects such as the Muda scheme (namely Alor Setar) or in the Kerian area (for instance, Bagan Serai) has risen considerably and is reflected in the building boom, urban land speculation, and an increase in the "social density" of urban life. But also Melaka, which experienced its first revival after the decline of its entrepôt trade in the rubber boom, appears to have received new impetus from the development of padi agriculture. In general the changes in the peasant economy have had considerable impact on the towns of the pekan and kota type that had already been linked with padi production in pre-colonial times.

Another factor that has promoted urbanization in the padi-producing areas is the decline and low level of subsistence production. According to a study of three double-cropping villages in Kedah, only 19.6 per cent of the average total farm income is retained for home consumption developed in Malaysia, peasants having to purchase domestic and similar items either in a local store or in a near-by town or city. What we are suggesting here is the hypothesis that a decrease in subsistence production is positively correlated with an increase in small town urbanization.[26]

---

[26]One might challenge this hypothesis by pointing out that the crucial factor may be transport technology. If adequate transport is available, peasants will ignore smaller towns and go to larger ones for their purchases (McGee, personal communication). This may indeed be true as far as the marketing of farm products is concerned but is not likely for the purchases made by peasants to supplement their decreasing subsistence products. In any case,

This hypothesis is, of course, even more relevant to the cash-crop producing sector of the peasant economy. This sector is rapidly increasing through the settlement programmes of the Federal Land Development Authority (FELDA), particularly in the larger regional development projects such as the Jengka Triangle, the Pahang Tenggara, or the Johor Kuantan join the ranks of boom towns, and newly planned or unplanned urban centres spring up and are likely to change the urban landscape of Malaysia drastically. The term "creeping urbanism" has been suggested to describe this process during this period (Guyot 1969).

As noted earlier, the number of padi producers has risen without an appropriate increase in the area under cultivation. In fact, the area under padi decreased from 1970 to 1975 (Third Malaysia Plan 1976:295). This adds another aspect to the change in peasant agriculture which is likely to have an important impact on urbanization (though probably a negative one), and which is going to cause considerable problems for urban administrators and planners. This aspect is the decreasing size of land holdings and the increasing shortage of padi land for farmers (Ooi 1963:194). According to the Third Malaysia Plan (1976:164), 55 per cent of all padi farmers had less than three acres and 80 per cent less than five acres of land. Tenancy is also quite high. A recalculation of the data resulting from a 1967/68 sample survey indicates that only 50.8 per cent of Malay small-holders owned their land, 23.2 per cent were tenant farmers, and 26 per cent agricultural wage-labourers (Chander 1970:90). The shortage of land is further aggravated by the extension of urban areas into former agriculture land and a displacement of peasants from their means of subsistence. Although some data are available to substantiate these claims, very little research has been done to link up the increasing shortage and increasing subdivision of land with the urbanization process. There are, however, indications that there is an increasing out-migration of Malay peasantry from the three major padi-producing areas mentioned earlier. Consequently it is likely that there will be an increase in squatters both in rural and urban areas. In fact, conflicts have arisen as spontaneous settlers from Kelantan have moved into the vicinity of planned, government-sponsored settlements in Pahang and Johor. How far the squatter areas that have developed in the Federal Territory (Pryor 1974, and others) on the outskirts of fast-growing towns like Ipoh or Butterworth (Goh and Evers 1978), or even Melaka, are occupied by direct migrants from the main padi-producing areas, by displaced estate-labourer populations, or by migrants from smaller towns, is not yet clear and needs to be researched further. The

---

a decline in subsistence production and a rising marketable surplus is a major contribution to urban economic growth.

contribution of the poverty-stricken fishing population to this kind of urbanization also needs further investigation.

Census figures at least indicate that Malay rural-urban migration has increased already during 1950-70. Pryor (1975:64) suggests that between 1957 and 1970 in absolute numbers Malay migration to towns of 10,000 and over was 32 per cent higher than that of Chinese and 69 per cent higher than that of Indians. The growing importance of Malay peasant society and economy for the fate of urban areas is further shown by recent political events in western Malaysia. On several occasions, most notably in Baling, Kedah, in 1974, and in Kota Bahru, Kelantan, in 1977, peasants marched into these towns in large numbers to demonstrate.

The growing interrelation between urban and rural areas can also be traced in social and economic terms. There appears to be a tendency for the new class of Malay bureaucrats to invest in rural land and thus become absentee land-owners. Although the acreage involved may still be small, this interrelation between urban, government employees, and rural areas is, nevertheless, significant. Similar trends are evident in the fishing industry. From a study of that industry in P. Penang and Kedah, Gibbons (1977) was able to contrast the tremendous growth of the industry with the small increase in the personal incomes of most fishermen. Most profits accrue to the owners of trawlers, most of whom are fish-dealers or businessmen formerly involved in the now defunct barter-trade with Indonesia, but civil servants and schoolteachers are also said to be involved as shareholders.

The change from the two urban circuits fueled by the economic dynamics of the two mercantile towns of Melaka and P. Penang towards a primate-city system influenced by the agrarian development of its hinterland signifies a major shift in the socio-political system of Malaysia on fairly general Southeast Asian. One might be tempted to refer to the basic topological difference and the resulting conflicts between commercial coastal states and inland empires, between pre-capitalist mercantilism and an Asiatic mode of production, between dependent and autocentric development. If we, like Denys Lombard in his "Sumbangan kepada sejarah kota-kota di Asia Tenggara", take a fairly long-term historical view, we might agree with his conclusion that "The investigator of problems of urbanization still observes in many Southeast Asian cities two underlying orientations to urban life: one, the ancient agrarian cultural orientation with the gentry civil-servant outlook on life, and two, the ancient harbour-town orientation with a more commercial outlook on life" (Lombard 1976:51). Though both outlooks are, of course, found in Malaysian cities and towns, the pendulum seems to be swinging back from the ancient harbour-towns orientation to the civil-servant outlook on life. The importance of peasant agriculture for urbanization, as outlined above, the "constant pie orientation" of Malaysian civil servants as described by Scott (1968), which appears to be similar to the "image of the limited good" described by other students of peasant societies, and the foundation of so many government-controlled and bureaucratically constituted organizations for agrarian development, all seem to substantiate this hypothesis.

Race and Class: The Structure of Malaysian Urban Society

No discussion of urbanization in Malaysia would be complete without consideration of its racial aspects, and practically all studies on the subjects refer to the ethnic distribution of Malaysia's urban population. Through the northern and southern circuits of urbanization described earlier, various immigrant communities were distributed throughout urban Malaya, and the percentage, though not the absolute number, of indigenous Malays declined until the 1950s. During the so-called "Emergency", a large section of the rural Chinese population was relocated in new villages, most of which were either located near urban areas or eventually became small towns themselves (Sandhu 1964). This massive rural-urban migration incorporated, however, a large proportion of Malays (Narayanan 1975:65). The depletion of Chinese in rural areas reduced Chinese rural-urban migration, and the creation of a population base of urban Malays eventually helped to reverse the general trend towards a complete sinicization of the urban population during the 1960s. Malaysian towns began to incorporate an ever larger group of urban Malays, particularly in the Federal Territory of Kuala Lumpur.

It is in this context that the racial riots of May 13th, 1969, which were largely confined to Kuala Lumpur City, have to be seen. This tragic incident has usually been analyzed as a race conflict between Malays and Chinese, and the slogan "Melayu boleh balik kampung" (let Malays go back to their villages), heard during the riots, has been cited as evidence that they were a conflict between Chinese urban dwellers and Malay rural-urban migrants (Goh 1971:21). Although there was definitely an essentially "racial" element involved, the social contrast between urbanites and migrants, or the political and economic difference between higher-income and lower-income groups (which was partly responsible for the defection of voters to the more radical opposition parties, namely the Democratic Action Party and Gerakan) indicates that more than race was involved. This leads to the question of the *Tiefenstruktur* (the infrastructure) of urban conflict in Malaysian towns. Is the plural character of Malaysian urban society or its social stratification, is race or class the basis of urban conflict? Although the political dimensions of this question are obvious, we shall only pursue its sociological content and try to formulate a hypothesis to guide us in our understanding of the structure of urban society in West Malaysia.

Most studies of ethnic relations in Malaysian cities deal with a relatively short period of time. In particular studies of residential segregation using the fairly broad census categories of Malays, Chinese, Indians, and others tend to emphasize stability instead of change (Lee 1977:234; Lee 1976b:55; McGee 1963:182). A more complex and long-term analysis would reveal a much more realistic pattern which, at the same time, might contribute to an explanation of the violent outbreaks of ethnic conflict that have troubled Malaysia from time to time.

"Segregation" can be understood not only in spatial but also in socio-economic, political, and cultural terms. Crucial indicators to measure these aspects would be residential proximity, degree of ethnic monopolization of occupation and income, miscegenation rates (i. e., the forming of multi-ethnic households), ethnic composition of the leadership, membership of political organizations, and the degree of assimilation of cultural traits such as language, customs, and religion. As ethnic segregation can operate differently in any of these dimensions and can change at different rates over time, the structure of Malaysia's urban plural society is very complex indeed. So far only anthropological studies of single communities in Malaysian cities have been able to reveal this complexity (e. g., Nagata 1974a).

Reverting to the earlier discussion of two circuits of urbanization in Malaysia, we are at least able to put forward a hypothesis on changing patterns of ethnic residential segregation. Again leaving aside the precolonial Malay towns, we can distinguish two basic types of urban ethnic structure, representing the centre and the periphery of the urban circuits. One may be called the "Melaka type" and the other the "pioneer city type".[27]

The Melaka type is characterized by a large number of ethnic groups, the persistence of residential quarters, high intermarriage rates, and "high degree of assimilation". The major ethnic groups themselves are highly differentiated and castes or speech groups maintain separate living quarters. Thus Mak (1977) shows how, in the Straits Settlements during the nineteenth century, Chinese speech groups were living in proximity but were separated and that secret societies and dialect associations helped to maintain territorial demarcations. Nevertheless, assimilation did occur, but it did not necessarily dissolve all the cultural differences between ethnic groups: sometimes it created a distinct culture different from the parent body of a particular ethnic group. The Baba Chinese in Melaka (as analyzed by Clammer), the Melaka Portuguese or the "Malay-Indian" (Jawi Pekan) community of P. Penang (Nagata 1974a, 1975)

---

[27]Nagata (1979) also distinguishes two types of cities and corresponding types of ethnic relations, namely traditional Malay towns (kota and pekan types) and heterogenetic colonial cities. Her prototypes are Alur Setar and Georgetown. The "pioneer city type" is distinct enough to be added here.

provide case studies of the type of ethnicity emerging in the "Melaka type" of urban ethnic structure. The situation in Bangkok also illustrates this type (Skinner 1958; Boonsanong 1971). In any case, both a certain consolidation of ethnic sub-groups and an assimilation between larger groups occurred which enabled greater cultural communication.

The "pioneer type" is characterized in the beginning by a smaller number of ethnic groups and the predominance of one. At the same time cultural and social interaction is minimal, and ethnic groups meet primarily "in the market place", as described in Furnivall's (1980) ideal typical analysis of plural society. Both types form the ends of a continuum in time and in space; they represent the centre and the periphery of the two urban circuits described earlier.

Table 1: Indices of Ethnic Diversity for Selected Towns in Peninsular Malaysia, 1833-1970.

Year	Melaka	Georgetown	Kuala Lumpur	Taiping
1833/5	(0.74)	(0.70)	-	-
1891	-	-	0.43	-
1901	-	-	0.45	0.55
1911	0.56	0.52	0.51	0.56
1921	0.52	0.50	0.56	0.57
1931	0.50	0.50	0.56	0.58
1947	0.42	0.44	0.54	0.56
1957	0.40	0.44	0.56	0.57
1970	0.41	0.45	0.60	0.58

Note: The index of ethnic diversity describes the "probability that randomly paired members of a population will be different on a specified characteristic" (Lieberson 1969:851). Zero indicates no diversity , i. e., a population consisting of one ethnic group only. See also Lee 1976a:42. The data are drawn from Census publications, Kuhne 1976, and Kuchler 1968.

When the immigrant population was distributed through the two urban circuits the new towns tended to be less ethnically diverse than the long-established centres of Melaka and Georgetown. Even within the sub-groups of the major communities, regional ethnic specialization took place and towns became dominated by one Chinese speech group or one Indian community. Over time the ethnic diversity of the pioneer towns must have risen in relation to that of the centres, though detailed studies on the subject still remain to be done. An ethnic diversity index used by Lee (1976b:42 and 1977:231-3) and here calculated for the period of earlier urban growth not covered by that author gives some confirmation that this hypothesis may indeed be tenable. Thus, the ethnic diversity index for the city of Melaka has fallen from the high value of a 0.74 in 1833 to 0.41 in 1970, whereas the diversity index for Kuala Lumpur has risen from 0.43 in 1891 to 0.60 in 1970. Even more pronounced is the picture if we look at one of the small mining towns in the Kinta Valley, Lahat for example. In 1901 this was an almost completely Chinese town with a diversity index of 0.1. However, by 1970, the index had risen to 0.4 (approximately the same as that for Melaka).

Whether or not ethnic diversity is still increasing, as we have noted for Kuala Lumpur and some other towns, it still needs to be studied. In any case, increasing diversity does not mean that residential segregation is declining at the same time. Thus, McGee (1963:182) notes with surprise that, in Kuala Lumpur between 1947 and 1957, "a period of rapid population growth and expansion of the city, the basic patterns of ecological segregation which existed in 1947 did not change very much". A similar conclusion is reached by Lee Boon Thong, who concludes, on the basis of a fairly sophisticated analysis of census data, that "Since independence in 1957, the basic ethnic structure of Peninsular Malaysian urban centres remained largely unchanged despite the greater involvement of the Malay population in the urbanization process. This is largely because of the strong tendency for the ethnic characteristics of the urban areas to be perpetuated over the years rather than diversified" (Lee 1977:234). But Lee also shows that urban centres differed in their trends towards ethnic homogeneity or heterogeneity. On the other hand, these authors cannot help noticing that during both intercensus periods "the ethnically more mixed middle and upper-class residential areas expanded" (McGee 1963:184; Lee 1976b:45). And it is precisely this trend that appears to be worth noticing. Residential quarters in which residence is determined not by race but by social class reflect a new principle of social and spatial organization in Malaysia and it is worthwhile to investigate how this development came about.

Before exact studies based on survey data are available, one might have to accept the argument presented in an earlier paper (Evers 1975b). The starting point of the argument is the process of rapid bureaucratization already described. As analyzed by Tilman (1964), British expatriates slowly vacated their positions and, at the same time, their high-status residence areas. The spacious colonial bungalows, set amidst landscaped lawns, were taken over by the new, indigenous bureaucratic élite. Although British officers were replaced mainly by Malays, other ethnic groups served as replacements, particularly in the technical services, so that a mixing of ethnic groups occurred. With the rapid growth of the civil service and related government agencies, particularly in the educational field, residential quarters for government employees also proliferated. The best known example is, of course, the satellite town of Petaling Jaya (McGee and McTaggart 1967; Kuhne 1971). In these new housing schemes, rank and position in the civil service rather than race became the determining factor for residential allocation. Industrialization, or at least the establishment of large firms or headquarters of multinational corporations, tended to have a similar impact. Living quarters for senior staff and housing estates for workers now tend to be racially integrated but distinct in terms of social class.[28]

Now one could argue that the ethnically mixed areas contain only a small proportion of the urban population (Lee 1976b:7), but still the individual areas tend to be large and therefore significant for the ecology of urban areas. Furthermore, the emergence of quite distinct ethnic patterns in upper-class and lower-class districts and the fast expansion of a new middle-class appears to support our earlier hypothesis that social class is becoming the more important factor in shaping the social and spatial structure of Malaysian and, indeed, Southeast Asian towns (Evers 1975b:785).

The third new factor in the urbanization process of Malaysia is the change in the peasant economy and the growing rural-urban migration. These migrants first flocked into areas occupied by their own ethnic group: thus, some inner kampung of Kota Bahru quickly deteriorated into slums (Clarke 1976). In the Malay settlement of Kampung Bahru, in the middle of Kuala Lumpur, overcrowding occurred, squatter settlements sprung up, and vacant land that had formerly separated ethnic groups was filled with new migrants. Ecological invasion by one ethnic group of the territory of another ethnic group became frequent. On the other hand, an analysis based on data from the 1970 census aggregated on an enumeration-block (EB) level shows that as yet only 7.3 per cent of Kuala Lumpur's 997 EBs are racially "integrated" in the sense that (a) representatives of all three major communities are found and (b) a majority community does not account for more than 60 per cent of the population per enumeration block (Oestereich 1978). As no comparative data from earlier years are provided, there is, however, no way of showing whether the 1970 situation presents a higher or lower degree of segregation in comparison to earlier years or to other towns.[29]

---

[28]As Cohen has pointed out, expatriates "tend to be ecologically segregated from their hosts, though not necessarily spatially concentrated" (Cohen 1976:32).They share their neighborhood with the Westernized upper class of their host countries and interact socially only with other expatriates or with local élites (Betke, Weitekamper and Grunewald 1978).

[29]There might also be a bias in drawing the EB boundaries to include ethnically homogeneous residential clusters within an EB.

The hypothesis of an increasing differentiation of urban areas by class seems to be well founded, though further studies are necessary to prove the point beyond doubt.[30] Nevertheless, the fact remains that, particularly in low-class areas, ethnic segregation, ethnic differences, and at times ethnic conflict remain. Class and ethnicity are thus both important aspects in explaining the internal structure and the social, economic, and political processes in Malaysian towns during the post-colonial phase.

Another issue that has so far received little attention from urban researchers might further highlight the issue of race and class in urban Malaysia. Although ethnic residential segregation both indicates and determines patterns of interaction, the legal ownership of land signifies control over urban space and urban resources. Land-ownership implies ownership and control over the means of living, an important aspect of class relations. The importance of land-ownership became evident when the increasing pressure on urban land led to waves of land speculation in the 1970s and to spiraling land prices (Evers 1976). The increase in land prices was, however, severely differentiated, and the gap between cheap and expensive land was widened. As soon as land prices rose in a favoured area, low-income tenants were removed and higher-income groups moved in. In general, the differentiation of land prices has further increased the residential segregation by ethnic groups. The integration tends to be much higher in upper middle and upper-class areas, where a Westernized style of life and a common consumption pattern reduce ethnic differences, as already analyzed in McGee and McTaggart's study of Petaling Jaya (1967:37). The situation is less favourable in the city centres, which tend to be owned and occupied by Chinese.

---

[30]Some recent studies have, however, pointed out that particularly Malay traditional values are set against the development of a class consciousness (Bador 1973; Nagata 1975; Provencher 1977). Another interpretation of ethnic cultural values in the urbanization process is provided in Evers (1977), where Malay and Chinese conceptions of space are analyzed.

Table 2: Ownership of Urban Land and Population by Ethnicity in West
Malaysian Towns, 1975-76 (Sample of Sixteen Towns)

Percentage of	Malays	Chinese	Indians	Others
Urban land owned	29	61	9	1
Population	30	58	11	1
Percentage balance	-1	+3	-2	-

Source: Urban Land-ownership Study, Centre for Policy Research, USM, directed by Hans-
Dieter Evers and Goh Ban Lee

Location and control over space is particularly important for the larger
participation of Malays in commercial activities. Only by acquiring access to
central business districts can Malays achieve commercial participation. As the
government has taken steps to give bumiputra access to urban land either
through rental arrangements or ownership, the results of this policy are definitely
felt. On the other hand, an increasing Malay urban population is faced with
decreasing Malay ownership of urban land during the 1970s, as has been shown
in a survey on urban land-ownership in sixteen Malaysian towns.[31] In 1975 of all
the land in these urban areas whose owners could be ethnically identified (i. e.,
excluding land owned by the government and by public corporations), 29 per
cent was owned by the Malays, 61 per cent by Chinese, 9 per cent by Indians,
and 1 per cent by other ethnic groups. Overall, this is more or less matched by
the ethnic distribution of the population in these towns, giving the Chinese only
a slightly higher share in the ownership of urban land than is warranted by their
population size. However, the situation differs considerably from town to town,
and the statistics have to be interpreted with caution because of the inclusion of
rural areas and Malay reservations (kawasan Melayu) within city boundaries.
There also appears to be a trend towards a higher concentration of land-
ownership in Chinese hands. Despite an increase in the Malay urban population,
Malays have lost land to Chinese during the 1970s (comparing present
ownership with ownership before the last transfer of land recorded). The other

[31]This study was carried out by H. - D. Evers and Goh Ban Lee under the auspices of the
Centre for Policy Research, Universiti Sains Malaysia, Penang. The sixteen towns studied
represent various settlement types but exclude the Federal Territory. Although the sample
cannot be regarded as representative in a strict methodological sense, the wide range of towns
selected from all over Peninsular Malaysia at least seems to indicate general trends and
patterns reasonably well. A comparison of the overall ethnic distribution of the urban
population in 1970 and the ethnic distribution of the population in our sample towns (the two
being almost identical) adds considerable credence to the suggestion that the data presented in
our urban-land-ownership study are roughly representative. See Goh and Evers (1977).

large ethnic group losing urban land are the Indians. It appears that a not insignificant part of urban land sold was formerly owned by Chettiar moneylenders (Evers 1978).

On the basis of the few available data we might thus conclude that the balance between urban land-ownership and urban population is only slightly tilted in favour of the Chinese. There is, however, increasing pressure on Malays and Indians, the two urban minority groups, to sell land to the Chinese, which may be the result of an extension of residential areas into the urban fringe and the building of housing estates for middle-income groups. Lower-income groups, to which a large section of the urban Malay population belongs, are forced to sell and either to move beyond the city limits to squatter areas or to become tenants in low-cost housing projects.

In this process the growing importance of class distinction becomes evident.[32] The rising cost of land and houses - the impact of which on residential segregation by class has already been mentioned above - leads to a considerable strengthening of an urban landowning class that comes into possession of a huge and constantly growing "urban capital stock" consisting of urban land and buildings. The concentration of land-ownership is indeed very high. Thus, the survey of urban land-ownership in sixteen Malaysian towns revealed that 5 per cent of the landowners owned 52.8 per cent of the urban land in these towns. 73.3 per cent of the top landowners were Chinese, 17.4 per cent Malays and 8.9 per cent Indians. Unfortunately, there are no figures available as yet to calculate the concentration of land-ownership in terms of land values rather than in acreages. But even without these figures it is obvious that an urban landowning class controls a large proportion of the nation's fixed urban capital. In general, our data give no cause to contradict a statement made by McTaggart and Teoh (1972:7): "If property ownership turns out to be significant as a device which ensures continued pre-eminence to whomsoever holds the most of the choicest urban land, efforts to improve the performance of the Malays may simply enhance the value of Chinese real estate."

---

[32]We maintain this position despite Shamsul's claim that the question of race or class is "caught in the epitemological space created and controlled by a framework of colonial knowledge" (Shamsul 1998: 44).

Table 3: Changes in urban land-ownership by ethnic groups in Peninsular Malaysia, 1975-6 (Sample of sixteen towns)

	MALAY	CHINESE	INDIAN
Sold (Acres)	506.9	354.4	718.7
Bought (Acres)	283.4	991.1	305.5
Balance	-223.5	+636.7	-413.2

Conclusions

The present chapter has attempted an interpretation of long-term processes of urbanization in Malaysia rather than a factual account based on census statistics. Three major hypotheses were advanced:

1. From the middle of the nineteenth century two major "circuits of urbanization" extended the new colonial mode of production to the west coast of Malaysia. Melaka and P. Penang were the original centres of these two circuits.

2. Bureaucratization, industrialization, and changes in the peasant economy have emerged as the major factors in the urbanization process in post-colonial Malaysia. Particularly the commercialization of peasant agriculture and a decline in subsistence production have fostered both small-town growth and migration to metropolitan centres.

3. Though ethnicity still remains a major factor in explaining the social ecology of Malaysian towns, social class has emerged as the major structuring principle of Malaysian urban society.

Though conclusive data are still lacking, it appears that a decrease in residential segregation by race in middle and upper-class areas, together with a general increase in residential segregation by occupation and income, that is by social class, can be discerned. There is, however, little evidence that ethnic cultural differences are being eliminated and that the "Melaka model" of assimilation is being followed. A high and possibly increasing concentration of urban land-ownership, a concentration of urban assets and pronounced income disparities all point to the consolidation of a social-class structure cutting across ethnic lines. We might, therefore, conclude that socio-economic or class differences represent the *Tiefenstruktur*, which is, however, overgrown and partly concealed by elaborate ethnic and cultural patterns. Simple correlations between census categories such as ethnicity and occupation do not do justice to the intricate relationship between race and class in urban Malaysia.

3. Meaning and Power in the Construction of Urban Space

The Cultural Construction of the Theravadha Buddhist City

Isaac (1961:12ff) differentiates between those religions in which the meaning of human existence derives from revelation, and those in which human order is believed to be brought into being at the creation of the world itself. In the first concept, underlying Christianity and Islam, no one place is intrinsically more holy than another. The divine is abstracted from the landscape, and any place can be made sacred through a ritual as a place for ceremonies. In Christianity, Jesus is with the believers wherever and whenever they pray. Heaven and earth are two opposing spheres which cannot be connected, except in an abstract way through praying. The connection between heaven, earth and hell is achieved at the end of time, after the final judgment. In the second concept, which prevails in Asia, it is possible to reproduce a version of the cosmos on earth. Sacred space is achieved through imitating cosmic archetypes. While in the first concept the religion has little impact on the transformation of the landscape, the second concept can become a powerful idea for the creation of landscape.

The cities, temples and monuments are attempts to replicate the cosmos. However, some locations are regarded as having already been created by the gods more sacred than others. Initially the intrinsic sacredness of the location had to be elucidated, and defined as a fixed central point from whence the sacredness spread in all directions. Through this point passes the world axis, usually symbolized as a world pillar, a lotus flower, a mountain etc. If no clear indications of an intrinsic sacredness exists, if, in other words, the location used to be "savage" and "chaos", the act of creation of the world has to be symbolically repeated (Eliade 1986:22).

To the same extent that the temple or city is constructed on the basis of archetypes, an architectural symbolism is connected to the centre. Following Eliade three major symbols are connected in the centre and combined there:

1. The sacred mountain where heaven and earth are articulated;

2. any temple, palace or ritual monument is a holy mountain and thus a centre;

3. the sacred city or the temple is the axis mundi and therefore the articulation between heaven, earth and underworld (Eliade 1986:25ff).

These concepts are not exclusively Asian, as Eliade shows. In fact the idea of the city as the centre, constructed on the basis of the idea of a heavenly city, a place for communication with the gods and therefore an articulation between heaven and earth, was probably crucial for the emergence of ceremonial ritual sites into centres and cities in all regions of generic urbanization (Wheatley 1967).[33] Wheatley concludes for the Asian city: "This central axis of the universe, of the kingdom, the city, or the temple could be moved to a more propitious site or duplicated whenever circumstances rendered this desirable, for it was an attribute of existential rather than of geometric space. From this point, the holy of holies at whichever hierarchical level it might occur, the four horizons were projected outwards to the cardinal points of the compass, thus assimilating the group's territory, whether tribal land, kingdom, or city to the cosmic order, and constructing a sanctified space or habitabilis. The sacred space delimited in this manner within the continuum of profane space provided the framework within which could be conducted the rituals necessary to ensure that intimate harmony between the macro-cosmos and the micro-cosmos without which there could be no prosperity in the world of men" (Wheatley 1972:417f). The discussion of the ritual construction of the Theravadha Buddhist city takes "dualism in its different social expressions" (J.P.B. de Josselin de Jong 1977:164-182) as starting-point. Popular Theravadha Buddhism is typified by an ethical dualism, not a cosmic one. The important opposition is that between lokottara, or otherworldly, that is, related to the next world, i. e. after rebirth, and laukika, or the mundane, worldly, pertaining to this world (Ames 1964:41; Evers 1972c:104; Dumont 1962:47-77). Lokottara and laukika are connected with a host of contrasting values. One stresses withdrawal from the activities of this world, the other active involvement; one stresses giving without hope of reward, the other exchange or bribes; one demands humility in this life, the other power and wealth; one demands abstention from sensual and sexual pleasures, the other sex and fertility.

The Buddha on the one hand and the gods on the other are clearly linked with these two contrasting value orientations. The king's position in this scheme is

---

[33]Outside Asia, in later cosmologies, namely Christianity and Islam, a new view of sacredness was developed though in which the city did not play a decisive role any more. In the monotheistic religions only one centre could exist, namely Rome or Jerusalem for Christianity and Mecca and Medina for Islam. As it is impossible for all believers to reside at this centre, communication with God is possible at any place, and it is sufficient to visit the centre more or less regularly through a specific meditative journey, the pilgrimage, notably if special wishes are to be granted. Although not included in the cosmology as such, the centre is regarded as a particularly auspicious location for the communication with God and the granting of wishes.

interesting. The term lokottara also designates a king or sovereign (Clough 1982:544), perhaps alluding to the component uttara (pre-eminent), but the common meaning of the term, "otherworldly", is certainly not lost. In practice the king was of course involved in the affairs of this world, i. e. his actions are laukika. On the other hand, he was referred to as lokottara (otherworldly). He was sometimes called a god, at other times a Bodhisattva or, at least in Burma, even a Buddha (Sarkisyanz 1965) and Chakkravarthin (world conqueror). The king was the protector of the Sangha, therefore he built monasteries and endowed them with land (Evers 1969b). On the other hand, fertility rites have been traditionally associated with kingship as evidenced by royal rainmaking ceremonies in Sri Lanka and Thailand. The king could thus be seen as a mediator or broker between laukika and lokottara; between the Buddha and the gods (Evers 1972c:104-125). The division between laukika and lokottara, mediated by the king, is spatially expressed in the royal cities and thus made visible and permanent.

The first cities constructed following Buddhist ritual concepts were built in Sri Lanka. Of particular interest is how Buddhist ideas lead to modifications of earlier, Brahmin urban concepts. These play a role not only in the earlier Sri Lankan cities, but have a strong impact on other Southeast Asian cities too.

The Ritual Structure of the Early Capitals of Sri Lanka

The first capital city of a state with island-wide significance emerged in Sri Lanka about three centuries before Christ, following the waves of Aryan settlers who invaded Sri Lanka from southern India. Anuradhapura became the capital when the economic and social development necessitated the concentration of skills and power for further spatial extension. According to the chronicles, Anuradhapura was founded by a hero and thereby history started (Wickremeratne 1987:48). For the establishment of those structures necessary for a state, the settlers depended on Indian concepts, craftsmen, artisans, etc. In addition, the royal consorts came principally from southern India. Until the rise of Buddhism the Brahmins were the predominant advisers of the élite and could provide clear concepts of administration and of selection of sites for cities and for building cities. "The central notion was the concept of the vastu or the site, and of its intrinsic sacrality. The proper divination of a site by means of omens, its sanctification, the propitiation of the vastupati or the deity of the site, notions of centrality or axiality, which determined what could be built at the cardinal points, were all integral elements of the ideology" (Ray 1964:49ff).

The major concept was the Mandala with Brahma, or the essence of the cosmos, in the centre. The arrangement of other squares in an outward direction were the locales for gods, in a descending order of importance. The main temple and the temples of other important gods within the broader temple complex was closely connected to the palace. The houses of other high state officials and those associated with the temple were clustered around the temple in accordance with their rank. As the streets were on the one hand the path through which cosmic power spread outwards into the kingdom, and on the other hand the path on which the profane gained access to the city, it was crucial to have specific protections for those structures of highest sacrality. Building walls and demarcating streets as royal streets which were forbidden to be used by commoners provided such a protection. "In political terms the walls dramatized the distinction between a sacredly ordained ruling élite and the common people" (Wickremeratne 1987:51).[34]

With the arrival of Buddhism in Sri Lanka the sacred structure of the capital had to be modified. Instead of Brahma, a centre had to be defined in line with Buddhist principles, and the sacredness of the city, on which the central power based its legitimacy, had to be defined in new terms. "The essence of the changes was the implanting of a new ideology. Its ontological, esoteriological, and eschatological dimensions postulated the relationship of the city dweller to the cosmos and to the transcendent realism beyond human perception and empirical experience. ... The sacred city had, as it were, to be re-established and the new metaphors of sacrality defined and internalized. Three processes were involved: first, the virtual extrapolation of a theory of sacrality drawn from within the matrix of the new ideology; secondly, the demonstration of its validity; and thirdly, the techniques and methodologies of its ritual validation" (Wickremeratne 1987:52). All this was achieved when Mahinda, the Buddhist monk, walked through the city and identified different spots as related to former visits of Buddha to Sri Lanka. The sacredness of the spots identified was validated by the shaking of the earth.

The new centre is indicated firstly by the place from where Mahinda starts his walks to identify the sacred sites. This spot is finally defined as centre through the bringing and planting of a branch of the original Bodhi tree under which Buddha received enlightenment. "It was the Bodhi tree which symbolized the reconciliation of the macrocosm with the microcosm. Therefore, in term of Buddhist cosmic notions it could lay just claim to being the true axis mundi. By bringing a branch of the Bodhi tree to Lanka, the island itself became part of this axiality. The site of Bodhi tree in Mahamegha Park thus became the central point in the sacral complex of Anuradhapura" (Wickremeratne 1987:55).

---

[34]This is reminiscent of the connection between Sangha and kingship as described for Pagan by Aung-Thwin (1987). However, the difference is that in Sri Lanka the political élite did not have close kinship ties to the religious élite.

But still, one problem remained to be solved. The Bodhi tree and most of the other sites identified as sacred were outside of the city. Accordingly, there are two centres: the Bodhi tree as sacred centre outside the city, and the royal palace as centre of the city. This duality resembles the dualism of secular power, centred around the palace, and spiritual power and order, centred around the Bodhi tree. This duality was resolved by the king conducting a ceremony of a ritual plowing of the surroundings of Anuradhapura, encompassing the city and the sacred sites, thus creating a symbiosis between kingship and religion or the Sangha (Wickremeratne 1987:56).

A problem arose when Anuradhapura had to be abandoned in the eleventh century as a result of attacks and invasions by the Cola empire. Although Polonaruva had many of the features of a universal sacred city, just like Anuradhapura, the Bodhi tree could no longer provide continuity as the centre of sacrality, as it was outside of the realm of Polonaruva. The tooth relic and the alms bowl relic fulfilled the function of defining the centre, which always implied the centre of the whole island, and continuity. "The Dalada (tooth relic) alone of all the relics ingeniously filled an obvious vacuum. More significantly, the political need for a symbol of legitimization was met by the Dalada. The simple fact that the Dalada, lone of all great relics of the Buddha in Sri Lanka, could be carried from place to place clearly enhanced its potentialities. As Singhalese Buddhist political power shifted to other parts of the island, one feature invariably recurred: the deliberate continuity of the palace of the Templum Sacrum. In time the abstraction of sacrality gave way to a simple formula: that whosoever possessed the Dalada had the right to rule the island" (Wickremeratne 1987:57). Thus the Dalada still up to the present allows the definition of a sacred centre (Kandy at present) and defines continuity.

The Kandyan kingdom emerged after a split from the Kotte kingdom at the beginning of the sixteenth century. In many respects, it can be regarded as the successor of the Anuradhapura and Polonaruva kingdoms. After the final fall of the Kotte kingdom in southern Sri Lanka to the Portuguese in 1597 (in 1551 the King of Kotte became a vassal of the Portuguese and in 1597 the Portuguese were the de jure rulers of Kotte), Kandy was the only place left in which the Buddhist tradition from Anuradhapura was continued in the temples of Malvatta, and in particular of Asgiriya. Furthermore, Kandy is the city of the Dalada Maligawa, the temple of the tooth.

In the Kandyan kingdom the Sangha and the state were closely connected. Besides the king as the protector and supporter of religion, the aristocracy and the Sangha were interrelated through kinship ties.[35] Only those monks who came from a "good" family could receive a high ordination, and the pupil, thereby the successor of the monk, was usually a blood relative of the teacher (Evers 1967a). The Sangha was not a force apart from the aristocracy but part and parcel of it (Dewaraja 1988:164ff).

On ascending the throne, the king sought the blessing of the guardian spirits, which were Hindu deities residing in a temple in front of the palace, and then received his name from these deities. Dewaraja interprets this ceremony as follows: "The naming ceremony seems to suggest that the ruler of the people's choice had received the approval and blessing of the guardian deities" (Dewaraja 1988:263). It did not imply that the king himself became an incarnation of a Hindu god. As Dewaraja points out, firstly, the idea of divinity is entirely foreign to Buddhism, and secondly "in countries like Siam and Sri Lanka, which claimed to adhere to the Theravadha Buddhist doctrine the Hindu gods were reduced to minor deities ministering the needs of the Buddha. It would not have been very flattering for a Buddhist king to be told he was an incarnation of a Hindu deity and nothing more. The conception of a king in Buddhist countries was that of a Bodhisatva or an incipient Buddha" (Dewaraja 1988:264).

As we have pointed out earlier (Evers, 1967b, 1972c) there is a parallelism of three structures in the socio-religious concepts used in Kandy, namely the Buddhist temple of the tooth (Dalada Maligawa), the temple for the Hindu deities, and the palace. These differing structures focus on either worldly or otherworldly aspects. The deities are related to involvement in everyday life while the Buddhist temple focuses on withdrawal from the activities of this world. The position of the king is most interesting as he "could be seen as the mediator between laukika and lokottara, between the Buddha and the gods and eventually between cosmos and world" (Evers 1972c:105). This argument is reminiscent of the proposition made by Wickremeratne in regard to the shift of the metaphors of sacrality in Anuradhapura. "The actual physical configuration of Anuradhapura seemed to reinforce the implied polarity. The walls of the city enclosed the palace and the original (Brahman, R. K.) Temple, whereas the more sacrally significant sites, ..., stand outside the city walls. ... The paradox is resolved by Devanampiyatissa when he furrows the land in a circle, encompassing in its broad sweep both the city and the sacred sites" (Wickremratne1987:55f).

---

[35]It is interesting that the Portuguese built a church behind the temples of the Hindu deities in the sixteenth century. Thus the whole complex combines state power through the palace, Buddhism and cosmological order through the temple of the tooth, Hinduism and Christianity

The "Temple of the Tooth" (Dalada Maligawa) is part of the original royal temple, it is not a monastery. Buddhist monks (bhikkhus) officiating at the temple are drawn from the two major monasteries: Malvatta and Asgiriya Vihara. The first and larger one (60 to over 100 monks during the time of my field work 1964-68) is situated within the town, close to the temples and the royal palace, the other up the hill just outside the former city limits. Though both belong to the same sect (Siyam Nikaya), their name and location indicate the division of the Buddhist order into gamavasin (village or town monks) and aranyavasin (forest monks) - or, in generalized terms of ritual space, the opposition between city and countryside, between habitat and wilderness.

In Kandy parallelism between the structures and their symbiosis is clearly expressed in the morphology of the city. On the slope of a mountain is the complex consisting of palace, temple of the tooth and temples of the guardian deities. The palace is located slightly higher than the temple of the tooth, separated from and connected to the temple by a common wall. On a lower level, separated from the palace-temple complex by walls and a street, are the enwalled temples of the guardian deities, frequented predominantly by women. Further down are the houses of the higher officials, and in the valley the market-place with the city proper. In morphological terms the palace-temple complex is separated from the city proper, overlooking and dominating the city from its higher position. This was enforced by the prohibition to build houses higher than two storeys. The appearance of the palace-temple complex as the most beautiful was achieved through the prohibition to use mud or tiles for the houses "so that the palace in Kandy, of very modest dimensions, appeared like a magnificent edifice to the highlanders who had seen nothing better" (Dewaraja 1988:268).

The capital city of Kandy had, indeed, a clearly discernible ritual structure, but the respective institutions were outward-directed. Unlike churches in European cities of the late middle ages the temples were not primarily institutions of the city, but of the realm in general. The deities in the temples of the gods (devala) were guardian deities in the city, but for Sri Lanka, the Dalada Maligava was a shrine for the most important relic of the Buddha whose magical power legitimized the king and protected the kingdom.

The Ritual Structure of the Mainland Southeast Asian City: Mandalay and Ayudhya

Turning to the mainland Southeast Asian scenario, in the Ayudhyan concept the king was a Buddhist Devaraja. As such he ceased to be regarded as a god, as this would be in contradiction to Buddhist belief, but was instead similar to a reborn Buddha. The Ayudhya idea in this regard fuses the Hindu view of the king as god or demigod with the Buddhist concept of the king as righteous ruler who through his righteousness and Kharma brings prosperity to the kingdom.

This idea follows quite closely the concept of the king who fulfills sacred functions and by this establishes and protects an ordered, prosperous cosmos.

The Burmese concept was based on the earlier Pagan idea of the king as Kharmaraja or Dharmaraja, a king who due to his Kharma and merit is in the position of kingship. Here as well, the righteousness of the king, his morality and justice are regarded as the basis for the prosperity of the kingdom. In the Burmese concept, however, the notion of Chakkravadhin (world conqueror) became important (Liebermann 1984:69ff).

Obviously in both cases the definition of the king as righteous ruler is insufficient, since on this basis any misfortune can be directly blamed on the king and his moral misdeeds; furthermore, righteousness does not provide any legitimization for domination of other centres and finally the legitimacy of the monarchy as an institution is based on the person of the king. The consequence is a strong integration of the king into the Sangha, thus making the symbiosis between sacrality and secularity difficult. Potentially the Sangha can become too powerful for the king, as actually did happen in Angor and Pagan.

The legitimacy of centrality and over-regional rule was derived from the king either as sacred ruler (Dharmaraja), or as world conqueror (Chakkravadhin). As sacred ruler the king was the only one able to engage in specific sacred rituals on which the prosperity of the realm and all his subjects depended, and who, in these rituals, harmonized the cosmos and the world. For the world conqueror, success in military conquest indicates the king's power and his merit. The position of king, i. e. his secular power as a conqueror, is legitimated through religion. The result in both cases is the same: only the person in the position of king is able to synthesize secular and sacred affairs, thereby bringing prosperity to the realm and bringing the world in harmony with the cosmos. Thus, a king is a necessity for the prosperity of the realm and the people in general, but who occupies this position is open. In the Burmese case, worldly power, i. e. success in warfare provides sacredness, in the Ayudhyan case sacred ritual, i. e. the ability to conduct certain rituals, provides worldly power.

The sacred ruler as the one gaining legitimacy from his singular ability to engage in sacred rituals depended on persons versed and knowledgeable in these rituals - the court Brahmins - and on the possession of the necessary symbols and paraphernalia for the rituals. One symbol in this context was the capital city as a sacred centre, with the necessary structures of sacredness and centrality like the world mountain, important relics, temples and the palace. The destruction of the capital and the deportation of the Brahmins accordingly was more than merely the fall of a city: it was a severe disruption and destruction of state organization, culture and society - in short, it was the destruction of a world.

In Burma, the sacredness of the capital and the palace derived from the power of the ruler. Accordingly, any place could become the exemplary centre through the power of the king. Only under the condition that the king in fact was powerful, was the exemplary centre a real centre. Special knowledgeable persons like the Brahmins were less necessary in Burma, as secular power was the precondition for sacredness. The main danger, however, was that any misfortune could directly be blamed on the king, and any loss of the king's power implied a loss of legitimacy. In this regard, the shift of the capital city can be viewed as an attempt by the king to bring his secular power and his sacrality into harmony again.

The Burmese concept places an importance on the dynasty, as the king is a successor of a "world conqueror", but little importance on the locality. Through the king, any place with a given sacrality can be defined as the centre. Thus shifts of the capital can easily be made, while the continuity of the dynasty is of greater importance. In contrast in the Ayudhyan concept the sacrality of the centre is of importance and its major construction, existing independent of the individual king. The result is constant dynastic changes but a continuity of the centre.

In Burma, during the period starting with the integration of the region into one kingdom until integration into the British colonial empire, there are only two dynasties but several shifts of the capital city. In Siam in contrast, Ayudhya was the centre for more than 400 years while the dynasties changed quite often. Shifts of dynasties in Burma were due to foreign intervention (fall of the Tougoo dynasty due to attacks from the Mon kingdom of Pegu, fall of Konbaug dynasty due to British colonial conquest).

Until the advent of British colonialism in Burma, most of the history of mainland Southeast Asia was defined by the struggle between these two mighty kingdoms, able to raise armies of up to a hundred thousand soldiers. In these struggles the conquest of the other was possible, but domination and control for a lasting period always proved impossible. The state organization of the two states bears several similarities and it is impossible to argue who borrowed and learned from whom. Clearly, there was a continuous diffusion between both resulting from the deportation of populations following the wars and through embassies. "Certainly the courts of Ava and Ayudhya in the early seventeenth century had reliable information on one another, through Mon intermediaries and diplomatic embassies" (Liebermann 1984:288). I would argue that the major difference concerns the position and role of the capital city in the process of state formation and conceptualization of kingship.

Mandalay: The Exemplary Centre of Burma

The founding of Mandalay by king Mindon in 1857 is related to two major issues. On the one hand, Mindon had in mind a prophecy of Buddha's that on the 2400th anniversary of Buddhism a metropolis and a centre for Buddhist teaching would be at the foot of Mandalay hill; on the other hand he intended to gain merit and thereby compensate for the injustices and atrocities which occurred in Amarapura. Mindon envisage a revitalization of Burma by strengthening his role as protector and sponsor of Buddhism. With astrologers the location for the new capital was selected and the city designed. This design is still clearly visible today in the palace complex, built as a huge square, and the layout of the living areas in the city in an axial gridwork pattern, with special quarters assigned for the different occupations.

The layout of the palace in a square form, with the walls facing the cardinal directions, and altogether twelve gates (one in the centre of the walls, two smaller ones flanking the main gate), reinforced by big towers resembles features of the Chinese city. Probably the general layout of Mandalay was influenced by Chinese concepts, which were used quite extensively in other cities in northern Southeast Asia like Chiang Mai, Chiang Saen etc. The pattern for the arrangement of the different structures within the palace complex, however, followed the Indian/Singhalese pattern. The entrance of the palace complex was in the east, and the main audience hall faced east (not to the south as in the Chinese city) and was located exactly in the centre. "While seated in the audience hall, the king faced east and from there could see straight down the main road through the east gate to the Shan Hills from where the sun would appear each morning at the first court session. When the king was seated there, princes of the blood were placed north (or left, the more auspicious side) while the ministers would stand in the south. The architectural angles created by the construction of the audience hall resembled (stylized) peacocks, symbol of the Solar Dynasty, to whose union with the (female) Lunar dynasty the Burmese kings traced their lineage. In fact, the figures of the peacock and the rabbit, symbols of the sun and moon, were carved on their respective sides on the seat of the Lion Throne" (Aung-Thwin 1987:91). As D.G.E. Hall (1977) points out, "to the Burmese Mandalay was Shwemyo, 'the golden city'; its official Pali name was Yadanabon, 'cluster of gems'" (Hall 1977:619).

Mandalay was, due to Mandalay hill, intrinsically sacred. The sacredness was enforced through the selection of the location for the palace and the main buildings by astrologers. The king, who due to his merit was king, resided on this sacred space and set the conditions for transforming the city into Jambudipa, the "take off point" for paradise. "This sacred energy also enabled the human world to be linked to the Burmese realm of the nats (spirits), thereby completing the relationship between heaven, earth and the supernatural world. The rituals that legitimated, legalized, 'officialized', and most clearly and conspicuously 'explained' this link occurred at the capital" (Aung-Thwin 1987:99).

What in the Singhalese concept were the Hindu guardian deities are in Mandalay the Burmese nats (spirits). Of these nats, thirty-seven are guardians of the state and royal family, under the overlordship of a female and male nat, resembling the human royal couple. Just as the king ruled the different provinces, these nats protected the supernatural territory of the capital city. The king regularly paid his respects to these nats in a special hall. "The homage relationship which occurred concurrently between the crown and its supernatural patrons and/or ancestors on the one hand and its human 'vassals' on the other, a ritual performed only at the capital city in this room, made clear that the capital was not only a model for human-supernatural relationships, but the most proper site whereby sacred space, sacred time, and sacred energy coalesced" (Aung-Thwin 1987:100).

On the foot of Mandalay Hill the Kuthodaw Pagoda (great work of royal merit Pagoda) was established and following the fifth Buddhist Synod in 1872, the Tripitaka (Buddhist teachings) was engraved into stone slabs, sheltered by small pagodas. Thus Mindon tried to emerge as the protector of Buddhism and as a righteous ruler through his support of Buddhism. Following the wars with the British and the loss of the commercially important territories, the Burmese king was unable to establish his position on the basis of military power. Accordingly, to legitimate himself as Chakkravadhin, he had to focus on the religious aspects. Thus Mandalay was the social, political, religious and ideological centre of Burma while real power increasingly centred around Rangoon, the centre of British colonial administration.

The centrality of Mandalay as the capital derives from its intrinsic sacrality which, however, does not by itself define it as a centre. Other places and pagodas in Burma are at least as sacred as Mandalay Hill. Mandalay became a centre through the combination of its intrinsic sacrality with the sacrality of the king, which had to be shown through success in conquest, righteousness and the protection and sponsorship of Buddhism.

In the Singhalese case continuity and centrality were defined by the symbiosis of kingship with sacrality, defined by relics (especially the Dalada or tooth relic), and secularity, based on Hindu guardian deities. As the relict could be carried along, the centres could shift. What was important though was that the newly established centre had to be arranged as an expression of the symbiosis. In the Burmese case the centres could shift due to the intrinsic sacrality of several places and the sacrality of the king. In both cases the centres functioned as "exemplary" centres, not necessarily as real centres. In fact, in Sri Lanka the real centre, after the British took over from the Dutch, was and up to now still is in Colombo, not in Kandy. In Burma, the real centre emerged at Rangoon, a city founded in the eighteenth century in the course of the conquest of the Mon territory, with an intrinsic sacrality indicated by the Shwedagon and Sule pagoda, not in Mandalay.

Ayudhya was the exemplary centre, like Mandalay, and the real centre as well. Rule was only possible from this centre and its legitimacy was based on the domination of this centre, i. e. access to the symbols and paraphernalia of sacrality. Accordingly, Ayudhya had to fulfill the requirements of an exemplary and a real centre for commerce and administration.

Ayudhya: Exemplary and Real Centre

Ayudhya was founded sometime in the middle of the fourteenth century by Uthong, according to Charnvit (1976) probably the son of a Chinese trader from Lopburi, married to a princess from Suphanburi. Ayudhya was located at the junction of the Chao Phraya and Lopburi rivers between Suphanburi and Lopburi, two important cities dominating the region, which were already regional centres during the Khmer empire. With the building of a small canal, the area of the city could be transformed into an island, thus providing protection. Aided by the tides ships from the sea could easily move up the Chao Phraya to Ayudhya. A harbour, surrounded by several quarters for different ethnic groups, was located at the southern edge of Ayudhya.

The shape of the island of Ayudhya was roughly square. The city itself was clearly clustered, with east-west and more strongly pronounced north-south axes. The enwalled royal palace and royal temple complex (Wat Phra Si Sanphet), as the biggest structure in the whole city, was located in the north of the island roughly in the middle of the east-west axes. The palace was north of the royal chapel which is reminiscent of the pattern of the Chinese city where palace and main temple also formed a north-south axis. Two temples are east of the palace complex connected with it by a straight street. To the north is the temple Wat Ratburana, built in the first half of the fifteenth century, to the south the huge Wat Mahathat (temple of the great relic). This temple is regarded as one of the earliest, if not the oldest, temple of Ayudhya, erected in the fourteenth century. The main chedi sheltered a relic of the Buddha, mysteriously found at that location. The ruins of this temple still today give an impression of it as a truly dominating mark on the city.

In between the complex of the two temples and the royal complex, slightly to the south of the axes, is another old temple, Wat Phra Ram, built in the fourteenth century. The story is that this temple was built to house the ashes of the founder of Ayudhya. Altogether the layout of Ayudhya shows a clear axiality. The royal complex (palace and royal chapel) is internally structured around a north-south axis while the relation between royal complex and main temple (Wat Mahathat) is along an east-west axis. The shape of the city resembles a rectangle, separated into clusters through straight streets and canals. Ayudhya was as much a city of canals as of streets.

From Joost Schouten, the director of the Dutch East India Company in Ayudhya, we find a brief description of Ayudhya during the early seventeenth century. "The country is generally well peopled, especially the lower part of it, being full of villages and towns; ... The city of Iudica, the metropolis of the kingdom and seat of the king and his chiefest nobles, is situated upon the river Menam, in a little round land, encompassed with a thick stone wall, about six miles round; the suburbs are on the other side of the river, closely builded, and full of temples and cloysters, lying in a flat fruitful country. The streets of the walled town are many of them large, straight and regular, with channels running through the, although for the most part of small narrow lanes, ditches, and creeks most confusedly placed; ... The building of the houfes (court) is according to the Indian fashion, flight, and covered with tiles; but the city is beautified with more than three hundred fair temples and cloysters, all curiously builded and adorned with many gilded towers, pyramids and pictures without number. ... This royal and admirable city is perfectly well seated, and populous to a wonder, being frequented by all Nations; and is likewise impregnable, as not to be besieged but six month in a year, by reason of inundations of the river" (Schouten 1671:125).

The estimations of the population of Ayudhya among the different writers who visited this city during the seventeenth century are between 300,000 to even 400,000 inhabitants. This is probably an exaggeration because the visitors estimated the population in total from the dense settlements alongside the canals. The area in between the canals was not fully settled though. However, the concentration of population in Siam was highest in the territory surrounding Ayudhya, under close administration from the capital. A further aspect referred to by all visitors to Ayudhya was the cosmopolitan character of the population. Besides Mon who migrated from lower Burma following revolts or warfare there, or who were searching for a better environment in Ayudhya, groups from Maccasar who fled Indonesia following the Dutch raids on Maccasar, Persians, Arabs, Japanese, Portuguese and other Europeans had their "camps" in Ayudhya outside the city wall or in the southern part of the city, close to the harbour. Here were also the palaces of those officials supervising trade.

Ayudhya is the combination of Indian/Singhalese urban concepts with Chinese concepts. The form of the city, resembling a rectangle with clustered streets, and the palace located north of the royal chapel, follows the pattern of the Chinese north-south axis. The Mahathat temple, in which the main relic is enshrined, resembles due to its relation to the palace of an east-west axis, the pattern of the Indian city. The major buildings were erected on the basis of those concepts, visible in the cityscape through tectonic marks in form of chedis and pagodas. But as Ayudhya was a commercial centre as well, a commercial city was directly linked and interwoven with the sacred city. Around the harbour and in the southern and eastern suburbs the different groups had their quarters and their sacral buildings, while the officials resided in the southern part of the enwalled city, close to the harbour, behind a fort dominating the harbour area (Kaempfer 1727/1987). Ayudhya as centre of trade, sacred city and centre of a territory is reflected in the inter-relatedness of different structures of the city itself.

The Buddhist ritual structure we made out in the case of Kandy, Mandalay and Ayudhya can also be discerned in Bangkok though with some (minor) deviations.[36] To the royal palace is also attached a Buddhist temple, the Wat Phra Kaeo, the functional equivalent of the Dalada Maligava. Instead of the Tooth Relic there is an emerald image of the Buddha. The temple of the gods (Bot Phram) is found at some distance near the "Great Swing", where an annual yearly ritual took place (Indra returns to Earth). The most important monastery, Wat Mahathat, is located close to the royal temple (Wat Phra Kaeo) and can be seen as the centre of the gamavasin monks. Whether the Temple of the Golden Mount (Wat Sakaet), just beyond the old city wall, might have symbolized the aranyavasin (forest monk) community, is difficult to establish, though some learned monks seem to favour this opinion.

Royal palace, Vishnu temple, royal Buddhist temple and the main monasteries structure ritual space according to Buddhist values. But in addition to this the cult of the city pillar (lak muang) adds a specific urban element to the ritual structure of Bangkok. Unlike the paku alam, the world axis, of Javanese realms, it is a symbol of Thai urbanism, which is also found in other cities like Chiang Mai, Korat or Nakhorn Sri Thammarat.

The Image of Bangkok

Bangkok serves as example for the discussion of how the construction of the city, the ideologies of the élites and the meaning assigned to the city are related and change over time. Bangkok is in so far an interesting example, as processes of state formation and the élite always had an urban base. In some regard one could even say that the Thai state used to be the extension of the Bangkok élite and state. Thus Bangkok as the capital city had a tremendous political, economic and symbolic importance for the state and the élites.

---

[36]The ritual structure of Bangkok will be discussed in detail in a later chapter.

From Sacred City to National Capital

After Rama I proclaimed himself King of Ayudhya on the sixth of April 1782, and decided to found a new capital city on the eastern Bank of the Chao Phraya river opposite Thonburi, on the 21st or 24th of April 1782, the city pillar (Lak Muang) was installed, and thereby Bangkok transformed into the capital of Siam. Two months later a small coronation ceremony was held, in which Rama I was crowned the King of Ayudhya. After the main buildings of the new capital had been erected or renovated (particularly the palace and the main temples), and an important symbol of Buddhism, the Emerald Buddha, was placed in the royal chapel, a big coronation ceremony was held, and the name of the capital city defined as "Krung Thep Rattanakosin Mahindra" ("City of the emerald Buddha beautiful palace of Indra") (Sulak 1985; Committee 1982).

Bangkok was a city planned following cosmological concepts. The existing structures, particularly the older temples, were integrated into these concepts and the cosmological order modified to account for what was available. the cosmological concepts behind the construction of Bangkok can be exemplified on the basis of three major structures:

1. The city pillar:

Quaritch-Wales (1931) regards the city pillar, i. e. the guardian deity of the city, as being in the same category as other locality spirits. I would not agree with this perspective. Certainly, the city spirit has a connection to animism, at least in regard to the way the people honour the spirit. However, the installation of the city pillar and the main ceremonies related to this are Brahmin. Furthermore, the city spirit is referred to as "Thevada" (angel), while locality spirits are referred to in general terms as "Phra Bhumi", or "Chao Di", with the particular spirit called "Chao Pho plus the name of the locality" (in case of a male spirit) or "Chao Mae plus name of locality" (in case of a female spirit). Although Quaritch-Wales is right in pointing out that the city spirit is respected by the people in a similar fashion to other locality spirits which showed their power (saksit), he himself indicates that the city spirit is officially sanctioned, and that in "the oath of allegiance taken by all officials, the Chao Lak Muang is still invoked, and his vengeance called down on any traitor. Thus it seems that the Guardian Spirit of the City is by no means forgotten, .., and in case of national danger no doubt he would come in for a considerably greater share of attention" (Quaritch-Wales 1931:303). Obviously, the city spirit is important for state ceremonies.

2. The royal chapel:

The royal chapel serves as the centre for important religious rites pertaining to the state and monarchy. In contrast to the city spirit, which is connected to Brahmin rites, the royal chapel is connected to Buddhist rites, and an expression of the king as a supporter of Buddhism. In this respect, Rama I built the Phra

Mondop in the complex of the royal temple to house the revised edition of the Buddhist canon of the Rattanakosin Era, the so-called "Royal Golden Edition". "The revision of the scriptures was one of the first tasks undertaken by Rama I on his accession to the throne" (Committee 1982).

3. Thung Phramen, or Sanam Luang:

This large square in the middle of Bangkok was (and still is) used for state ceremonies, namely the plowing ceremony and cremations of kings and queens. For the cremation wooden structures were erected, thus transforming the plain field into a world mountain.

City pillar, royal temple, and Sanam Luang form a triangle of three interdependent centres and express the simultaneity of them. The city pillar is the centre of the capital city, and the residence of the Guardian deity of the city, thus connecting the city with the supernatural. The royal temple, with the most auspicious Buddhist symbol of the country, is the centre of the country, and the expression of the king as supporter of Buddhism. The Phra Meru (Sanam Luang), when used for cremations, is the world mountain. All these three structures together connect city, country, world and cosmos, through centreing all on the same spot. In this configuration the guardian deity of the city bears power which can be applied to the secular world in the present. In case of treason, he is the potential avenger. The royal temple symbolizes morality and a righteous life to harmonize world and cosmos. Finally, the Sanam Luang symbolizes the power of the king, who, as a serene being, is able to engage in specific rituals which bring prosperity to the people. The king conducting state ceremonies on the Sanam Luang merges the present and supernatural power (symbolized by the city pillar and the Brahmins) with sacrality and moral order (symbolized by the royal temple and the monks) to bring prosperity to the realm.

In an interview, the court Brahmins, direct successors of the first "city planners" of Bangkok, explained the concept and rites underlying the founding of Bangkok.

When it was decided that a new capital city should be established, initially the Gods had to be made aware of this, and their support had to be requested. This was achieved through a ceremony, in which the founding of the world by Brahma was re-enacted. The story goes that after Brahma founded the world, he asked Shiva to test its strength. For this, Shiva asked the Naga (the giant snake) for help. Shiva sat down with only one leg on the ground, while the Naga bent itself around two mountains and tried to shake these. If Shiva can remain seated with only one leg on the ground, the world is strong enough. This was recapitulated in an initial swinging ceremony at the Giant Swing, in which a person selected by the King symbolizes Shiva, while others are symbolizing the attempts to shake the world by the Naga through the swinging. Until 1932, the year of the revolt leading to the abolition of absolutist monarchy, this ceremony was held annually, indicating the strength of the "world" and its ruler. Following this ceremony, a place was selected as the centre from which the world could be structured. This centre was to be the location of the guardian deity. The Brahmins defined a name for the deity, and a high official walked along in the area, orating the name. The first person who reacted to this name was taken, and given all the privileges due to a deity. On the auspicious day, when the pillar was to be erected, the person was put below and the pillar pushed through the body, thus transforming the human being into a deity protecting the city. As Quaritch-Wales points out, this has nothing to do with sacrifices. "The victims were themselves more or less deified" (Quaritch-Wales 1931:306). With this ceremony, a centre was clearly marked and by the pillar a connection between world, underworld and heaven was established.

During the swinging ceremony, the processions went through Bamrung Muang (translatable as nourishing/nurturing and civilizing the country/city) and Ganlajan Maidri (translatable as beautiful friendship/sympathy/amicability) Road, the street connecting the Giant Swing and the Brahmin temple with the royal complex. It can be regarded as the main road of Bangkok, as the main axis of the city, which received its importance from royal ritual.

From this point of view Bangkok displays the features of a sacred city. The sacrality of the space used for the new capital was defined on the one hand by the installation of the Emerald Buddha in the city, on the other through an elaborate Brahmin ritual by which "chaos" or unstructured space is transformed into an order, thus structured and thereby sacred space (Eliade) The further development of Bangkok followed quite clearly this meaning of the city and the reflected the power of the élite.

Up to the nineteenth century, the construction of the royal palace, and palaces for the nobility, the renovation of temples existing already in the area and defensive works were the main works. All these constructions, with the exception of the building of a fort in Samut Prakan at the entrance of the river, were located in Bangkok. During the long reign of Rama III (1824 - 1851) many architectural works initiated by his predecessors were finished. Still, temples, palaces and defense works were the main constructions. However, these were increasingly built outside Bangkok proper. Rama IV (1852 - 1868) initiated in particular the restoration of temples in the provinces, and the building of new palaces outside of Bangkok. In this reign, for the first time, infrastructure was constructed under royal command, such as three bridges, new canals and roads within and outside the enwalled city of Bangkok. Bangkok developed as a city of temples and palaces. Until the middle of the nineteenth century, it was the only place were the élite had a strong power base, while the provinces remained rather independent.

Turning to the development of Bangkok in the later half of the nineteenth century, i. e. the process of the formation of Bangkok as the centre of a centralized administration, several changes in the pattern of urban development can be recognized. Increasingly the king sponsored the construction of public buildings, particularly those used for education (Chulalongkorn University, Maha Monghkut College, Sirirat Hospital and Medical College) and administration (post and telegraph office, Ministry of Justice etc.), and the establishment of a modern infrastructure through roads, bridges, and the railway, covering not only Bangkok but connecting the capital with the provinces.

The constructions in Bangkok reflect the development of the city as the administrative and commercial centre of Siam as a whole. Still, new palaces and temples were founded or existing temples renovated, but the city was no longer shaped by the palaces and temples only, but increasingly by public buildings, shops and offices of companies. The architectural styles became diverse, with western-style buildings standing side by side with Chinese-style shophouses and Thai-style temples and palaces. But even the palaces and temples received a strong influence from western architecture, particularly classicism and Jugendstil. The public buildings, in particular the ministries, followed European architectural concepts, and look quite similar to the buildings used for colonial administration in other cities, or buildings in the capital cities of Europe. What is interesting is the combination of Thai architectural elements with European elements in the building of the educational institutions. The dominance of European architectural styles reflects the attempt to modernize the country and make the capital city comparable to western capitals. But the traditional concepts were kept up. Rama V did not only build the Pahnumatchamrun Palace, which could be located anywhere in Germany, but also a palace constructed entirely of teak following classical Thai lines.

Bangkok looked like a colonial city. The difference to Jakarta, Manila and Singapore was that the colonial élite were not the European administrators, but the Thai élite itself. Thus, the architecture is a mixture between styles reflecting the position of the Thai élite by the application of Thai architectural concepts and by sponsoring buildings following European styles. Just as the villas of the well-to-do Europeans in Jakarta were influenced by the Priyayi style, and the houses of the British in Malaya by Indian architecture, in Bangkok the houses of the Siamese élite were influenced by European architectural concepts. The shophouses alongside the new roads were mixtures between Chinese and European styles, while the consulates and legations generally followed a colonial tropical architecture.

In the twentieth century several additional roads were built. Along these roads, shops and the offices of trading houses were erected, like the first "department store" of Bangkok, Harry Batman and Co. When the royal palace was shifted to the northern quarter of Dusit, a new road used for parades and ceremonies was built to connect this area and the new palace with the old city centre and royal complex. Radamnoen road (great/royal procession road), as it was called, was by far the biggest street in Bangkok, with different lanes for cars, carts, and smaller vehicles. The whole street was lined by mahagony trees, and the different lanes separated by trees and lawns. Radamnoen road was a "royal" road, alongside which palaces, temples and public buildings were located, not a road to be lined with shops, workshops or residences of common people.

Alongside Radamnoen Road and the new royal palace, the administrative centre of Siam evolved, forming a specific "administrative" quarter of Bangkok. Bangkok still remained a sacred city, but a new meaning was added to it: Bangkok as centre for the administration of the country. The streets referring to the civilization and amicability of the city (Bamrung Muang Road, Ganjanmaidri Road) became overshadowed by the "Royal Procession Road". Cosmology was replaced by the monarch administering the country from a "modern" capital city.

When the aristocratic élite lost its political power to the bureaucratic élite following the revolt of 1932, the structure of Bangkok was changed. Radamnoen road, which indicated that the monarch was the only one able to bring modernity and prosperity to the kingdom, was to be re-constructed. In 1940 it was transformed into an avenue, with the Democracy monument in its centre. Alongside the street modern buildings in European style were constructed, and became the location of companies, shops, theatres, hotels and modern nightclubs. The palaces lining the road were transformed into public buildings. The royal palace became the parliament building. At the northern end was a big square for military parades overlooked by the parliament building. The straight street was lined by the ministries, and, after crossing the old city moat, the name changed to Radamnoen Klang or central Radamnoen. Here classicist buildings were constructed, sometimes in front of older temples. In the centre of "central" Radamnoen avenue was the democracy monument. The style of the democracy monument is reminiscent of monuments built in Italy during the thirties. Crossing another canal, which formerly demarcated the old royal centre of Bangkok, the name changes to Radamnoen Nai (inside). At this end of the street was the Ministry of Justice, the Ministry of Defense, the city pillar, Sanam Luang and the newly founded University for Politics and Ethics: Thammasat University.

It is obvious that Radamnoen avenue was intended as the new centre of a "democratic" and modern Bangkok, in contrast to the former royal and traditional centres, thus the central part of it had to be lined by constructions reflecting in their function and their architecture the new modern period. The poles of this street are interesting. In the north is the parliament building with a big plaza in front, used for military parades. The southern pole is formed by the old royal complex (Royal Palace and royal temple), with the Sanam Luang in front, used for royal state ceremonies. Radamnoen thus forms an axis between the new centre of power (parliament, buildings of the ministries), and the old centre (Royal Palace, city pillar, Sanam Luang). Radamnoen Klang (the central part of the avenue) is roughly parallel to the old Bamrung Muang Road connecting the Royal Palace with the Giant Swing. This used to be the major road of Bangkok, where bigger shops and stores were located, like the Batman and Co. department store. It was furthermore a road used in state ceremonies, namely the Swinging ceremony, which was abandoned in 1933. In this regard, Radamnoen indicates the attempt to shift the main axis of the city.

Bangkok was founded by an élite whose legitimacy was based on religious concepts and demonstrated in its ability to bring prosperity to the country. The capital city was the centre of power and of sacrality, and as such directly connected to the country as a whole and the king and the ruling élite. Any attempt to modify the definition of Bangkok as the sacred centre implied challenging the worldly and the cosmic order, and accordingly would have had worldly as well as supernatural repercussions.

The profane, however, required that the economy was organized, thus providing revenue for the state and profits for the élite, and that the country was administered. Successful territorial expansion, integration of the provinces, and integration into trading networks required that an efficient administration was established. In a long process during the second half of the eighteenth century, such an efficient administration was established with Bangkok as its centre by one faction of the ruling élite under the domination of a powerful king. The meaning of Bangkok was modified from that of a sacred centre, to the centre for the administration of the country. This already provided the base for the emergence of Bangkok as "national centre". At the time when the development of Bangkok as administrative centre changed its meaning as sacred centre, when the bureaucracy replaced the nobility as the new élite, sacredness, which was connected with the king, was transformed into nationalism, which was connected with the central administration and the officials. Bangkok was defined as national capital.

Ideological Constructions: Bangkok as Symbiosis of Tradition and Modernity

The ideology of present-day Bangkok is the articulation of tradition and identity with development and modernity, as was already argued in the official yearbook of Thailand in 1968: "Bangkok is a curious amalgam of ancient pomp and ceremony contrasting with an extremely active programme of modernization. Bangkok is a bustling metropolis, yet in the midst of its up-to-date hotels and modern homes are monasteries and palaces of fairy-tale magnificence. ... In Bangkok, there is a remarkable blending of the old and the new, of East and

West" (Government of Thailand 1968:680). The people were to be proud of both the glorious past and the successful present. Exemplifications of this ideology can be found in descriptions of Thai identity and Thai world view, particularly those given by the Board of National Identity. A good example of this is a series of English language lectures in the radio, which have also been published as language training books. The situation on which the lectures are based is that a group of tourists is visiting Thailand and the guides explain life, culture, religion etc. to the tourists (volume "Wonderful Thailand"), and two American Ph.D. students visit Thailand for their fieldwork and a Thai student explains Thai world views etc. to them (volume Thai National Identity).

Three major aspects are brought together and combined in the ideology of Bangkok. Firstly, places and buildings (palaces and temples) in Bangkok indicate the glorious past of the Thai people:

The tourists are visiting the Royal Palace and are impressed by the buildings there.

Tourist: All of the buildings provide such a beautiful, romantic glimpse of Thailand's glorious past. The Thai people must be very proud of them.

Tour guide: Yes we are. They are a living reminder of our roots.

Secondly, Bangkok is still based on tradition:

When the American students visited the house of the Thai counterpart:

American student: I'm glad I could oblige. Your home is really marvellous, you know. You're lucky to be living in a traditional Thai house right in the heart of Bangkok

Thai student: Yes, we are. Traditional Thai houses in Bangkok are rare, indeed. We consider ourselves fortunate, but I would have thought that you would prefer a more western-style house.

American student: Not in the least, although I must admit that Thai architects have managed to blend the best of both worlds into some of the houses I've seen in Bangkok.

In the language drills which follow the sentence "Thai architects have managed to blend the best of two worlds" is repeated. Looking at the architecture in Bangkok, this is astonishing. A leading Thai architect argued in a newspaper series that the current architecture is best described as "punk" architecture, which he did not regard as a compliment.

Thirdly, Bangkok is an impressive modern city with all the facilities of other modern cities, but this modernization did not imply a far-reaching change of beliefs and "identity".

American student:	Bangkok certainly seems to be a bustling metropolis.
Thai student:	Yes. The city is developing at a very rapid pace. New and larger complexes are going up daily.
American student:	Do you think the development has had any effect upon the people. I mean, has it changed them in any significant way?
Thai student:	Well, certainly, progress changes life styles as well as cities. But I think that you will find that in spite of the seeming westernization, Thai culture and traditions are still alive and well. Old beliefs die hard, especially among Thais who are proud of their heritage and thus have no desire to change their basic identity.

Fourthly, the modernization of Bangkok implies problems, but these are coped with.

After the tourist has been informed that the canals were filled to make space for the large roads:

Tourist:	What a shame! Instead of maintaining peaceful canals throughout the city, Bangkok has kept up with progress and transformed itself into a traffic nightmare.
Tour guide:	Well, progress does have its price, ...

Finally, there is an ambiguous difference between Bangkok and rural Thailand. Rural Thailand is more genuinely Thai, because many of those living in Bangkok are Chinese, but a little bit "backward" as well.

When looking at the building housing a Chinese association the Thai student explains:

Thai student:	It's the headquarters of a Chinese regional association. I believe that this one was founded by the Teochiu Chinese. There are many of these associations in Bangkok, because there are so many Chinese.

American
student:
Have the Chinese been assimilated successfully into Thai culture, would you say, or have they kept their own cultural identity?

Thai student:
Well, it's a little bit of both. The Chinese tend to be very clan-centred. But they've intermarried a great deal with the Thais, and some Chinese families have even taken Thai surnames. In fact, many Chinese-Thai young people don't even speak Chinese - only Thai.

When going to a wedding in a remote village:

American
student:
It's fascinating. It's also totally unlike the wedding I attended at a Bangkok hotel.

Thai student:
Everything is different here, Chris. Rural Thailand is almost a different world from a city like Bangkok. These people still adhere to many old customs.

In conclusion, Bangkok is, from the perspective of this ideology, a symbol and expression of pride in national history: this is the secondary function and meaning of the old buildings, especially the major temples and the Grand Palace, which are impressive to the visitor, and Bangkok is symbol and expression of Thailand's success in development towards a modern country, a country at the edge of becoming a Newly Industrialized Country. Bangkok is no longer the articulation of the cosmos and the world, but the articulation of modernity and tradition, the past of the Thai nation and its bright future.

O'Connor's (1983) approach to an "indigenous theory of urbanization" in Southeast Asia follows this ideology quite closely. O'Connor argues that urbanism in Southeast Asia focuses around two complexes which he refers to as "community" and "hierarchy". Community is the personal relations among people in the city, be it within the neighbourhood and locality, or the network of acquaintances and friends among social groups. Thus "communities" do not necessarily have to have a spatial correspondence. Communities "can be unorganized, though they always have the order of a single self-fulfilling assumption: everyone has some community just as everyone has a family. Southeast Asian urbanites thus learn that you need friends and connections to get by, and so they turn their energies to building communities" (O'Connor 1983:5). Contrasted to these communities are the hierarchies in which everybody and every community has its ranks. While commonality is a traditional feature of Southeast Asian society, hierarchization and urbanization were introduced by Indianization. The modern Southeast Asian city consists of a kaleidoscope of communities on different levels, ordered by hierarchy, which now has its base in symbols of modernity instead of the cult of the devaraja. He concludes: "Community and hierarchy are the dominant organizing principles of urban life, although of the two only hierarchy is intrinsically urban. Within the larger society hierarchy ensures urban rule. It sets the capital above other cities and the lot above the countryside, not just in institutionalized power but in social prestige as well" (O'Connor 1983:118).

O'Connor's finding that community still plays a major role in the Southeast Asian city undoubtedly has its base. The problem is, however, that he does not distinguish between the brief personal encounters, particularly within localities, and the comparatively stabilized relations among strategic groups. To argue that the present-day city consists of both, does not, however, provide any perspective for a critical assessment of what the Southeast Asian city could be. If community is translated into tradition, and hierarchy into modernization and westernization (which O'Connor does of course not do), the approach appears to be very close to the ideology of the city as the symbiosis of old and new, as "the blend of the best of two worlds" etc.

The situation in regard to present-day Bangkok is that inappropriate ideologies confront each other while Bangkok follows a course of development based on the market. Bangkok is definitely not the "symbiosis" of tradition and modernity, nor is the village an alternative to Bangkok (this is rather neo-romantic escapism). The alternative to present-day Bangkok is neither the village, nor the Thevadha (guardian deity of Bangkok), nor "modernity". Instead of confronting the market with an idealized picture of the village or an ideologized picture of the city, a new urban imagination beyond the market is needed.

Everyday Life Constructions of Bangkok

Although to the casual visitor it might seem that Bangkok lacks a centre, the inhabitants have a clear perception of centres and central locations within Bangkok. What makes a difference is that different centres corresponding to different aspects coexist. Clearly, the old city centre around Sanam Luang, Wat Phra Khaeu and the Royal Palace still is a centre of Bangkok. Radamoen Road is undeniably another centre. What is interesting are the other centres and important locations indicated, namely the area around Phaholyothin Road and the Victory Monument, Siam Square and Sukhumvit region, and Silom - Rama IV region. Here we find a combination between axes (the major roads leading out of or into the city) and squares (Victory Monument as the node of the public transportation system, and Siam Square as the commercial centre and node of public transportation).

The centres with their associated axes, organized in a constellation with Sanam Luang, Royal complex and Radamoen Road as the major centre, are associated with differing aspects. Sanam Luang, Royal complex and Radamnoen Road are linked with state ritual and politics. Radamoen Road, lined primarily by public buildings, is used for parades and demonstrations. Sanam Luang and the royal complex are based on the ritual structure of Bangkok. These rituals brought legitimacy to rule and as such they were linked with politics. Some of these ceremonies (plowing ceremony, funerals etc.) are still held at Sanam Luang. The main centre has primarily a political, culturally associative and communicative meaning. It is in some respects not only the centre of Bangkok but the centre of the Thai nation, as all symbols of nationhood are concentrated here: The Emerald Buddha as symbol for religion, the Royal Palace as symbol for the monarchy and Sanam Luang, Radamnoen Road and buildings along this road as symbols of the state.

The area around Silom Road in contrast has not much to do with politics or culture. It is regarded as the centre of big business in Bangkok, indicated by the location of the headquarters of banks, including most foreign banks and airline offices, in this street. Silom Road is thus not primarily a commercial centre for Bangkok, but rather a centre for nation-wide and international commerce. Since in 1986/87 the telephone and electricity wires have been laid underground, it is the only street in Thailand not lined by masts and wires. In addition, several of the highest office towers and apartment houses are located in this area. Finally, in the Silom area land prices and rents are highest.

Siam Square and the Radamri area, together with Sukhumvit Road, incorporate the commercial centre of Bangkok; the place where most shopping centres and department stores are located. It is not an area associated with international commerce but with shopping in Bangkok, fashion and modernity. Siam Square and Radamri are not without symbolic meaning though. They are show-cases of economic success and modernity.

Whiphawadhy - Rangsit Road and Phaholyothin Road are the major roads linking Bangkok proper with the airport, the industrial suburbs and the north and northeast of Thailand. Thus it is the "gateway" through which migrants commonly enter Bangkok. Like Siam Square or Sanam Luang, the Victory Monument is a node of the public transportation network. The area around is a busy commercial area, not catering for the fashionable Yuppy, like Siam Square, but catering for normal shoppers. The bus stop area is lined with hawkers' stalls. Behind are two cheaper department stores. For anybody not very well acquainted with Bangkok, Victory Monument can easily be taken as a centre of the city.

The association with centrality and shopping centres is interesting. Sanam Luang, Radamnoen, the palace and temples are not areas which have any particular commercial activities associated with them. In some respects, these central locations relate to Bangkok as a cultural and political centre, and to a ritual structure of the city, while the reference to shopping "centres" hints at the characteristic of Bangkok, like any other city, as a centre of commerce. The interesting point is that in Bangkok the commercial centre and economic structure of the city and the symbolic centre and ritual structure do not have the same focus. Within Bangkok distinct cities exist: the traditional Theravadha Buddhist capital city, the national capital and the centre of commerce and modernity in Thailand.

Among the different groups the concept of Bangkok is similar. There are no larger differences, only slight tendencies. Among the migrants, the ritual aspects of Bangkok are more strongly pronounced than the aspect of Bangkok as centre of modernity in Thailand. For them Bangkok is still mainly the city of the Emerlad Buddha (Wat Phra Khaeu), the Royal Palace and of state ceremonies. For the Bangkokians and those having a positive attitude towards Bangkok, the commercial aspects are more strongly pronounced. Among the migrants the distribution is concentrated on three major roads (Radamnoen, Sukhumvit and Silom), while the Bangkokians tend to differentiate between more axes.

In addition to the centres and main axes of Bangkok, which are all part of the inner city, or roads linking the inner city with the fringe, we have the centres at the fringe and the axes of the fringe, and then, finally, there are the minor centres of localities, the axes associated with these, and the streets linking localities with the other parts of the city. Bangkok is conceptualized in a differentiated form by the people. They distinguish between the centres of city-wide, even nation-wide significance and the centres of local significance with the axes connecting the different centres and places.

Bangkok in fact does not have one centre, or a structure with a specific centre. Bangkok has several structures coexisting with different centres. There are the temples, the palace, the roads used for parades, demonstrations and mass meetings, and there are the commercial centres. The relevance of the one derives from their intrinsic meaning, or what Eco (1988). discusses as secondary meaning, while the commercial centres derive their importance from their integration into the everyday life of the inhabitants. In addition, there are the centres of the localities where most of the lives of the people are spent.

The Construction of the Personality of the Bangkokian

Turning to stereotypes of what are the characteristics of the "Bangkokian", two issues are evident. Firstly, the people clearly differentiate between the personality of those in Bangkok and those not living in Bangkok, which implies that a rural-urban differentiation plays a role for them. Secondly, it becomes evident that Bangkok is perceived as "modern" and confronted with a neo-romantic idealization of a "traditional" rural life.

Obviously, there are large differences between an "urban" personality stereotype and a "provincial" personality stereotype. Interestingly, the urban stereotype shows many features mentioned already by Wirth as characteristics of urbanism. The characteristics of the Bangkokians have a clear negative valuation, even though some characteristics are mentioned which can be evaluated as positive. First of all, people in Bangkok are selfish, insincere, unkind, greedy and hasty. As all Bangkokians have these characteristics there is a struggle and competition going on in the city, in which only those who are enthusiastic, efficient, industrious and brilliant can win. These winners show their success in their extravagance. No wonder that the people are lonely in such an environment.

The "non"-Bangkokians are very different. They are helpful and kind. As they are honest, one can rely on them. In contrast to the struggle in Bangkok, they are easy-going and sociable rather than struggling and competing with each other. The atmosphere outside Bangkok seems to be quite cozy.

It is interesting that a stereotype of an "urban" life-style is contrasted with a stereotype of a rural lifestyle. In the questionnaire it was not asked, "What are the characteristics of Thai peasants", but "what are the characteristics of people not living in Bangkok", which of course includes those in the middle-sized towns and the provincial centres. Obviously, these are completely ignored by the people and anything besides Bangkok is directly identified with rural. There are no larger differences in the stereotypes between people preferring to live in Bangkok and defining themselves as Bangkokian and migrants and/or people preferring to live elsewhere than in Bangkok and not regarding themselves as Bangkokians. The only difference is a kind of secondary valuation depending on what the person himself regards as positive and negative. The industriousness of the Bangkokian thus can contrast with the "laziness" of the peasant, or the kind and helpful peasant is contrasted with the hurrying and struggling Bangkokian, or the sophisticated, brilliant and extravagant Bangkokian looks down on the naive country bumpkin from outside Bangkok.

The above data differ from findings of a study on values in Thai society by Suntaree (1985). Suntaree's study had its focus on values, not on projected characteristics, thus the findings cannot directly be compared. In the study the following values were differentiated for urban and rural Thais:

Her conclusion is: "All of the instrumental values that the rural Thai held significantly higher than the urban Thais are of an interpersonal moral value focus, stressing high concern for gratitude, caring and consideration of others, ... Whereas almost all of the instrumental values that were more significant for the urban Thai are of the personal competence and achievement orientation focus"

(Suntaree 1985:187). With her focus on positive values, ignoring negative characteristics, she can argue that the Thai world view provides the people with an outlook on life which prepares them to accommodate varying states of change. This world view rests on the attempt to harmonize and smoothen interpersonal relations. "The Thai world view on man-to-man relations seems to be one of harmonious co-existence combined with pragmatism of adaptability and flexibility" (Suntaree 1985:190). This conclusion is astonishing in view of the above data, particularly on the urban personality. It seems as if a strong discrepancy between world view (which is primarily ideological) and stereotypes constructed from experience exists. In terms of values harmony, smoothness etc. are held in high esteem, while these find no echoes in the ascribed characteristics. Only the non-Bangkok characteristics resemble features associated with an ideological "Thai world view", which could explain why the peasant society is regarded by some people as the genuine representative of Thai culture. The main problem with Suntaree's conclusion is that she does not distinguish between ideal conceptions and reality, and thus her argument concerning smoothness and adaptability has to be taken with caution.

In regard to the characteristics, the person either identifies with the modern style of life, interprets it in a "modern world view" and develops those characteristics which suit circumstances in Bangkok, or prefers to follow a "traditional" lifestyle identified with life in the villages.

World views, values and stereotypes of personality are projections which do not have to reflect reality. Obviously, the projection of values and stereotypes is not coherent in Bangkok. It seems as if the Thai world view does not fit Bangkok reality. This is one reason, I would argue, for the ascription of rather negative characteristics to the Bangkok personality stereotype and the idealization of the Non-Bangkok stereotype. From this perspective it is understandable that most of those living in Bangkok have a negative attitude towards Bangkok.

Conclusions

When Bangkok was founded, it followed closely the idea of a Theravadha Buddhist city in which heaven and world are articulated. Bangkok was an exemplary centre, a regalia for monarchic rule. At the end of the nineteenth century, Bangkok was transformed into a "colonial city", with an absolutist king following policies of modernization to bring the kingdom in line with the European states. Still the meaning of Bangkok was defined as centre of monarchic rule. The monarch, however, was no longer a Bodhisatva, as in the Theravadha Buddhist city, but an absolutist king with a strongly centralized government apparatus. The abolition of absolutist rule in 1932 required a new definition of Bangkok. Bangkok changed from monarchic centre to "national" centre. The rites of the Devaraja conducted by Brahmin priests were replaced, as McGee argues, by the rites of nationalism conducted by a state bureaucracy.

The policies of modernization followed since the sixties had an impact on the composition of the élite and the structure of Bangkok. The market increasingly defined where what could be built. This put the urban ideology, especially from the bureaucratic élite, in some difficulty. The more the western-designed high-rise apartment houses, shopping centres, hotels and office buildings, "expressways" and "fly-overs" overshadowed the temples, ministries and Procession Roads, the more difficult it became to define Bangkok as the traditional centre of Thai culture and society. A new ideology, in which the market, nationalism and tradition is connected was formed, defining Bangkok as a synthesis of tradition and modernity, reflecting the state ideology of Thailand as a traditional country now at the threshold of becoming a Newly Industrialized Country. But, with the market as main mechanism of urban development, the meaning of the city is increasingly dissolving. Bangkok is becoming a department store of localities, open for those who can afford it. Interestingly, simultaneously with the dissolution of a generally defined meaning of Bangkok, the architecture became post-modernist.

Instead of a symbiosis, there is a rather a divorce between "tradition" and "modernity". In fact, the ideology stating the symbiosis implies already that a coherent meaning does not exist. Instead of a city with one structure and one centre, several structures with differing centres emerged. This makes orientation within the city difficult. This applies to social orientation as well. In regard to world views, Bangkok reality obviously does not fit the projections of a Thai world view. Bangkok ceases to be a definable as a symbol of the Thai state and the Thai élite but emerges as a metropolis.

Urbanism and Local Traditions: The Example of Korat

Local traditions bear an ambivalence. As a means to achieve social cohesion and forms of solidarity in a limited space, beyond differences and distinctions in terms of social status, cultural prestige and economic possibilities, they enforce social integration but at the same time give rise to new borders and demarcations. Local traditions can thus become important for policies of decentralization and the development of local élites, but might also put obstacles in the way of national integration or even lead to separatists movements.

Like any tradition, local traditions cannot be verified by their historical plausibility, but rather by their effects in the context of power relations and struggles. Local[37] traditions are connected to specific symbols and artifacts which do not have an implicit meaning, but are selected and defined by social groups and the figuration of these groups. In the paper we will develop the argument that the local traditions created in Korat, a city in north-eastern Thailand, play a crucial role in integrating very diverse local élites and strategic groups in their competition with Bangkok-based strategic groups. In particular, the modern local traditions firstly limit the movement of Korat élites towards Bangkok to become part of Bangkok-based strategic groups, as has commonly been the case (Korff 1989). In contrast, at present the local élites are pursuing strongly an ideology of developing their own province of Korat. Secondly, the modern local traditions provide forms of local integration and social cohesion which is necessary to be able to compete with the Bangkok strategic groups. Thus through local traditions local linkages are strengthened, while linkages based on other interests become less pronounced.

From this perspective, the construction of local traditions and the role of local élites is closely linked and mutually reinforcing. At least at present, these developments are connected to globalization processes. In Thailand globalization is leading to social, economic and political changes, like the rise of new middle classes demanding political influence and democratization, by which the dominance of centralized strategic groups has been reduced. Thereby an openness is created in the political, economic and cultural space of Thailand, which local élites can enter. Bangkok is undeniably the political power centre of Thailand and in the focus of national politics, but power has been decentralized as local power for local affairs. The local élites do not attempt to enter politically influential positions in the national state apparatus, but try to keep their local affairs under local control.

This pattern differs firstly from a "warlord"-pattern in which local "warlords" use their local position to gain access to political power positions within the national state. An example is the current Thai prime minister Banharn Silapha Archa, the "Godfather" of Saraburi province. Secondly it is different from a pattern in which those groups and persons who lost their influence in the Bangkok struggle try to regain it by establishing linkages to certain localities and regions (Korff 1991). Here vote-buying and the differentials of democratic consciousness between Bangkok, other urban areas and the rural areas is relevant. Through vote-buying it is possible to become a member of parliament,

---

[37]With "local" we imply more than a geographical reference to a certain limited area. Local is a limited social, economic, political, administrative and cultural space beyond the national level. In real terms the local traditions we are going to discuss are traditions in the city and province of Korat.

minister etc. and thereby gain or regain a power position in Bangkok. In both cases the local connections are resources in the struggle between strategic groups in Bangkok. We regard Chathchai Choonhavon as example for this pattern.

Although economic and social development has been concentrated in Bangkok, its success has led to spatial limitations on the further extension of the city, which has increasingly negative effects like traffic jams, expensive labour etc. In fact, within Bangkok decentralization is taking place with the rise of new centres in the surroundings of the city proper. While finances and commerce are still strongly concentrated in the inner city, further industrialization has required the development of regional growth poles and centres. Thus the dynamic described by Scott (1988) according to whom labour intensive investment tends to be located in central places, while capital intensive investment is spatially concentrated at the fringes of cities, is taking place in Bangkok too, initially in the form of transforming the rural surroundings of the city into industrial suburbs, and currently in the form of regional centres closely linked with a modern infrastructure to Bangkok.

Keeping this dynamic of spatial differentiation through industrialization in mind, the question is, whether the newly developing growth poles and regional centres are mere industrial suburbs of Bangkok or centres in their own right. Certainly, the development of regional growth poles and their industrialization provides new resources, which can potentially be used by local élites.[38] However, as the decentral industrialization process itself is based on central planning and the interests of central élites, these certainly have good chances of keeping or establishing their access to these resources. This advantage is strengthened through their better information.[39]

In the case of local traditions in Korat their strength in bringing groups with rather diverse interests together is astonishing. Furthermore, it is interesting that this does not lead towards separatism, but something like a local/provincial self-awareness. The traditions are thus an asset in that they imply a distinction from Bangkok and the construction of their own identity, connected to an ideology of

---

[38]Most obvious is the rise of land prices as new, more profitable forms of land use are possible. Where does the money from land speculation go to? Is it gained by local landowners, or are these tricked out of the market beforehand? If locals gain from it, do they spend it on luxury consumption or on investments? Are they in fact able to invest or not?

[39]The best example is the Eastern Seaboard Project. The investment has been made nearly exclusively by Bangkok big business and speculators. Even the profits from selling the land went to these groups, as before the plans were implemented, most land had been bought already by Bangkok speculators.

development, and providing cultural continuity. Thus Korat is developing towards a genuine regional centre in its own right and not as a suburb of Bangkok located further away.

Aspects of Korat as a Secondary Centre

The present day city of Nakorn Ratshasima, the official name of Korat, was founded during the end of the 17th century as the border station of the Ayudhya Empire by King Narai. The construction followed plans made by a French constructor of fortresses who was working in the kingdom.[40] Although the city was newly founded, it was based on the ruins and the population of two older cities founded by the Khmer in the 10th century (Koratana or Korapura and Muang Sena).[41] Nakorn Ratshasima was a border town with the main function of protecting the central provinces of Siam in the lower Chao Phraya plains from attacks coming out of the Laotian wilderness. Furthermore, Nakorn Ratshasima was the starting point for colonizing and controlling this wilderness. The status of Korat was as a provincial capital of the second order (muang dho). More important border towns of the first order (muang aek) were Nakhorn Sri Thamarat in the South and Phitsanulok in the north. These two towns are also of a much greater strategic importance, as the Burmese armies usually passed through them in their approach towards the capital city. As a border town Korat was a "melting pot" at the junction of several cultural flows, namely the old Khmer influence, Laotian influences and of course strong influences from the central power. In addition, in Korat Loatian prisoners-of-war were settled and Mon refugees from southern Burma moved to Korat. Still today this is reflected in the "Korat" language which is close to central Thai, but includes many Khmer and Laotian words.

In the history of Siam Korat is mentioned only seldom, in connection with either raids from Laos or revolts. These revolts led to short-lived attempts towards independence, which were crushed in due course by the armies from the centre. The city used to be a distantly located place without much significance, be it economic, cultural or political.[42] This changed when Siam's position was

---

[40]During the reign of King Narai close contacts were established between France and Siam. The intention of Narai was to balance the increasing influence of the British East-India-Company with the French.

[41]These two cities already had the function of border towns. The province of Korat used to be the most northeastern extension of the old Khmer empire. The most important city during that time was Phimai and the temple-fortresses of Phanom Rung.

[42]Only once, after the fall of Ayudhya, did Korat have larger significance, when it was used as a base by a noble of the old Ayudhya aristocracy to fight against Taksin, who had

challenged by the French colonialization of Cambodia and later Laos. It became necessary to define and protect the borders of the kingdom, and integrate these far away regions into the Thai administration.[43] Thus Korat became the capital of the Monthon Isaharn late in the nineteenth century. This Monthon covered the whole of the Northeast of modern Thailand and those parts of Cambodia belonging to Siam at that time. A large military base was set up in Korat for the protection of the borders and for internal control. In 1900 a railway was built from Bangkok up to Korat, which triggered off a first economic boom. Rice mills were established and up to 20 % of the overall rice export of Thailand was handled through Korat, before being sent to Bangkok. Many of the railway workers were Chinese, who settled in the city to use and create economic opportunities. Although Korat was the second largest town in Thailand it still remained a rather sleepy outpost. Business like rice mills, later followed by cassava mills etc. was based on and connected to agriculture.

Another boom took place in the sixties in connection with the American war in Vietnam. The large military base was used for bombing Cambodia and Vietnam. Partly to support the military infrastructure, partly as counter-insurgency measures, development projects were sponsored and an infrastructure built, namely a large road was constructed, the so-called friendship highway, leading from Bangkok and passing through Korat up to Nong Khai at the Laotian border. Combined with military spending and the stationing of American soldiers, an economic boom was fueled in the sixties which lasted up to the early seventies.

In the seventies and eighties other regional centres like Chiang Mai in the North, Haad Yai/Songhkla in the South, Cholburi in the East and Kon Khaen in the Northeast gained in importance, while Korat was left far behind. For example, the first university of the Northeast was established in Khon Khaen, a rather new city, and not Korat. The description of Korat in a travel guide as a place where there is nothing to see or to do, except use it as a starting point to visit the Khmer ruins of Phimai, captures the situation quite well.

When Chatchai Chonhavoon became prime minister of Thailand in 1988, this situation changed again. Chatchai had the city of Korat as his electorate and won with a clear majority. Commonly, the elected member of parliament, especially

---

shifted the capital to Thonburi. In the end, Taksin's army conquered Korat and the city was integrated into the new Siamese kingdom.

[43]In the traditional Siamese concept, a state was defined by the centre, be it the palace or the capital city, not by borders. In fact, defined borders would have contradicted the idea of "world conqueror". Thus these borders were never clearly defined. Only when European colonialism entered, did it become a necessity to fix borders and integrate the territories belonging to the state.

if he becomes a minister and even more so when he is the prime minister, is expected to provide resources and support for his province. Although this by no means explains the success and boom of the region, the projects initiated during the prime-ministership of Chathchai provided a base for rapid economic development.

Initially the existing friendship highway was extended to a four-lane highway. Then a new street was built to link the province of Korat with the industrial zones of the eastern seaboard and the new harbour there. Thereby Korat gained a direct link to the sea and to international markets. In addition the connections with the cities in the north were extended and improved by building new highways like the one to Phitsanulok. Currently a large container depot is planned; it will become the centre for the Northeast of Thailand, Laos, Cambodia and parts of Vietnam. In addition, as this container depot has a link to the new harbour on the eastern seaboard, and it is also expected to be a turnover point for the traffic in goods to the north of Thailand, to reduce the traffic flow in Bangkok. Finally, two large export processing industrial estates have been set up and several more are planned.

While these developments are taking place mainly at the periphery of the city proper, within the inner city, three department stores have been established and more are planned and under construction. Several first class hotels have been built, although Korat still hardly has any attraction for tourists. At the fringe of the inner city, connected to the larger roads, housing estates for middle and higher-income groups have been built. All Bangkok-based banks have several branches in Korat. As an expression of the current boom and the intention to develop Nakorn Ratshasima into a centre beyond the Northeast, in December a "World Tech" show was held close to the recently established Technical University, the first "Technical University" outside of Bangkok. Today Korat is no longer a sleepy provincial city, but rather a rapidly growing and extending boom town with construction taking place anywhere.

Social Cohesion of Local Elites

As in any other larger town, the élite of Korat is far from homogenous but consists of bureaucrats, intellectuals, professionals and businessmen. These have different and even diverging interests and personal connections beyond the region. Thus local cohesion and co-operation is difficult to achieve. Why should for example a rich businessman building department stores and hotels in Korat co-operate with a local intellectual writing critical articles in leftist publications? Why should an entrepreneur join hands with a local environmental NGO? To complicate matters even further, Korat is a city of migrants with very diverse ethnic and social backgrounds.

An indicator of social cohesion are personal linkages and membership of associations. In Korat the astonishing situation is that associations which usually follow conflicting interests co-operate and that diverse groups and persons with different interests belong to the same association. Two associations form something like a core and will be described as examples: the Korat Chamber of Commerce (CoC) and the Local Information Centre for Development (LICD).

The Korat Chamber of Commerce is an umbrella organization for different local groups and other associations. The vice chairman is also chairman of a large local environmental NGO and another leading member of the Chamber of Commerce is the vice rector of the Rajabat Institute, and is a member of a Chinese language club as well. The Local Information Centre for Development belongs to the Rajabat Institute[44] and is an umbrella organization for local and regional NGOs. The leading members of the LICD are also members of the CoC and of alumni clubs of Bangkok Universities. The LICD and the CoC regularly organize seminars in one of the larger hotels to which academics, businessmen, NGO-representatives, the provincial governor and members of the city council etc. are invited, on topics like: "Decentralization of Power", "Development Potentials of Nakorn Ratshasima" etc.

Although the local groups, especially business groups, compete with Bangkok-based groups, competition alone does not imply or lead to locally-based social cohesion and co-operation. The competition and conflicts do not dissolve the local conflicts. Korat's big business could improve its position vis-à-vis the local bureaucracy and NGOs with alliances to Bangkok's big business, playing an important political role. In a similar vein, the Korat NGOs can co-operate with Bangkok-based NGOs with their political influence and access to foreign funding, to strengthen their own position vis-à-vis opposing local groups. In Korat, however, the local orientation overrides other interest conflicts to a considerable degree. Interviews with different people indicate such a strong local orientation in terms like "we are the people of Korat", "we have to develop our province" etc. Even people who studied in Bangkok or abroad went back to Korat for the reason that "this is my home province".[45] Especially among

---

[44]The Rajabat Institute, which has now the same status as other national institutes in Thailand like the King Monghut Institute of Technology or the National Institute for Development Administration, developed out of a teacher's college. Besides the LICD a Centre for Local Culture belongs to the Rajabat Institute.

[45]That young well-educated persons go back to their home province is still unusual in Thailand. In a talk with a spokesman of the provincial assembly of Nakorn Sawan, he pointed out the problem that the children, after studying in Bangkok, do not want to come back to the "outback", boring places full of bureaucratic corruption, mafia structures etc. Many businesses had problems continuing due to this drain.

younger businessmen, a strong motive is to modernize and beautify the city. Their idea is to make Korat a modern city with all "modern" amenities, without the problems of Bangkok. From this starting point, the creation of local traditions, symbols and identity-markers is important to achieve solidarity and to build up bonds with the locality.

In the centre of these local traditions and as a major symbol of local identity is the Ya Mo (Grandmother Mo) cult.

The Ya Mo Tradition

Like any tradition, the cult is connected with historical incidents. In the early nineteenth century, a revolt in Vientiane, Laos broke out and an army was heading towards Bangkok. In the course of the approach, the city of Korat was besieged, conquered and all inhabitants taken prisoner. According to Chakrabongse (1960), "Every night while the men were in close captivity, the women were ordered to serve the Laotian officers and men with food and drink. One night the wife of the murdered governor of Korat led other women in luring their Laotian captors into a kind of drunken orgy, after which they were able to free their menfolk, who fought and killed some 2,000 of the Vientiane troops and were thus able to free themselves and rejoined the Thais" (Chakrabongse 1960:161). Manich Jumsai (1977), who takes pride in being versed in Thai tales argues, "Among the people swept away to Vientiane was the Deputy-Governor's wife, Mo, and all her women colleagues. At night Mo led her women and other compatriots to rise against the Lao gardes [sic] who were killed. ... This led Anu (the commander) to believe that the Thai were coming up and he retreated to find a better place to hold up" (Manich 1977:470). Due to her braveness, Mo was given the title of honor "Thao Suranari".[46]

Historically approved is the fact of an attack from Laos in course of which Korat was conquered. This revolt was defeated by Bangkok troops and in the end Laos became a vassal of the Bangkok state (Hall 1977:468). Recently, in an M.A. thesis at Thammasat University, the argument was developed that the whole Ya Mo story is completely fictitious, which led to an uproar and large-scale demonstrations in Korat, demanding that the whole province to be closed to the woman who wrote the thesis. Unfortunately, she was working as a teacher in Korat and it was demanded that she be deported from the province.[47]

---

[46]It is interesting that the governor's role in this story is limited to being the husband of Mo. What did he do during the fight? What did he do to protect the city?

[47]This "scandal" indicates the sensitivity of history in Thailand. Not only in local traditions is the attempt made to construct historical continuities but even more so in official state ideology. In quite a similar vein several scandals occurred, when basic assumptions of

This story of Mo or Suranari reminds one of a Chinese Opera play or the story of Judith in the bible and does not end here. Suranari died a natural death in 1847, and her bones were kept in a special urn in a temple (Wat Salaloi). This urn broke for unknown reasons and her bones were transferred to another temple, where again the urn broke. The explanation was that so far her remains have not been properly kept and her spirit thus cannot find peace. Here is an alteration from the usual pattern in recounting how protective spirits are born. Commonly, protective spirits are humans who died a violent death, especially pregnant women.[48] So her natural death would certainly not indicate that she has become a spirit, especially not a powerful one. Thus the story of the broken urns may compensate this shortcoming. Finally a monument was built in 1934 and she has become the protective spirit of the province and city of Korat.

In the Ya Mo story several cultural elements are connected. Firstly Mo appears to be a local woman married to the centrally installed governor of the province. Thus a linkage between "local - female" and "central - male" is expressed. The governor was the leading representative of the state in Korat and thus installed with power to keep order. This connection between "central - powerful - ordered" is weakened in course of the story, as the Thai soldiers were defeated or could not protect the city against the Laotians. Thus in the final struggle, the "local - female" became the powerful defender against the barbarian invaders.[49] Furthermore, in Thailand female spirits are usually regarded as more powerful and fierce than male spirits.

Obviously, the Ya Mo story was kept alive in local traditions. I think that during the nationalist phase in the reign of Rama VI, when heroic local traditions of fights against invading armies were revived, the Ya Mo story was made popular again.[50] In 1934 a monument was built to commemorate Suranari, financed by the state through the provincial governor and local donations mainly from the

---

the state ideology were challenged as fiction and not historic facts. Most important in this context was the discussion whether the Ramkhamhaeng inscription was a fake made by King Monghut or not.

[48]See in this context Quaritch-Wales (1931).

[49]An interesting side story concerns the girlfriend of Mo, who helped her in attacking the Laotian soldiers. Her remains are kept in a temple away from the city. The place is hardly known by the people of Korat. The reason given is that she either had an affair with a Laotian soldier or was raped, thus lost her innocence and could not be styled as Jeanne D'Arc of Korat.

[50]These local stories were used to express the close linkages and nationalism between the different regions of Thailand and the central state. There are no monuments for local heroes who fought against armies from Bangkok or Ayudhya.

Chinese population. The monument was designed by Sil Bhirasi, an Italian artist who was working at Silaphakorn University.[51] In 1987 the foundation collapsed and it was rebuilt, this time by a local architect. The money for the renovation came from local donations.

The Suranari monument is in front of the western city gate of Korat, adjacent to "Suranari Road". This road connects the "new" city, where the railway station is located, with the old quadrangular city. This new city grew after the railway was built early in the nineteenth century. It was extended during the sixties, when shops, hotels, brothels and bars were set up there for the R and R of the American soldiers in the sixties. When passing along the monument, the people pay respect to the spirit of Suranari and worship her regularly. Stories of how her spirit helped people who did pay homage to her abound. Around the monument are several stalls selling flowers and sandalwood sticks for those who want to pay homage or beg for help.

The statue, designed in European fashion, is facing to the west with her back to the old city of Korat. Across the street is a Chinese temple (San). On the land belonging to this temple a stage is erected where the so-called Korat song and play is performed. It is said that the spirit of Suranari enjoys these shows which are sponsored by people whose wishes have been fulfilled.

The spirit of Suranari is not regarded as a "god", but as a locality spirit, a very powerful one though. In this respect, Suranari is similar to the spirit of the city pillar or other locality spirits. Usually the power of these spirits is limited to the locality and its direct vicinity. In the case of Suranari, the locality is regarded as being the whole province and its inhabitants.

Currently, a large Suranari Memorial with several showpieces belonging to her is under construction and in some shops photographs of her can be bought, even though she lived in the first half of the nineteenth century. This memorial faces some opposition from the locals. One reason probably is that a market has been destroyed to make space for the memorial and that the governor is promoting the construction. One argument is that the memorial is supposed to be the governor's memorial, not the memorial of the Korat people.

To quite a large degree, Ya Mo structures the city spatially as well as spiritually. The monument located at the edge of the old city and the new city is in the middle of the modern city of Korat and the province of Korat. It is a point of reference. In addition, it is a central place for urban traffic and most busses pass

---

[51]At about the same time, a similar monument was erected in Phuket to commemorate the heroic acts of two women protecting the island of Phuket against Burmese invaders. In Phuket this did not lead to the establishment of a cult though.

it. Thus the place and its surroundings are always very busy. To locate business close to the monument is regarded as advantageous for spiritual as well as economic reasons, and the streets in the vicinity form the major business districts. The owner of a large department store (Klang Plaza II) argued that it is very important to locate the department store close to the monument to gain additional spiritual protection. Thus he wants to extend the existing department store towards the monument.

The name Suranari is often used. Besides the Suranari Road, there is a Suranari Hotel, the Suranari industrial estate, the Yamo market and the new university is named Suranari University. In a publication of the Chamber of Commerce's, reference is made to Suranari when Korat is described as the "province and city of brave women". Through activities by those groups who have the potential for investment, giving names to Universities etc. the importance of Suranari is strengthened.

Ya Mo certainly is "the centre" of Korat and the whole province. In a survey in the city of Korat, 90 % of the respondents regard the monument as the centre of Korat. About one third regularly go to the monument to pay homage to Ya Mo or ask for favours. Although in Korat two other locations are connected to powerful locality spirits (the city pillar and the San Chang Puak or temple of the white elephant) 90 % of the respondents regard the monument as most important and most powerful. A survey among those paying homage at the Suranari monument indicated a large number of people coming from the provinces and even other provinces of Thailand. Thus the reputation of Ya Mo is far beyond the city and even the province and not limited to special social or ethnic groups.[52]

Although local traditions are not limited to the Ya Mo cult, it forms a core and point of reference, providing a self-awareness and pride. Thus other local traditions (language, food) are elevated as well, strengthening local integration. Several examples can be cited:

The province of Nakorn Rashasima is by far the largest province of Thailand and it was planned to split it into three. At least two other cities grew rapidly during the last decade: Chokchai and Phak Chong/Si Khiau and was to be promoted to the status of provincial capital. Such a promotion implies a largely

---

[52]This has to be put into a context though. Although Korat is a city of migrants, most are Buddhists and have no religious problems with engaging in spirit cults. There is only a very small Islamic and Christian minority in Korat that does not participate in the cult or participates only marginally. Most migrants are Chinese, Khmer and people from Laos. Recently, due to the boom, people from the north and south and parts of the central provinces moved to Korat. For many years a larger minority of Mon has lived in Korat.

improved status and several advantages like having one's own budget. Astonishingly, this plan faced strong resistance from the people of the whole province, who wanted to remain "the children of grandmother (Ya) Mo".

Another indicator is the name of the province and the city. The old name, dating back to the Khmer empire, is "Korat", which is also the geographical name for the whole region: the "Korat Plateau". The official name of the city and province is "Nakorn Ratshasima". Inside the province, everybody speaks only of Korat, not of Nakorn Ratshasima. The people define themselves as people of Korat, certainly not as people of Nakorn Ratshasima. Even most migrants soon regard themselves as "people of Korat".

Finally. in the province a special Thai dialect is spoken, consisting of several words from the Khmer and Laotian language and with a pronunciation different from central Thai. Locally this dialect is referred to as "Korat language". For a long time it was regarded as a sign of underdevelopment to speak local dialects and not proper central Thai, especially not a dialect that could be identified with "Laotian". Now Korat Thai is widely spoken in the province and it is pointed out that it is not at all Laotian, although different from Bangkok Thai. One woman felt quite insulted when her language was referred to as Korat Laotian in Bangkok. Her argument was that the Bangkok people have no idea about Laotian and Korat language.

How could such a strong local orientation emerge in the context of a strongly centralized state, where especially culture is defined by the centre?

Syncretism of the Ya Mo Cult as Background and Result of Local Integration

Following Eisenstadt (1979), modernization demands new forms of integration in which tradition, change and modernity are combined. Thus the "reconstruction" of traditions and symbols of collective identification through which cultural continuity is achieved, is part of modernization (Eisenstadt 1979:364-365). The Ya Mo cult can be described as such a "constructed tradition", integrating diverse cultural elements and social groups on a local level. The cult is successful in achieving the local integration of diverse groups, because it consists of many elements that make it possible for diverse groups to identify with it.

The monument was built to symbolize the spirit of Suranari and her braveness in protecting the city of Korat. It was built by an Italian architect following European artistic views and values and could be located in any European city. The building was financed by the Thai state and local donations from mainly Chinese businessmen. The order for the monument was made by the governor of the Province who was sent there from the Ministry of Interior. Thus the first monument is a monument of Bangkok support of the province, a monument of the governor and the artist and also of local strength to collect sufficient funds for such a monument. The renovation in 1987 was financed entirely by local donations with the names of the donors inscribed in the base of the monument. Thereby Suranari became more of a local symbol taken care of by locals.

It is interesting that there is a wide-spread Chinese-based symbolism. Although at the monument no Chinese signs are written, on the opposite side of the street, where the stage used for the Korat song and play is located, Chinese signs are wide-spread and a Chinese temple is located there. The temple is regularly used in Chinese ceremonies.

The local context is expressed particularly in the Korat song and play. The song and play is a traditional Thai dance, into which aspects of Khmer and Laotian folk dance and music are integrated. In the songs local myths, sometimes funny affairs and stories from the life of Buddha are told. The special Korat song has existed since the thirties, when the monument was built and the Ya Mo cult had a strong revival. The stories are written by locals, as only they are able to interpret the story of Ya Mo in the correct way.

Obviously, the Ya Mo cult is highly syncretist. In this respect, the cult provides something for most inhabitants of the city and the province. It points at the desire for freedom and independence, the strength to fight for it, the relation to Bangkok, the distance to the Laotian wilderness from where the army came, modernism in the form of a European-style statue, and integration of the Chinese. Furthermore it provides a local self-awareness in that the people of Korat can fight for themselves, as Ya Mo showed them in her struggle with the Laotian army.

Conclusions

The current boom of Korat is to a great extent due to policies and interests of Bangkok-based strategic groups in the context of the globalization of the Thai economy. However, conditions exist in Korat and traditions have been created by which the local élite is able to develop strong social cohesion and solidarity. The local traditions as exemplified by the extremely popular Ya Mo cult are syncretist enough so that on the local level, nearly any group and person can identify with it. Thus the ideology of "we are the children of Ya Mo" overshadows other interest conflicts in favour of local cooperation. This allows the local élites to gain or keep a certain degree of independence in local and provincial affairs. Korat today is neither a satellite of Bangkok, nor a province aiming at independence or local autonomy. It is a province integrated into Thailand where the local élites try quite successfully to gain from the available opportunities.

The Cultural Construction of Malay Cities

In contrast to the Theravadha Buddhist cities in Sri Lanka and mainland Southeast Asia, the early Indonesian or Javanese capitals do not seem to have had an urban image. Thus, an Arab writer at the beginning of the tenth century goes so far as to assert that "in India (i. e. Indonesia) there are no towns." (Wolters 1976:18). Quite unlike Ayudhya and seventeenth century Bangkok, the capital of Majapahit was, as described in the fourteenth century Nagarakertagama, not necessarily a walled city (Pigeaud 1962:IV, 11-18, V, 467-552). Whether or not there was a wall of any importance or military use, whether it marked a significant cultural boundary between town and countryside is doubtful, but deserves further study (Reid 1980:242). In fact, the major division appears to have been that between the walled palace of the ruler (kraton) surrounded by a royal district (nagaragung), much larger than the town itself, and the neighbouring regions (mancanegara) and the coastal provinces (pasisir). The spatial perception is centrifocal, and the centre is the kraton or istana of the ruler rather than a capital city (Evers 1977, Evers 1984b).

The lack of a linkage between city and palace is visible up to now in Malaysia. The centre of political power in the Malay states was the palace (istana) of the king or sultan. The istana was, very much like the Javanese kraton, surrounded by royal villages, inhabited by retailers and craftsmen serving the royal court. A central square (padang) opens towards the Sultan's palace (istana) and the living quarters of the Sultan's extended family and their descendants. The main mosque is found next to the padang in immediate proximity to the palace, whereas the market and the Chinese settlement are some way off the centre of religious and political power.

Kota Bahru (Evers and Goh 1976; Clarke 1976) and Kuala Trengganu conform very much to this pattern, as do several Javanese towns (Siddique 1977). In Malaysia, market places are often separated from the palace by some distance. It is, however, here that cities developed primarily through Chinese and Indian immigration. Up to today the Malay image of the town is one of the market place rather than a residential area. In fact, bandar means, strictly speaking, a port or harbour town. Kota, another term frequently connected with town names, means fort or stockade. There is no precise Malay expression for town or city. Malays, by popular definition, live in villages (kampong), even if these villages now administratively fall within the boundaries of a municipality. Malay life is focused on the istana and the mosque, but not on the city.

It is, therefore, not so much Kuala Lumpur, the colonial capital city, but the national mosque, the Mesjid Negara, and the king, the Yang di-Pertuan Agong, elected from among the sultans of the Malay states, that form the focus of Malay national sentiment and identity. In fact, a truly urban conception of space is perhaps only expressed in the "chinatowns" of Malaysian and Indonesian cities.

Conflicting Constructions: Space in a Multicultural Society

Though most Chinese immigrants to Malaysia and Indonesia originally came from rural areas in Southern China, they nevertheless brought with them the image of life centred on the city. As Skinner (1964) has pointed out in a lengthy study, Chinese rural social structure cannot be understood without reference to towns. Clusters of small villages surrounding a locally important town formed a discrete social and territorial unit, which Skinner terms a "standard marketing area". Occupational and religious associations as well as kinship ties combined to turn this area into a tightly knit socio-political unit.

Chinese social life, even in rural areas, was centred on the city and it is likely that this image of the city was also brought over to Malaysia by Southern Chinese migrants. At least the Chinese secret societies that dominated Chinese society in the Straits Settlements and the Malay states perpetuated the urban image and enshrined it in their most important ritual, the initiation of new members. These rites were held in a Chinese temple, representing "an imaginary walled city through which the candidate was to take a symbolic journey" (Purcell 1956:165). A Chinese city itself was a highly structured spatial entity with definite boundaries, directions and functional areas (Wheatley 1972). Though no walled Chinese city was ever built in Malaysia or Indonesia, the concept of dense urban living in bounded, clearly defined space was certainly known and utilized as a "mental map", or blueprint, in Nanyang Chinese urbanism (Evers 1977).

Malaysian society is multiracial and countless observers have drawn attention to the unequal geographical distribution of its two major ethnic groups, Malays and Chinese. Overall population statistics of Peninsular Malaysia clearly show that the majority of urban areas are mainly populated by Chinese. whereas Malays are mainly concentrated in the rural hinterland. There are of course exceptions to this. A few major towns, particularly on the east coast, have a majority of Malays, but even here the city core tends to be inhabited and owned by Chinese. Those ecological areas of towns that convey a typically "urban" character are Chinese, whereas the Malay areas maintain a typical "rural" appearance. It is not without justification that Malay areas within Malaysian towns are usually called kampong, whereas Chinese areas are given place names and street names, or are in some cases just called Chinatown. There are also Chinese villages with a predominantly agricultural population, and single Chinese families in Malay villages. But even then Chinese houses tend to have a more urban appearance. They tend to be built of stone more often than of timber and they sit squarely on the ground, whereas Malay houses are raised on stilts, built of planks, and thatched or covered with corrugated iron sheets.

The rural character of the Malays and the urban mode of living of the Chinese have often been noted, described and explained. Malays always have been, so the argument goes, a rural people, who have adopted their style of life to the tropical climate to find an ecological niche left by the Malays. They came into Malaya with the expansion of modern capitalism, partly even before colonial rule was firmly established. It was left to them to extend markets, to provide labour for tin mining and for the capitalist plantation economy, and to found and settle the communication centres of the new political and economic system, namely, the town and cities. Thus a colonial plural society emerged with a division of labour based on ethnic lines. All these reasons given for the unequal geographical distribution of Malays and Chinese are true, but not necessarily sufficient to explain present day urbanization taking place under changed circumstances. This is because the cultural aspect has so far been neglected and the ideological superstructure, as it were, disregarded. Even if the basic socioeconomic structure changes, even if the development policy of rectifying the racial imbalance within the occupational and residential structure meets with success, Malays are unlikely to change their way of life immediately nor is the ethnic structure of Malaysian cities likely to be reversed in the near future. Even those Malays who have been lured into the cities by the efforts of the Malaysian government to open up urban job opportunities for rural Malays appear to be still maintaining a rural ideology. Malay politicians are known to have admonished Malay civil servants to stay in town after retirement instead of returning to their home villages. Even within cities, areas with a concentration of Malay population tend to preserve their rural character in at least a symbolic fashion. Despite very often crowded conditions houses are still built on stilts and a few coconut trees are planted and chickens are raised.

Now it could be argued and statistically "proven" that the economic, educational, and occupational differences between Chinese and Malays are nonexistent if one keeps place of residence (rural or urban) constant. Consequently, there are said to be no real differences between Chinese and Malays except place of residence. If Malays move to the city, differences between them and Chinese would disappear. This argument is, of course, nonsensical and based on a complete misunderstanding of both the political economy and the culture of Malaysia. It is precisely the fact that rural urban migration is still very low (except in Kuala Lumpur; Fernandez et al. 1975:40) and that Malays tend to stay in the rural areas and maintain a rural style of life even in cities, whereas the Chinese tend to concentrate in cities and maintain an urban way of life, which needs explanation. To keep the dependent variable constant or to eliminate it statistically from one's paradigm begs the question and renders the possibility of explaining the structure and dynamics of Malaysian society impossible.

British colonial policy has created a socioeconomic base on which a cultural superstructure could flourish, creating, selecting, and maintaining traditional Chinese and Malay values that otherwise might have vanished. In the following paragraphs I wish to explicate an important aspect of these Chinese and Malay cultural values, which appears to be a most relevant factor in shaping the process of Malaysian urbanization and the ecological structure of Malaysian urban areas.

Differing Conceptions of Space and the Image of the City

In the following explications we use a phenomenological approach. The data are primarily observations ordered in a more or less systematic fashion, a number of linguistic facts (or patterns of verbal behaviour) from free interviews and written records, and the results of a survey of land-ownership in 18 Malaysian towns.

Upon entering Malay rural or urban kampong (villages) one is faced with the problem of orientation. There is usually no main street, no plaza or main square, but only an apparently arbitrary system of winding footpaths leading from house to house, becoming narrower at times or ending in blind alleys. There appears to be no clear pattern, no "readability" of the urban or rural scene, which according to Kevin Lynch's well-known study, "The Image of the City", is so important for the image of a town or settlement (Lynch 1960). Malay houses themselves are built according to a clear pattern. They have a veranda (serambi), a main room (ibu rumah) from which one or two sleeping rooms may be divided (bilek), and a kitchen attached to the back of the house (dapur). The veranda usually (but not necessarily) faces the east or south to keep it cool in the afternoon, but apart from this there are no rules or regulations about how houses ought to relate to each other. There appears to be a tendency to keep them apart as far as possible and in such a way that the view is never blocked by houses alone. This creates an impression of wide-open space even if villages become more densely settled due to growing population and the rule of neo-local residence after marriage. Boundaries between the house lots are in no way demarcated, and residents find it difficult to point out the exact shape of the plot of land on which the house is built. Importance is only attached to the usufructuary rights to coconut trees or fruit trees; otherwise, boundaries do not seem to matter. Though Malaysia has had, since British times, a fairly well-organized cadastre system, Malay villagers quite often do not bother to register changes in the ownership of their housing lots. If new settlers come in from other areas or new families are created by marriage, permission to put up a house is fairly easily granted by the owner and no rent is charged for the land (Goh and Evers 1976). Houses, however, are rented or sold separately irrespective of the National Land Code, which does not allow a legal separation of land and building structures.

The nature of the conception of geographical space or land is demonstrated by a case from a village. A man moved into the village to earn a living as a sate vendor. He asked an absentee landlord to rent him a house. When the latter visited the village, he found to his surprise that the tenant was occupying a house on a lot adjacent to the property he was supposed to be renting. The actual owner, on learning of the situation, reacted only by exhibiting the common "never-mind attitude" (tidak apa-apa). Discussions with villagers to verify boundaries on cadastre maps proved to be very difficult and often futile. There appeared to be no clearly developed conception of bounded space and of clear-cut boundaries in general.

The same attitude is found when trying to delineate the boundaries of a kampong or village. A kampong is usually defined by the relationship of its inhabitants to the mosque or prayer house. As Clarke (1976:63) pointed out in an analysis of the spatial order of Kota Bahru, Kelantan, "most areas have a central identifying physical feature and from this the areas radiate in various directions. Boundaries are indistinct ... " All those taking part in the election of the mosque committee belong to one kampong, irrespective of where they actually live. The kampong is therefore in essence not a residential group in the sense the term is defined in sociology text books. The definition of the village as a territorial group is based on the European image of a settlement and is not strictly applicable to the Malay situation.[53]

Boundaries in the rice fields are more clearly defined, as rice fields are divided by dams and irrigation channels. But even here conception of space or area is rather diffuse. Originally, the size of paddy field was measured in sowing extent (i. e., according to a fixed measure of rice that was used to sow a plot of land, which could vary in size according to the availability of water and the quality of soil). Nowadays traditional Malay measures of rice land have their equivalent in English measures (acres, usually), but the equivalent acreage varies from area to area or from state to state. It is only in the area of small-holding rubber plantations that fairly fixed conceptions of areas are maintained.

---

[53]Soja (1971:9-10) has drawn attention to the fact that "conventional western perspectives on spatial organization are powerfully shaped by the concept of property" and that "property has become rigidly and territorially defined." This is certainly true though rigid territoriality is by no means an exclusively Western concept, as we are going to argue in the Chinese case. The dichotomy between "Western" and "native" conceptions of space, found in studies in other societies as well (e. g. Bohannan 1964:174-176) does not appear useful in these general terms. Some related issues are discussed in Evers (1975a, 1976) and in Cohen (n. d.). The Indians had to be left out of this study.

The Chinese conception of space differs greatly from that of the Malays. On entering a Chinese village one is sure where it begins and where it ends. Whereas Malay houses stand on stilts and are suspended above ground, Chinese houses sit squarely on the soil. There tends to be one main footpath or street passing through the village, which in most cases is usually clearly discernible even on a cadastre map because plots of land tend to be small but regular. Members of a Chinese family will be able to say exactly where their land ends and their neighbour's begins. Quite often a fence is put up creating an inner yard attached to the house.

Whereas Malays tend to add the names of family members as owners of a plot of land on intestate inheritance, Chinese tend to subdivide or sell land. Working on land registry data we often came across plots of Malay-owned land that were divided into shares of one seventh, one twelfth, or up to several hundredth shares. Islamic law is partly responsible for this, but the fact remains that effective individual ownership is no longer possible. Though joint ownership is also common among Chinese, it seldom extends to unmanageable proportions.

The importance of the ownership of land and the concomitant clear-cut conception of geographical space is further emphasized by the fact that Chinese have developed a special science of boundaries, namely geomancy. The measures of a plot of land and the direction a house should face were traditionally determined by a ritual specialist, a geomancer. Though his services are not necessarily employed any more, there is still a rudimentary knowledge of the science of geomancy (feng shui) and clear understanding of the importance of spatial arrangements. Great attention is still paid to the direction of the main door and the positioning of houses in general. On occasion the outlay of cities and the fortune of their inhabitants are related to geomantic principles. One informant even tried to explain the initial success of British rule over Malay by pointing out, in terms of geogmancy, the highly appropriate position of the living quarters of British residents and district officers, which tended to be located on hills, their backs to mountain ranges.

The difference between Chinese and Malay conceptions of space becomes particularly visible when comparing Chinese and Malay Moslem graveyards. Chinese attach a great importance to the exact location and the boundaries of a grave, which are, as long as the family can afford it, indicated by strong walls surrounding the tomb. Ritual specialists are employed to measure and determine a good location for an ancestral grave. Chinese graveyards are therefore spatially highly structured and permanent. A Malay graveyard is in contrast very loosely structured. The two boundary stones put on each grave are scattered and extend into the surrounding areas, provided that building regulations in cities have not made this impossible. No great importance is attached to the location of the grave. Wherever there is some space left the burial can take place. The only exceptions are graves said to posses magic powers (kuburan keramat) and the mosques themselves, which have a clearly defined ritually pure area.

But even here the Malay conception of space has made inroads. A frequently found form of holy grave in Malaysia is the so-called kuburan panjang (long grave). The holy man buried here is said to have grown, thus pushing the boundary stones of the grave down. The grave stones have to be re-erected from time to time, extending the length of the grave in the process.

Even in the area of non-orthodox religion the differences between the Chinese and Malay conceptions of space become apparent. The Chinese attach great importance to the earth goddess. Villages or town quarters tend to have a local guardian deity, a Datok. Malay ghosts, however, are not attached to a particular place of worship.[54] Though the Malays also know guardian ghosts whose power emanates from a certain place, their power does not apply to a clearly defined area; they do not rule defined territories.

Our analysis of the differences between Chinese and Malay conceptions of geographical and religious space can also be extended to conceptions of social space. With very few exceptions the population of the Malay peninsula consists of immigrants. This holds true both for Malays, many of whom originated from Sumatra, Java, or other Indonesian islands, and for Chinese. Nevertheless, Malays would attach very little importance to their place of origin. Migrants from Sumatra or Java are quickly acculturated to a uniform Malay society. Second generation migrants usually do not speak the dialect or language of their parents any more and would claim, on being interviewed, that they are local people (asal dari sini). On being questioned further, they might have some hazy conceptions of where their ancestors came from but will usually not know or be interested in the exact place of origin. Exceptions to this general rule tend to be people of Minangkabau origin, as long as they live together in close settlements and maintain a system of matrilineal descent (Evers 1975a).

In contrast, Chinese tend to have a very clear conception not only of their general area of origin. This knowledge is to a certain extent still transmitted from generation to generation. Whereas Malay identity is established by social and cultural facts - namely, by being a Muslim, speaking the Malay language, and being in very general, locally undefined terms a "bumiputra" (son of the soil) - Chinese determine their ethnic identity primarily by their dialect and their

---

[54]See Mulder (1975:77) for a relevant discussion on domesticated and non-domesticated ghosts (hantu).

place of origin in China.[55] A strict system of patrilineal descent, lineages, and clans defined by common ancestors, common geographical origin, and common localized places of worship is based on an identity between social and geographical space.

The localized bias in the Malay conception of social space could also be demonstrated in a study of the "mental maps" of Malaysian students in a northern town (Gould and White 1974:167-169). On being asked where they would prefer to find employment, most Malays gave the name of their home town and to a lesser degree the surrounding area, whereas Chinese students preferred various urban centres along the west coast as far south as Singapore.

The Chinese mental map was clearly focused on major urban areas whereas the Malay one was centred on the primarily rural home districts. These differing conceptions of space form in a general way the basis of another culturally defined complex, namely, the image of an urban area, a town, or a city. It is the combination of the conception of space and the image of an urban area that, I submit, still influences the urbanization process and urban ecology of Malaysia.

In contrast, the Malay perception of political space and of the city was quite different. It seems to go back to or at least to show great similarity to Indonesian predecessors. In the empires of Majapahit and Mataram "territory was concerted as radiating in three concentric circles with the Kraton of the prince at the centre: (1) the nagaragung or core regions, (2) the mantjanegara, or neighbouring regions and (3) the pasisir, or coastal provinces" (Siddique 1977). The spatial perception is centrifocal and the centre is the palace of the ruler rather than the city.[56] The Malay conception of political space appears to have been quite similar.

In the ecological structure of some of the Malay cities the principles of an Islamized and Malayanized image of the Indian city of ancient Southeast Asia are still to be seen. A central square (padang) opens toward the sultan's palace (istana) and the living quarters of the sultan's extended family and their descendants. The main mosque is found next to the padang in the immediate proximity of the istana, whereas the market and the Chinese settlement are some

---

[55]For a very perceptive discussion on the ethnographic meaning of Malay see Judith Nagata's essay (Nagata 1974a).

[56]According to the 14th-century Nagarakertagama, the capital city of Majapahit had a brick wall, which is archeologically confirmed (Krom 1923:174). Also Bantam, Jakarta, and Cirebon were walled cities in pre-Dutch times. More important however, is the wall surrounding the Sultan's palace (Kraton), which sets off the political and ritual centre from the rest of the town. The kraton walls are still maintained in the remaining sultan's residence in Java.

way off the centre of religious and political power. Kota Bahru (Evers and Goh 1976; Clarke 1976) and Kuala Trengganu conform very much to this pattern. A similar pattern could also be shown to exist in the physical outlay of the National University of Malaysia (Evers 1997). But whereas some Javanese cities up to the 16th century were still surrounded by a wall, the Malayanized town consistently exhibits the centrifocal conception of space. The centre (padang, istana, and mesjid besar) is clearly defined but beyond this area the spatial structures peter out and become less and less clear. The town is in cultural and social terms not a bounded area and it is completely undefined where the town ends and the villages begin.

Even among the modern Malay urban middle class[57], consisting of civil servants and professionals, the original conception of space and of the city is still maintained, whenever a chance is given. It is first of all expressed in a certain uneasiness and reluctance to move into the new middle-class housing estates that are springing up in practically all Malaysian cities. A massive increase in Malay urban population living primarily in these estates has so far been noted only for the Federal Territory surrounding Kuala Lumpur. This may signal a change, but still the housing estates are normally designed by Chinese architects, built by Chinese contractors, and conform to the Chinese cultural conception of space and housing. Most of these housing estates consist of modernized versions of the Chinese shophouse, where the shop is replaced by a parking space for a small car. Mostly these houses are semidetached or row houses with a narrow back lane and very small backyards surrounded by a wall. The maintenance of boundaries is very important and clearly expressed in iron gates and stone walls. Not so in Malay areas designed and constructed by Malays themselves; here still kampong type houses are found, though the lower, formerly open part tends to be walled in and used by younger or newly married children of the family. But still, wherever possible, the boundary to the neighbour's house is not marked by a fence or a stone wall but is left open. If there are hedges or fences at all, they tend to have holes or passages, not primarily from neglect, but because maintaining such a visible boundary does not conform to Malay conceptions of space and reciprocal relations with neighbours.

This point is very clearly documented in a detailed ethnography of Kota Bahru, the capital city of the state of Kelantan. According to this study, a "neighbour is one who makes himself available to other neighbours when he is at home. One of the most significant features of this is that a neighbour's house should be both visible and accessible to other neighbours who may wish to call. Informants frequently relate that persons they consider to be rich people (orang kaya) build

---

[57]For a review on the discussion of the middle class in Malaysia see Kahn 1996.

houses which are surrounded by fences with bolted gates and lots of shrubbery ... Persons classed as rich people are not neighbours" (Clarke 1976:167).

The Example of Jakarta

But let us turn to Jakarta, which has grown in geographical extension and population to a size which makes it extremely difficult to discern any clear-cut ritual structure.

Though mosques have been built more or less continuously since Dutch times, a Mesjid Agung has been completed only recently. Situated north of the Medan Merdeka (Freedom Square), it occupies a central position in the hierarchy of Muslim ritual places. The presidential palace (istana presiden) is still important, but less so than in Sukarno's time. Important ceremonies (upacara) and meetings are regularly held in special ceremonial halls or meeting places, which, despite their modern facilities from air-conditioning to loudspeaker facilities, seem to fulfill the functions of the pemdopo (assembly hall) of Javanese empires.

The Taman Mini Indonesia, a tourist attraction created by the wife of former President Suharto, depicts the whole of Indonesia in a miniature lake. Despite its modern facilities, including, of course, a large conference hall for the above-mentioned ceremonies, one is reminded of the model of Angkor Wat found in the Wat Phra Kaeo, the royal temple of Bangkok. Certainly the impression of the whole of Indonesia being represented in the capital city is not lost on the Javanese mystical mind.

Since the 1970s many multistoried buildings have sprung up in the centre of Jakarta, mainly along Jalan Tamrin, the so-called "gold coast", very much like in other Southeast Asian cities. What might escape the casual observer is, however, the proudly presented big-lettered names of various Indonesian institutions like Arthaloka, Graha Purna Yudha, Bina Graha, Ariyaduta. These terms are not really part of modern Indonesian, but are mostly derived straight from Sanskrit. The skyscrapers of Jakarta are, one might venture, the modern candi of the new rulers!

A last indication of the newly emerging ritual complex is the Lobang Buaya (crocodile hole), where in 1965 several Indonesian generals were murdered by communist paramilitary forces and thrown into the aforementioned well by communist paramilitary. Their images now overlook a ceremonial place, where annually, in the presence of the President and the diplomatic corps, a ceremony is held and the state ideology of Pancasila proclaimed (Nas 1992). It would be difficult to argue that the New Order ritual structure fosters Indonesian urbanism. It is a ritual structure dominated by Javanese values designed to integrate the realm, but not a city.

Conclusions

Taking a holistic approach and applying it to the Southeast Asian urban areas, we discern two distinct concepts of space. One is the urbanism of the Buddhist cities of Sri Lanka and Mainland Southeast Asia, characterized by Buddhist dualism (not necessarily cosmic, though) both in the Buddha-God, laukika-lokottara and the nature-culture, gamavasin-aranyavasin opposition. Comparison within this field shows some variations (or transformations). Thai cities show a high degree of "urbanism", ritually established and spatially expressed through city walls, gates and monks.

The (ancient) large Indonesian settlements show cosmic dualism, as pointed out by Peter Nas, but little "urbanism". Not a city but a kraton or istana is ritually defined and forms the centre of a centrifocal spatial system. The earlier cosmic dualism has changed into a political-cultural opposition, symbolized by palace (kraton or istana) and mosque (mesjid agung). The new Javanese ritual structure of Jakarta is not directed at the city, but the realm, the national territory. Modern Jakarta is, to paraphrase Oswald Spengler (1923:662), "a very large settlement but, nevertheless, not a city". The lack of urbanism is further shown by the fact that relatively highly developed Indonesian societies, like the Minangkabau, were societies without cities.

The two patterns of spatial structuration coexist historically in different societies, namely those of mainland Southeast Asia, and those of the Malay archipelago, where the large urban places like Melacca or Banten were, as Boeke argues, harbour principalities with a limited impact on urban traditions of the empires. This changed with colonialism and immigration, especially of Chinese migrants, into the archipelago. Whereas the Malay conception of geographical, social, religious, and political space is centrifocal, the Chinese conception of space is bounded. Chinese, even rural Chinese, have a clear-cut image of the "city" and of urban life, whereas Malays centre their spatial attention on central institutions like the istana or the mesjid, both of which are not necessarily urban or connected with urbanism. Malay living quarters are defined as kampongs (villages) even if they happen to be part of a city.

We hope to have shown that the two differing conceptions of space are consistent and can be traced in different aspects of social organization and culture of Malays and Chinese. Such consistent socio-cultural patterns reinforcing each other account for the persistence of culture over long periods of time. This also means that they are difficult to alter even if the underlying socioeconomic system changes. This poses a dilemma.

The policy of the Malaysian government under the so-called New Economic Policy of the Second and Third Malaysia Plan has been to draw more Malays into urban occupations and to "urbanize" the Malay peasant. As most urban centres are Chinese in terms of inhabitants and in terms of culture, the attempt to urbanize Malays amounts to a policy of sinization of parts of Malay culture. Though this is, of course, a policy that may be followed, it is indeed hard to believe that this is the intention of the present Malaysian government. What then are the alternatives? The alternative appears to be the development of an image of a Malay or at least Malaysian city in which Malay conceptions of space are translated into urban planning. So far local and foreign architects and urban planners have either copied Western models or provided slightly modernized versions of the Chinese shophouse city.

At present, the different urban traditions seem to have lost their importance. Colonialism, immigration and lately, integration into a world economy and globalization certainly implied an increased homogenization of the morphology of the cities. The sky-line of Bangkok, Manila, Jakarta and Singapore looks quite similar to the postmodernist high-rise architecture, which hides the temples, palaces and masjids. However, the traditional concepts of the city still play a role as they define specific views of urbanism, specific contested genii loci within the city that quite often form the "hot" spots of urban conflicts. These may be ceremonial places like the Sanam Luang in Bangkok, but can also be conflicts associated with kampung demolition, or, urban re-construction in general. For the understanding of present-day urbanism in Southeast Asia, these concepts have to be taken into consideration.

Images of a Sumatran Town

The Growth of Urban Symbols

The rapid growth of urban symbols is, as some other studies have shown, common throughout Indonesia and some of its neighbouring countries (Anderson 1990; Clammer 1983; Nas 1992; Evers and Gerke 1991; Korff 1993). All over Indonesia we can observe a construction boom in statues (patung), "traditional" roofs, monuments and buildings of high symbolic significance.

Why did Indonesia experience a rapid growth of urban symbols in the 1980s? Do we at present witness a struggle for cultural hegemony between the Javanese-dominated central government, the army, Islam, and regional groups? Or is it just plain public affluence and an easy way to complete a "project" with the attached financial benefits? Was the struggle for symbolic space a foreboding for the conflicts and separatist movements after the fall of President Suharto?

At present we can only pose questions rather than provide satisfactory answers. A case study of Padang, the provincial capital of West Sumatra, attempts to lay an empirical foundation for a further analysis of the ramifications of urban images and urban symbolism in Southeast Asia.

Even the occasional visitor to the provincial capital of West Sumatra is impressed by the signs of economic vitality, the density of traffic, the hustle and bustle of the market places. Like many other medium-sized cities in Indonesia, Padang has been transformed during the past two decades from a sleepy backwater to a vibrant centre of commerce and administration. At least so it appears when traversing the city from the harbour of Teluk Bayur in the South to the international airport of Tabing in the North.

Comparing our personal image of the city as we had experienced it during field research in 1969 - 1970 with observations in 1991, three areas of change become obvious: religion, trade and state.[58] Each is expressed in new buildings, which have since been erected or modified. There are several new mosques, the central market has been greatly expanded, and a number of magnificent government offices have been constructed. In addition the character of trade and its manifestations have been altered and expanded. In front of the old central market a four-storey shopping complex and department store has been erected (currently empty and bankrupt) and the city centre is full of rather over-dimensional bank buildings.

However, what strikes us most is the abundance of traditional Minangkabau roofs *(atap bergonjong)* attached to most of the public buildings. In some instances a dummy *adat* roof has been added to span an entrance or an arch. These curving roofs up to now used to adorn only matrilineal homesteads in the Minangkabau highlands, but were never found in coastal villages, let alone in towns.[59] Government buildings were designed to carry Minangkabau roofs from the early 1980s onward and pressure was brought on private investors with strong links to the government to also use Minangkabau roofs.[60]

The urbanization of Padang is expressed in public buildings, like government offices, post offices, hotels or private and government banks, whose functions

---

[58]Fieldwork was carried out in Padang for twelve months in 1969 - 1970 and for two months each in 1973 and 1991. This study is the result of a cooperation between the Faculty of Humanities, Andalas University (Prof. Dr. Aziz Saleh) and the Sociology of Development Research Centre, University of Bielefeld. See Evers 1975a; Arbeitsgruppe Bielefelder Entwicklungssoziologen 1991.

[59]As a matter of fact, Padang had developed its own traditional type of wooden house with a large verandah, beautifully carved gables and a straight roof. Today modern homes are often adorned with Greek columns, referred to as "Spanish" by Padangese.

[60]There was also a fair number of new monuments constructed, which will, however, not be discussed at the moment.

are disguised by symbols of a matrilineal peasant society. There are, however, significant exceptions. One type of public building, namely mosques, are rarely adorned with Minangkabau roofs, despite the identification of the Minangkabaus as strict adherents to Islam. The often conflicting but symbiotic differentiation between Minangkabau customs *(adat)* and Islam is maintained even in modern architecture and its urban symbols. Also department stores, shopping complexes and shops, mostly owned by ethnic Chinese, are largely exempted from the obvious Minangkabau symbolism.

The symbolic universe[61] of the city of Padang therefore appears to be mixed. Islam, Minangkabau, nationalism and modernity are four obvious divisions of the world of meaning, but the boundaries are often blurred or overlapping. The symbols by themselves convey immediate meaning. The curved roof refers to the regional identity of West Sumatra and its predominant Minangkabau society. The cupola and the minarets of mosques refer to the world of Islam, and "Spanish-style" Greek columns appear to express a new type of Southeast Asian post-modern urbanism, shared by Thailand, the Philippines, and Indonesia. In addition there are numerous monuments ranging from soldiers storming an imaginary hill to a huge fruit supposed to symbolize the specific culinary delights of the Padangese *(orang Padang)*. But what do the urban symbols mean in the context of a symbolic universe?

The Symbolic Universe

The symbolic universe of cities is changing over time, both in terms of the number, volume, size and variety of symbols as well as in the meaning attached to symbols. Social and cultural development is reflected or even governed by urban symbols which by their very physical nature add a touch of permanence to the rapidly changing urban society. This double nature of urban symbols heralding change as well as permanence adds to their significance. On the one hand the visitor may express his bewilderment because of "so many new buildings" that have been erected since his last visit, but on the other hand he can be assured that these buildings, strong and permanent as they are, will still be there for many years to come.

It can be argued that each man-made physical structure has a "meaning" and therefore is a symbol. On the other hand some structures are more meaningful than others and the symbolic content of some signs or shapes is negligible. Padang is a "city full of symbols" (as is Jakarta, see Nas 1992), but most of the

---

[61]Berger and Luckmann (1966:95) refer to a "symbolic universe" as "bodies of theoretical tradition that integrate different provinces of meaning and encompass the institutional order in a symbolic totality".

officially erected monuments are hardly noticed by Padangese, or their meaning is forgotten or grossly misinterpreted, like the statue of the ape-god Hanuman in Jakarta, who is alternately seen as a parachutist or as an advertisement for a bottled drink. In contrast to monuments, public buildings are connected with institutions. Precisely because of their utilitarian property and their "use value", they enable the urban population to interact with them and thus force a reproduction of their "symbolic value".

What determines the relevance of symbols? We regard those symbols as relevant that help to construct the socio-spatial image of a city. Specific buildings are symbols and signs, identity markers and cornerstones for the construction of urban images. Symbols demarcate boundaries or lines of division and provide, as Mary Douglas (1970) has argued, the basis for cultural classification and social order. This is also valid with regard to the form of cities. "The culture and social structure of a society are reflected in the shape of its cities" (Nas 1984:129). In empirical terms that means: an "image of the city" determines which symbolic structures are noticed, remembered and declared important by various groups of city dwellers or sojourners. In turn, symbols stabilize or even determine the urban mental map. Only those who have internalized the "socio-spatial image of the city" are able to orient themselves within it. Those with diverging views and images of the city "get lost" socially as well as spatially.

Domains of Meaning

The symbolic universe is made up of more or less coherent sets of macro and micro symbols, which are related to distinct sets of cultural values, to domains of meaning ("Sinnprovinzen" according to Schütz [1981] or "fields" in the sense of Bourdieu [1974]) which have a certain degree of autonomy. However, the divisions are not fixed, but are subject to a pluralization of life-worlds, particularly in an urban setting (Berger, Berger and Kellner 1974:62). Whereas formerly domains were fairly stable, well-delineated and integrated into a symbolic universe and stabilized through widely accepted meta-narratives, they are now following their own dynamics, compete with each other in an urban forum and encroach on each other's territory. Domains of meaning (Sinnprovinzen) may disappear, may be refashioned, combine or fall prey to "hybridization", i. e. to an unstable combination of incompatible values, meanings and symbols.[62]

We have earlier identified four domains: Islam, Minangkabau *adat,* modernity and nationalism. These domains attach meaning to urban institutions and urban

---

[62]The concept of hybridization is taken from strategic group theory; see Evers and Schiel (1988).

public buildings, and turn them into urban symbols. Individual symbols, which are physically attached to public buildings like Minangkabau roofs, are obvious means to transfer meaning to utilitarian structures or institutions. Architectural forms, like columns, wood carvings, or the sheer size of a building are instruments of the creation of meaning.

Fieldwork in Padang has focused on the following groups of urban institutions which are connected with the functions of central places in general.

They are:

- local marketplaces

- places of religious worship (e. g. mosques)

- buildings and institutions serving the modern economy

  (like banks, department stores, computer shops, etc.)

- government offices.

We can distinguish which kinds of buildings belong to each domain, what symbolism is attached to the respective institution, and how the content of each category changes over time. In short, the classification of the symbolic universe serves the function of analyzing the process of modernization as "meaningful" cultural change (on Methods and Data see note.[63]).

Markets

Economic goods are part of the cultural system and the acquisition of goods is a means to anchor meaning in social life (Douglas and Isherwood 1979:12). Therefore the market, where goods are bought and sold, is also a place for the production and reproduction of meaning and a powerful symbol of urban life.

Sketch maps drawn by informants in Padang invariably focus on the market. All other quarters, places or buildings are depicted in relation to the main pasar. The market rather than the governor's office is the "exemplary centre" on which attention is focused. This contradicts the image of an "average regency seat"

---

[63]The data for this paper were collected in 1991 from official sources (the Department of Religion, the Municipal Government, the Provincial Statistical Office) and through field observations and unstructured interviews. The time series in table 1 are absolute figures and show the number of urban institutions and buildings in operation at any particular year. The first diagram is based on a composite index of modernity (banks, international hotels, department stores and computer shops), an index of Islamic places of worship and of market stalls in the municipal markets. Table 3 is based on table 1, but data are set to 100 for 1965 to show the relative growth of public buildings as symbols.

from a Dutch colonial point of view[64], and the quite similar description of a Javanese town by an American anthropologist (Geertz 1963:10), in which the town square *(alun-alun)* and the offices and houses of the chief government officers constitute the centre of the town. In Padang the town square and the town hall also occupy the geographical centre of town, but they are culturally not defined as central, except in official documents.

The central market is the "structural core" of the town and has shifted its location with urban development. Its small cubicles filled with goods of various kinds and above all the throng of customers crowding through the narrow lanes create a feeling of community, closeness and belonging that symbolizes Indonesian city life. This was already the case during our first stay in Padang in 1969 - 1970, but measured in terms of the number of trading enterprises in the municipal markets, expansion was rapid between 1970 and 1985. In fact, this market expansion was typical for the first phase of the economic recovery after the change of government in 1965 - 1967. Its symbolism is traditional and the expansion of market activities does not signify a departure from a known and culturally well-established way of life.

Modernity and change is, however, symbolized by modern economic institutions and by the construction of new buildings connected with a modern, formalized economy. Table 1 shows the total number of selected categories of buildings and institutions for each year. Banks, international hotels, department stores and computer shops were selected by respondents in Padang as the most significant symbols of modernity.

---

[64]See the map of 1938 drawn by the Dutch geographer H. Ph. Th. Witkamp with a commentary by H. F. Tillema in Wertheim et al. 1958:81-82. For a theoretical discussion see Barnes et al. 1991 and Hamm 1982, chapter 8 on Räumliche Semiotik.

Table 1: Growth of Urban Symbols, Padang 1965 - 1991.

Year	Mosques	Surau	Banks	Internat. hotels	Depart- ment Stores	Com- puter- shops	Market- stalls
65	150	267	5	2	0	0	474
66	156	272	6	2	0	0	474
67	161	278	8	2	0	0	474
68	165	287	8	2	0	0	474
69	169	298	8	2	0	0	474
70	176	322	8	2	0	0	474
71	177	328	8	2	0	0	646
72	178	338	8	2	0	0	646
73	179	347	8	2	0	0	937
74	186	355	8	2	0	0	1097
75	194	370	8	2	0	0	1320
76	198	385	8	2	0	0	1697
77	203	393	8	2	0	0	1758
78	208	410	8	5	0	0	1758
79	210	421	8	5	0	0	1870
80	214	441	8	10	0	0	1986
82	231	463	8	10	0	0	2094
83	241	479	9	10	0	0	2094
84	244	504	10	10	0	0	2186
85	259	523	16	10	1	0	2344
86	265	539	16	16	1	0	2648
87	271	554	16	16	1	3	2648
88	275	558	16	16	1	3	2712
89	279	565	23	23	4	3	2712
90	281	570	23	23	5	7	2579
91	281	570	23	23	6	9	2669

The Modern Economy

Perhaps the most obvious example of modern economy is a huge department store put up in front of the old central market. Its dark glass-covered facade overshadows both the colonial building of the town hall and the modernized two-storey market buildings. But the purely symbolic character of this building is perhaps best demonstrated by the fact that it was more or less empty at the time of my field research in 1991, as traders and customers prefer the coziness and intense social interaction of the old *pasar* to the modern and costly shopping centre.

But there are also other modern buildings that have recently been erected, e. g. commercial banks. Banks are symbols of the capitalist market economy, of modernity and, in the Indonesian context, of continued security and progress. Their architecture usually expresses this meaning in a most forceful way.

In Padang banks and bank branches were opened rapidly after the policy of deregulating the economy was put into practice 1 June 1983. The centre of Padang, on all counts a modest provincial town of less than 300 thousand inhabitants in the built-up area (and 631 thousand in 1990, after a large part of its rural hinterland had been integrated into the city limits), is now dominated by a number of fairly large bank buildings, creating a "banking district" somewhat out of proportion to the rest. A comparison of some statistical data reveals this "over-banking" from an economic point of view, but in turn emphasizes the symbolic importance.

Table 2: Banks per 100,000 Urban Population, 1990.

Padang[65]	8,089
Yogyakarta	7,083
Jakarta	4,968

The Religious Domain

The religious domain finds its visible symbolic expression in mosques, Islamic prayer houses, churches and Chinese temples. Mosques in particular are numerous and are frequently repaired, extended or newly constructed. Even the spread of "electronic prayers", i. e. the use of tapes, tape decks and loudspeakers does not seem to have impaired the construction of mosques, but has rather boosted the symbolic impact through amplified sound power.

---

[65]Figures for Padang are in all tables based on the city limits in 1980. Singapore, the region's premier financial centre, would range in the region of 14,815 and outdo all Indonesian cities.

The Minangkabau are known as ardent Muslims, but mosques may have different meanings.

There are three central mosques in Padang:

- The mosque of old Padang (Ganting)

- The Muhammadiya mosque on the corner of the main market

- The "presidential mosque" on the city square.

The oldest mosque, now rather off-stage, is regarded as the centre of conservative Minangkabau clan leaders. It is a beautiful example of Sumatran mosque architecture. Located in what used to be the Minangkabau centre of Padang during the 18th and 19th centuries, it is found up-river from the Chinese settlement, not far from the now almost abandoned market Pasar Mudik (Amran 1986:22, 92). The new mosque (Mesjid Taqwa) next to the central market is connected with the modernist Muhammadiya movement and, at the same time, caters primarily to the merchant community, with whose contributions it was built. A large and quite modern mosque (Mesjid Narul Imam) was built close by on the central square, an army- controlled piece of valuable urban property. The central government and the army contributed to the construction costs as people were reluctant to contribute because of the invasion of central government troops to crush a regional rebellion in 1958.[66] Today informants point out that the President of the Republic of Indonesia, General Suharto, will pray here, if he happens to visit West Sumatra - hence the name "presidential mosque". During 1965 - 1970 there was intense competition for the rank of premier mosque (mesjid agung), though informants were undecided which mosque deserved the title. Building a mosque next to the market in the centre of the city was apparently regarded as important. The symbolic value of the location was clearly recognized when construction began around 1970 as soon as the market economy started to expand. Symbols of Islam and Western modernity are combined to demonstrate the modernity of Islamic religious revival (Evers 1991).

Seats of Power

Along one of the two main roads, Protocol Road, so-called because of its use for military parades and other official functions, a number of important government offices have been built or used: the office and residence of the provincial governor, the headquarters and residence of the regional military commander *(panglima),* and various other government offices. The buildings are often

---

[66]Interview with Colonel S., May 1970. The construction of the two mosques was a major issue during field work in 1970.

somewhat over-dimensional and grandiose: nation building is conducted through the construction of government offices.

Recently most public buildings have been adorned with a "traditional" Minangkabau roof. Officials are slow to offer an explanation for this costly and architecturally not always happy marriage between cement and *adat*. The objective is, to our mind, obvious. It is an attempt to transfer meanging from Minangkabau *adat* to the national culture and to legitimize the central government. As also in other Indonesian provinces the government bureaucracy and the military have used local cultural symbols and turned them into symbols of state-power in a province, i. e. a sub-unit of the highly centralized state.

Competing Symbolic Domains

The following statistical time series may serve as indicators of the expansion or contraction of the respective symbolic domains.

Table 3: Growth of Urban Symbols, Padang 1965 - 1990 (Index 1965 = 100).

Year	Mosques	Banks	Markets
65	100	100	100
70	117	160	100
75	129	160	279
80	143	160	419
85	173	320	495
90	187	460	544

Buildings as symbolic structures can be counted, compared and analyzed. But figures and statistical data are signs or symbols as well whose interpretation is subject to cultural codes (Eco 1988:59).[67] The statistical figures are hopefully "correct" in the sense that they indeed give a positively accurate picture of the number of certain buildings in our sample city. But this is not really what we are after. The important aspect is that the symbolic meaning of buildings is transferred to the statistical data. It is assumed that an increase in the number of buildings also represents an increase of symbolism, i. e. a growth of a certain field or domain of meaning.

---

[67]As Betke (1988) has shown in a study on Indonesian statistics and bureaucratic symbolism, the meaning attached to the number seven, four or five in Javanese numerology deeply influences the order of government reports and, at times, the outcome of arithmetic operations.

Interpreting these statistical time series we have to bear in mind that we are looking at buildings symbolizing distinct cultural complexes of values and meanings that extend beyond their utilitarian use. Meaning is transferred to these structures but conversely these buildings act as symbols that transmit powerful signals to the urban population. A mosque reminds the onlooker of the world of Islam and the religious values that go with it. The banks and department stores show that modernity and economic rationality are firmly established and are, symbolized by *adat* roofs, compatible with traditional Minangkabau culture. The markets depict urbanism, life, activity and the multifarious world of commodities, including their cultural meaning.

The growing symbolic universe, of which only a fraction - but a significant one - is shown in our diagram, exhibits some remarkable features. Mosques and Islamic prayer houses *(surau)* have grown almost parallel to the urban population. If there has been any religious revivalism during this past quarter century at all (Evers 1991), it has not found its expression in excessive mosque building or, in other words, in an extension of Islamic symbols. In contrast economic institutions and symbols show rapid and erratic growth. There is, however, a distinct sequence in the growth of the indicators. First the traditional, small-scale market sector takes off in the early 1970s, then symbols of modernity and an expanding modern market economy increasingly determine the symbolic scene in the form of banks, department stores, international hotels and related modern structures from 1983 onwards.

The provincial capital of West Sumatra has served as an example how to analyze the change of urban symbols through a methodology of objective hermeneutics (Oevermann et al. 1979:352). The results of our exercise have yielded some insights which are not confined to Padang alone.

The town centre is marked by a high density of concrete symbols. Within a short distance we find the central market, a large department store, the municipal office and the fortified police station, two large mosques and a tall bank building. Since 1970 the symbolic scenery has changed considerably, as the two mosques, the department store and the bank are recent constructions. The struggle for symbolic predominance is all too obvious.

We may now return to the question posed at the beginning of this paper. Is the rise of urban symbolism in Indonesia an expression of a new regionalism, of a revival of ethnic identity? A solution to this question has to be sought in the context of modern Indonesian statecraft. From the early days of Indonesian nationalism, a united Indonesia and a unitary state with one language has been the aim of national leaders. "Bhinneka Tunggal Ika", Unity in Diversity, is the motto of the Republic of Indonesia. Frequently, the central government has resorted to armed intervention to bring recalcitrant independence movements to their heels,[68] but by and large the multi-ethnic state has been integrated by a consistent cultural policy. The national language and national culture must not be connected with one particular ethnic group and its cultural tradition, but must derive its unifying force from its status as a meta-culture, transcending ethnic and local boundaries (Anderson 1983). Each province has been allotted an official symbol, a "typical" dance and form of music. The cultural diversity of Indonesia is in official policy reduced to a standardized difference between the officially created provinces. Cultural and ethnic differences are transformed into an essential collective representation of the Indonesian state. Regionalism is contained and urbanism becomes part and parcel of a national identity.

---

[68]The reactions to the abortive attempt to establish an independent South Moluccan Republic after 1949, the Permesta Revolt in North Sulawesi, the Sumatran PRRI (Pemerintah Revolusioner Republik Indonesia) revolt in 1958, and the current insurgencies in East Timor, Irian Jaya and Aceh are examples.

4. Strategies of Survival in the Cities

Strategies of Articulation: Subsistence Production, Informal Sector and the Market Economy

Hardly any theme in the discussions on "economy and society" caused more confusion and reactions than the rediscovery of the shadow economy. To their surprise the authors of relevant anthologies ascertained that there are economic activities which so far have not been considered worth being included in national economic accounts. A "shadow economy" was postulated in which all sorts of activities were put together into one category, ranging from quite usual household activities and unpaid women's labour to tax evasion, unregistered labour and economic crimes.[69]

It seems appropriate to look at past social-scientific developments first, in order to place the topic within a wider scope. At the same time we shall try to introduce more precise definitions, as far as this is possible with regard to such a broad phenomenon.

To start with, we shall define the central notions as follows: (1) The "shadow economy" covers all those economic activities which are not included in the official statistics, and which are therefore withdrawn from government regulations and taxation (2) The "informal sector" consists of that part of the shadow economy in which small units produce for the market or render services (3) "Subsistence production" comprises all consumption-oriented economic

---

[69]In spite of decades of discussions on the so-called "informal sector", new "home economy" and on the results from criminology, the reader of this article will be surprised to take note of the fact that already in 1977 the American economist P. M. Gunman pointed out the existence of a "subterranean economy" that comprised 10 % of the America GNP and that also German economist Schmolders has been occupied with this theme and has used the term *Schattenwirtschaft* (shadow economy) (Gretschmann et al. 1984:5). These and similar contributions (like Schrage 1984:11 among others) show clearly how the disciplinary partition within economic science has caused the neglect of the topic that is now being actualized through the concept of the "shadow economy".

activities intended for private use and consumption outside of market economic relations.

The shadow economy is thus an economic field which tries to withdraw itself from state influence, or else is excluded from the state system. In a certain sense the informal sector is rather an antipode of nation building and bureaucratization than of the formal sector, as we shall argue below. Similarly, subsistence production can be seen as an economy (and its general medium of exchange, money). What does this fundamental state of affairs represent in the light of sociological theory-building?

At first we are tempted to relate the analytical dichotomy between the formal official economy on the one hand, and the shadow economy on the other hand, to other dualisms so common within sociology. Are we not dealing here with the thesis, well known within organization sociology, of the tense relation between formal organizational structures and informal behaviour? Is the shadow economy not simply an elabouration of deviant behaviour, which can be analyzed with corresponding criminological theories? Or is the opposition between the consumption-oriented economy of subsistence production and the market-oriented production of the formal sector not simply a special case of the opposing pairs "traditional" versus "modern society", "community and society", or even "social environment and system"?

We don't believe this to be the case. However, to prove this, we should explain the fields covered by the shadow economy, the informal sector, and the subsistence economy more accurately.

Theoretical Approaches to the Analysis of a Casual Economy

The entire field covered by the shadow economy, informal sector and subsistence production combined, is associated with things illegal, old-fashioned, pre-industrial and in fact, with bygone times. Indeed, there has been consensus between Marxists and structural functionalists on the inevitability of the "expropriation of actual producers" and the incorporation of an extending sphere of life in large formal organizations, for a long time. The accompanying increasing commonness of wage-labour, the decline of unpaid family labour, the proletarization of farmers and the disappearance of social class structures - either in a socialist or a post-industrial welfare state - is postulated as an inevitable evolutionary trend. The culmination of this way of thinking was formed by the so-called convergence thesis, which predicts a world-wide unified industrial culture and society. Since the late eighties, this convergence thesis has received a new twist. The "informal sector" and casual economy is obviously not a (temporary) feature of Third World cities, but a characteristic of highly developed cities as well, as the studies of New York indicate (Castells 1989, 1997b, Portes et al. 1989, Sassen 1994, 1998).

Already at an early date Karl Polanyi (1978, orig. 1944) turned against this thesis. He considered the development of the self-regulating market a "turning point" in world history, but did not give this rare and degenerated type of socio-economic organization a long-term chance to survive. In his opinion, an economy which is completely dis-embedded from social ties is condemned to (self)destruction. Whether hereby the work of Polanyi also undermines more recent theories on the evolutionary differentiation of the economy into self-regulating subsystems remains to be seen.[70] The classification of economic activities into reciprocity, redistribution, market-exchange and subsistence production proposed by Polanyi is however of vital importance for our topic.

Another perspective, generated by criticism of Polanyi's economic classification, has been given by the French historian Braudel. He distinguishes three economic sectors. In his opinion, the two sectors "market economy" and "capitalism" must not be considered new phenomena which emerged after the industrial revolution but as essential structures in Europe since the Middle Ages. His classification, elucidated with historical facts, conforms in our view largely to today's usual division of the economy into an "informal" and a "formal sector". Braudel mentions still another, third sector, namely the "non-economy", the base in which the market mechanism is rooted, without however being able to penetrate this sector completely. On top of this still immense base the actual zone of the market economy is situated, in which many small producers offer their goods. Spread over this zone is the zone of the "contra-market", where the smart and powerful are in command. This is the actual capitalist domain, in the past and in the present, before as well as after the industrial revolution (Braudel 1986a:245-246). Braudel's three sectors, material life (non-economy), market economy and capitalism, are thus not stages within an evolutionary scheme, but exist side by side, in ever-changing figurations.

Indeed, capitalism and the nation-state, the two main structuring forces of modern times, have formed all societies in the world, without succeeding however in fully penetrating them. A larger domain is withdrawn from direct influence by the state and/or the capitalist market, and not only in Third World countries. Up to the present it has been impossible to give an unambiguous answer, based on empirical research, to the question whether we have reached another turning point, and whether at least a partial economy is taking place. But we can nevertheless allow ourselves to ask the question whether "free" wage-

---

[70]Elwert (1985:509) argues that precisely the connection between the capitalist economy and a moral economy explains its success. One could also argue, as we shall do later on, that the preservation of subsistence production outside the economy of commodities and outside of Elwert's venality is an essential condition for the success of capitalism.

labour is actually expanding on a world-wide scale (Evers and Schiel 1979) and whether the formal sector is in fact forcing back the informal sector. Or could it be possible that subsistence production for private use, unregistered labour and illegal businesses are expanding world-wide instead?

The Etatiste Approach: The Underground Economy

The withdrawal of an increasing amount of economic activities from state control, and from tax-collection in particular, induced a series of investigations into the "subterranean" or "underground economy" in the United States at the end of the seventies (US Congress, Committee on Ways and Means, Underground Economy 1980). Among other things it was estimated that the unregistered contribution of the American underground economy amounted to some 100 to 200 billion US $. More recent estimations go as far as 563,3 billion US $ for 1980 (Feige 1987:93). Similar attempts by exchequers in Germany led to comparable estimations (for 1980 between 3.7 and 27 % of the GNP); in this case the tackling of illegal labour formed the core of the discussions.[71] The underground economy is thus comprehensively defined as comprising those economic activities which are illegal and not registered or controlled by the state. The heavy tax burden imposed by the state on entrepreneurs and employees is held responsible for the increase of illegal labour and businesses without book-keeping (Heinze, Schedl and Vogler-Ludwig 1986:5).

Often this illegal underground economy is not well distinguished from other legal forms of the so-called shadow economy, while both fields have merely failing state control in common.

Dualism Theories and the Informal Sector

As early as the thirties, Julius Herman Boeke referred to a sector of the then colonial economy which resisted the penetration of the colonial state. In his opinion a dual economy had developed, in which each sector showed unmistakable characteristics of its own. On the one hand there were the trading companies and large enterprises, part of a sector operating on capitalist principles, while the other sector, consisting of farmers and craftsmen, was pervaded with an "oriental mentality" (Boeke 1980). Since then dualism theories have appeared in several versions, concerning developing countries as well as industrial societies (Berger et al. 1985). The most influential was the concept of the "informal sector", which has been elaborated in several studies by the ILO (for a summary, see Sethuraman 1974, for a critical view, see Schiel 1987).

---

[71]The estimations for West Germany vary between 3.7 and 27 %, depending on the method of calculation used for Italy between 10 and 30 % and for Great Britain between 2.5 and 15 % of the GDP (Gretschmann, Heinze and Mettelsiefen 1984:29-30).

In these studies the informal sector is defined as the field in which the production of goods and rendering of services are largely withdrawn from state control and registration. Street vendors, small enterprises using family labour, pedicab drivers, shoe-shiners and scavengers are considered typical manifestations of this informal sector.

Meanwhile, the concept of the "informal sector" has also been adopted to characterize certain fields of the West German industrial society, without paying attention, however, to the critical discussions which are being carried on internationally within development sociology. Thus, activities of the formal sector which are fully in the market and integrated into the money economy have frequently been mixed up with consumption aimed at private use, which we shall discuss later on. Further confusion has been caused by authors who, like Berger and Weber-Voigt (1982:13-14), consider all economic activities which are managed and defrayed personally and which do not use labour contracts, enterprises belonging to the informal sector. According to this definition, not only all farmers and small entrepreneurs belong to the informal sector, but many doctors and lawyers too!

Up till now, all attempts to use the concept of the "informal sector" not just in a descriptive way but as an analytical tool, by putting it within a theoretical context, have failed. Therefore we have argued that the informal sector - which we can indeed observe - should be regarded from the sociological side. We pointed out that a stratum of society which has a very precarious basis of subsistence will try to survive and secure its reproduction by using all possible economic niches, by high mobility in the search for work, and by combining several production and income sources (Elwert, Evers and Wilkens 1983).[72] This explains the expanding of the informal sector in times of crisis when the unemployment in the formal sector increases.

The heterogeneity of large cities is often discussed as a dichotomy between an "informal" and "formal sector".[73] In fact, the economy of most cities in the Third World seems to be made up of two rather distinct and separate sectors or circuits (Santos 1979): A formal or modern sector, to which the big enterprises, banks, shopping centres belong, and an informal sector of hawkers, peddlers,

---

[72]The criticism of Spiegel (1986) that the "Bielefeld approach" has ignored the masses of the people and class conflicts seems unjustified to us.

[73]Recently the concept of the informal sector has become popular in the discussion of the European city as well. Usually it is ignored that this concept was developed in the twenties of this century by a Dutch colonial administrator (Boeke 1980), who describes the economy of the Dutch East Indies as a "Dual Economy". Although the concept of dualism was correctly criticized, it seems that it still bears a lot of fascination.

petty commodity producers, whores and scavengers. Walking along the roads and streets, especially in Southeast Asia, one passes lines of stalls selling food, fake watches and designer clothes, noodle soup etc. But we see the high-rise office towers, modern hotels, department stores and shopping centres too. At first sight, a separation of the above type seems to make sense. One is puzzled though. The numerous shops and stalls within the air conditioned shopping centres, built following the latest post-modernist architecture, can they really be defined as a "formal sector"? What about the jewelry shop beside an overcrowded lane, too small for a car to pass through? It seems to be easily defined as "informal"; however, the owner is one of the leading exporters of gems. Obviously, a simple division into two sectors does not provide a proper tool for the analysis or description of the economy of a big city. The economy is more heterogeneous than such a distinction would indicate; and the economy is not separated through certain arbitrary criteria into distinct sectors, however they are referred to, but unified. Success or failure of the business endeavour is measured for hawker and banker in the same unit-money.

Until now, aspects of the informal sector which have received little attention are "social environment", "everyday experience" and "moral economy"; yet these could be useful for the explanation of protest behaviour emerging in the informal sector (Stauth 1982; Semsek 1986). The Islamic revolution of Ayatollah Khomeini, which was essentially supported by bazaar traders in Teheran, may function as proof of the political significance of the informal sector.

The Subsistence Production Approach: Non-Market-Oriented Production

Although the economy, especially in a modern industrial society, is largely determined by market mechanism or state legislation, there is a significant sphere of every day life that takes place outside of market and state. The maintenance of human life consists first of all of a multitude of activities for the sake of a person and his immediate social environment itself. Production for others and for an anonymous market in particular, is unthinkable without this subsistence production.[74]

Food-stuff production for one's own consumption determines agricultural subsistence production. This is however by no means limited to rural areas, but takes place in backyards and allotment gardens in the cities as well. In addition,

---

[74] "Production in order to survive encompasses a multitude of activities in all sectors and in all possible combinations ... housewife labour, small farmers' production, small handicrafts... are examples of such activities combined by members of these "units of production" (kinship groups, nuclear families, individuals etc.) (Arbeitsgruppe Bielefelder Entwicklungssoziologen 1981:5).

the main part of housing in the cities of the Third World is produced and consumed by the tenants themselves. We are dealing here with a kind of urban subsistence production, in which the house owner together with the members of his household, usually his nuclear family, manufactures his accommodation himself, by continually applying unpaid labour (Evers and Schiel 1979:313ff.).[75]

However, this type of urban subsistence production is not solely carried out by slum dwellers in developing countries. A study by Berekoven shows that only 23 % of the households in West Germany that modernized their home in 1979 used a professional builder, "The typical do-it-your-self amateur is younger than 30, employee or civil servant, and lives in a small house in the country" (Berekoven 1983:210).

Although the running of the household, and specially housewife activities, constitute one of the most important forms of subsistence production, a limitation to this alone would fall short. Even in developed industrial societies, tasks performed for the community like assistance at celebrations, care of children, attending the old and the sick, helping neighbours with house construction etc., play a prominent role. In developing countries, the mending of tools, the weaving of cloth, the gathering of fuel, the sinking of wells, intensive breeding of small livestock, laying-out of gardens, draining and irrigation, transportation and house building etc., are of great supplementary importance for the rural subsistence economy. But here also, despite some exceptions, it is the women who carry the burden of subsistence production.

Problems of the Measurement of Subsistence Production

It was no coincidence that the first attempt to measure subsistence production took place before and during the world-wide economic crisis in the twenties and thirties of this century. During that time unpaid domestic labour amounted probably to a quarter or more of the Gross National Product of the United States. Similar figures have been adopted for the Scandinavian countries. Early estimations for West Germany range from 32 to 39 % of the GDP in 1953/54 (Furst 1956). In those early studies, the value of hours dedicated to household activities was appraised in terms of wages of domestic servants. If one uses more appropriate standards however, like opportunity costs of fixed wages, the value of these household activities increases proportionally. The figures for the USA amounted to approximately 30 - 60 % of the GDP in 1976 (Petersen 1984:121) and for West Germany around 38 % in 1971 (Langfeldt 1984:187).

---

[75]This urban "habitat reproduction and subsistence production is investigated in bigger empirical studies in the slums of Recife (Augel 1985), Bangkok (Korff 1986), Jakarta (Evers 1981a) and Cairo (Stauth 1982; Semsek 1986).

The increasing political attention to this topic is proportional to the increase of the estimated value. In West Germany this had already reached 68 % of the GDP in 1982, i. e. 1,1 billion DM. These estimations are based on a household time allocation and budget study conducted by Krusselberg, Auge and Hilzenbecher, in which household activities are appraised by means of an achievement index and categorized according to the scale of wages established by the Federal Republic of Germany (Handelsblatt 13./14.2.87).

Meanwhile economists have made many suggestions about the measurement and appraisement of unpaid household activities (Goldschmidt-Clermont 1982). In most studies that attempt to measure subsistence labour, the time allocation and budget method is used. The hours worked are converted either into comparable labour costs or into opportunity costs, i. e. based on the loss of income of the members of the household. Since the price of labour in industrialized countries is high, the total value of subsistence production (or household activities) is high too. Until now, only a few studies of developing countries are known that present comprehensive estimations of the extent and growth of subsistence production or the entire shadow economy.[76]

Another method to measure subsistence production follows the labourious path of considering all consumed goods and services of household. By doing so, one should distinguish clearly between services rendered by members of the household or group themselves, or else self-produced goods, and goods and services obtained from the market. Only then does a complete insight into the subsistence production become possible. However, it is difficult to appraise the consumed goods and services. Since subsistence production is precisely use-value-oriented it has strictly speaking no market price, which becomes clear if we look at the astronomically high production costs of bio-dynamic tomatoes and radishes, which the author of this article yearly wrests from his kitchen-garden. A way out may be the determination of "shadow prices", which correspond to the lowest market price instead of opportunity costs of applied labour. In our research on Indonesia, which we shall elaborate later on, this method was used.

The Articulation of Subsistence and Commodity Production

In many developing countries survival is dependent on what combination of activities and sources of income persons or groups concerned decide on (Arbeitsgruppe Bielefelder Entwicklungssoziologen 1981:5). But also in industrial societies the intertwining of several sources of income and different

---

[76]An exception is formed by the study of Fisk on Papua New Guinea, see Fisk (1975a, 1975b).

kinds of labour is by no means unimportant, although over-looked by most studies. In particular the demand to organize an alternative economic system, something that has been influenced by ideas of dualism, has emphasized the distinctions rather than the systematic interweaving of the subsistence economy and the production of goods, of wage labour and unpaid labour.

Thus, Johannes Berger (1985:33-48) makes the at first sight interesting proposal of bringing all matters covered by the dual economy, shadow economy, informal sector etc., together into one category of alternatives to "wage-labour", and to choose "society" as the basic configuration of registered wage-labour instead of government surveys as point of reference. But what is a "wage-labourer"? Berger, like others, overlooks the very close connection between subsistence labour and wage-labour - which for the latter is plainly constituting. The true proletarian, who reproduces himself solely on the "yuppie" (Young Urban Professional) who, as a leading executive climbing the hierarchical ladder of the multi-national company he works for, orders a sandwich for lunch, and in the evening meets his "yuppie"-wife (who is likely to be a professor or a stockbroker) over dinner in a restaurant, while at the couple's rented apartment the maid is doing the household chare. The normal wage-labourer, on the other hand, is being reproduced by his wife, or he actively takes part in the subsistence production himself. In this connection we also have to pay attention to the increase of new forms of employment like publishing houses, part-time employment or home employment, which represent paid labour within the framework of the house-economy and which are mixed together with subsistence production.

The recently much-discussed concept of the labour society (Offe 1984) indicates that milieu, social environment and chances in society are fully dependent on occupation. This is by no means a new idea, but has for a long time been the basis of numerous surveys using SES (socio-economic status) indicators, which elevated occupation as the yardstick of all things. That in the process the residual category "housewife" disappeared has caused the SES researcher indeed occasionally worries, due to the fact that the status of housewives was rather difficult to measure. In most cases the professional status of the husband was substituted, without resulting in the necessary theoretical conclusion that unpaid female housework or subsistence labour is absolutely necessary to secure the subsistence of the male wage-earner. Paid labour without subsistence labour is simply unthinkable. The exclusively subsistence producer Robinson Crusoe is as much a literary fiction as Charlie Chaplin in his role of wage-earner in the movie "Modern Times", in which even his food is taken away from him by a machine.

A dualistic separation or a dichotomization of subsistence economy and market economy is as unjustifiable as the evolutionist doctrine on the transition of one economic system into the other, adhered to by old and newer theories of modernization. Subsistence production and market production are always closely intertwined, although in regionally and historically different configurations. "There is practically no such thing as a subsistence economy in which everything produced is also consumed by the producers. Similarly, there is no such thing as market economy in which all goods and services are distributed solely through market outlets. No economy or society can function without subsistence production in small entities" (Evers, Clauss and Wong 1984:29).

From the point of view of a small farmer or an urban slum dweller, the close intertwinement of production for one's own consumption and production for the market is perfectly clear. French social anthropologists (Meillassoux and J. P. Rey among others) already during the 1960s pointed out the intertwinement of African ethnic economies and the mining economy of South Africa. Moreover, two basic types of this unequal intertwinement have been distinguished, and even a mixed production, in which production of simple goods as well as subsistence production is performed, and the migration from a "subsistence production-dominated configuration into a capitalist mode of production" (Elwert and Wong 1979:263). The subsequently ensuing debate on the intertwinement of modes of production has proven to be a wrong track, since not separate economic systems but instead the very same members of society are involved in market as well as own consumption-oriented production. Fundamental to the analysis is not the articulation of modes of production, but rather the intertwinement of various forms of production within one single, i. e. capitalist mode of production. Field surveys have indicated however that the intertwinement of subsistence production and the production of goods can be enormously complex and that its organization can be socially very distinct.

The combination of activities and income source and its effects has been studied in detail by us through a questionnaire covering over 1000 households in Jakarta (cf. Evers 1981a and Evers, Betke and Pitomo 1983). Our original hypothesis that subsistence production will relatively achieve more significance with declining household income, was only partially confirmed. Indeed, for very poor households subsistence labour, although absolutely necessary for their survival, constituted a smaller consumption compared to somewhat "richer" households. The access to land and resources, or the availability of "basic tools" for domestic production like the sewing machine, the cooking stove or a bicycle, is as important as the contribution of income earners of the household with wage-labour in the formal or informal sector.

For these reasons the total value of subsistence production rises with increasing household income, while its relative value drops. Or in other words, as wage-labour contributes increasingly to the household income, the monetary input provides access to resources which can be utilized for subsistence production which has become so important that the basic needs of housing and livelihood are substantially provided for from this source alone.

In the following we will present data from two surveys in slum areas in Jakarta and Bangkok to substantiate our arguments.

The Combination of Subsistence Production and Wage Labour in a Jakarta Slum

Our research on lower income groups in urban areas of Southeast Asia has shown that generally wage-labour covers around 50 %, labour in the informal sector around 30 % and subsistence labour around 20 % of the consumption needs of the average household (Korff 1986; Evers 1981a; Evers, Betke and Pitomo 1983). In line with our previous arguments it seems however to be quite meaningless to observe the three sectors separately. Which of the 64 theoretical possible combinations will come out, and which intertwinement of labour allocation in the formal, informal and subsistence sector will offer the possibility of survival and the satisfaction of basic needs?

If we disregard insignificant contributions to household consumption, we come across the following intertwinement types:

(1) F-Type (Formal Sector Type): predominance of income from wage-labour with less importance of subsistence production and no income from the informal sector;

(2) FS-Type (Formal and Subsistence Sector Type): high importance of income from wage-labour in the formal sector, consumption from subsistence production;

(3) FIS-Type (Formal plus Informal plus Subsistence Sector Type): a high degree of intertwinement in which all three sources of reproduction are important;

(4) FI-Type (Formal and Informal Sector Type): beside the equally important incomes from wage-labour in the formal sector and activities in the informal sector, subsistence production is insignificant. As with the F-Type, household income and expenditures are settled mainly through the market.

(5) IS-Type (Informal and Subsistence Sector Type): the informal sector is the dominant source of income but is closely intertwined with subsistence production. Wage-labour in the formal sector appears only sporadically.

Since a good education is the requirement for employment in the formal sector, households with better educated members are more likely to be found in the intertwinement types F and F+I and receive higher incomes. The F-Type, with the highest average income, consists primarily of small households with young, relatively well-educated members, whereas the F+I+S+Type consists mainly of the biggest households of this type with a low educational level, where it is hard to satisfy basic needs. They have to try, in their struggle to survive, to take up all kinds of work and at the same time use a high input from subsistence labour. It is decisive, as has been established in a study by Neubert (1986:254) on Nairobi, whether the opportunity for available changes is taken or not: "It is tried, as far as possible, to keep multiple alternatives for action open".

Up till now it can only be speculated how these intertwinement types shift through time and from society to society. But it can in no way be taken for granted that a clear trend away from the IS-Type occurs.

Also in peasant societies, of which the economy has often been wrongly described as a subsistence economy, a strategic intertwinement of market- and own consumption-oriented action is taking place (Elwert, Evers and Wilkens 1983).

Table 7: Intertwinement type and average income of household (Jakarta 1979)

	F	F+S	F+I	F+S+I	I+S
Average household					
Income (Rp 1,000)	127.0	54.4	81.1	59.5	41.6
Household above					
the poverty					
Line (%)	87 %	76 %	75 %	40 %	40 %
Households (n=120)	7 %	39 %	19 %	3 %	32 %

F: Income derived mostly from the formal sector

I: Income derived mostly from the informal sector

S: Income derived mostly from the subsistence sector

Thus research undertaken in Venezuela's middle west has shown that the so-called "subsistence peasants" [conqueros], depicted in the literature as a classic example of a typical subsistence economy, are closely intertwined with the goods economy through seasonal labour in the sugar plantations as well as through female housework (Werlhof 1985:87-102). Even tribal societies living isolated in remote jungle areas, like for example the Dayak of Borneo, have been closely connected for hundreds of years with the world economy. Many spices, as well as rubber, were and are commodities gathered in the tropical rain forest.

There are, however, cases where we have a clear separation of the planting of commodities for own consumption and for sale, as for example is shown by research on the Chiapas/Rio Grande region of Mexico, conducted by Bennholdt-Thomsen (1982). Something similar has been reported by Clauss (1982) on North Sumatra, Indonesia. However, it would be wrong to conclude on the basis of the separation of cultivated land that there is also a separation of subsistence production and goods production: "For the producers, they belong inseparably together; it is a matter of relations of production" (Bennholdt-Thomsen 1982:80).

Reproduction of Labour Power and Trade: An Example from Klong Thoey Slum

A slum, which can be defined as a workers' quarter rather than either a "community" or a place of despair, (Korff 1985; Evers and Korff 1986), is integrated into the urban economy. The reproduction of the households depends on a monetary income generated through work in different occupations and different social relations, and an urban subsistence production[77]. The monetary income is necessary to be able to purchase the consumer goods needed, while subsistence production, defined as the production of goods and the procurement of services for direct consumption or usage, allows the reduction of expenditures. The combination of subsistence production and of income sources is crucial for the households to generate a regular and sufficient income under the overall condition of irregular employment and generally low wages.

Subsistence production means, cooking, washing, taking care of children, housekeeping in general etc., but also production organized on a scale beyond the household, like house building with the help of friends, joint organization of ceremonies etc. It depends on a sufficient amount of labour power within the household. Subsistence production is directly linked to "everyday life". As the connection between producer(s) and consumer(s) is not based on money, social relations and social exchange is important. These social relations play another important role for the survival of the households, because access to work and access to a place to set up a stall or shop depends on them. Furthermore, social relations provide access to money through different means.

From a survey of monetary receipts of households in Klong Thoey slum[78], it was found that nearly 20 % of the money used in the households is derived through debts, share games,[79] and gambling (see Korff 1988:300). Although these

---

[77]For the concept of subsistence production see Arbeitsgruppe Bielefelder Entwicklungssoziologen (1979); Evers, Clauss and Wong (1984); Evers and Korff (1986).

[78]A daily household budget was recorded for 18 families over one month.

[79]Share games are a form of saving common all over Southeast Asia. At regular intervals (daily, weekly etc.) a group meets and everybody pays a fixed sum of money into the pool.

monetary receipts cannot be defined as "income" in a strict sense, they determine the purchasing capacity of the household. Under the condition of an irregular income, the money in the pocket today can be spent today. Debts, although they have to be paid back, can temporarily compensate for unemployment. In a similar way, share games provide an opportunity for savings and easy access to credit.

To generate a regular income, income sources are combined. Either the individual works in different occupations, so that if he does not find work in one, he works in another, or within the household several distinct sources are combined, with the aim of securing a more or less regular and sufficient household income.[80] The combination is not specific to slum areas, but is a general strategy of most households in Bangkok. Different forms of trade are for many households and individuals used as income sources in addition to other work.

Although the data indicate that quite a substantial number of people is engaged in trade, and as the labour force survey of Bangkok shows (National Statistical Office 1986), more than sixty percent of the labour force is in commerce and services, this does not imply that access to the market as a trader is free, as for example Sethuraman (1981) argues. To set up a stall at an attractive location, like the bigger markets, one has to buy or rent it or even to buy a rent contract.[81] To rent a stall at a central place in Bangkok (Siam Square) an initial amount of 250,000 Baht has to be paid for a contract to rent the location for three years. The monthly rent is between ten and fifteen thousand Baht. At the smaller markets, or along the streets in front of a shop, the investment is much lower; however there the space has already been occupied for a long time and the income is small. The easiest way, to which access is in fact rather free, is either to set up a stall in front of the hut, or to walk around with baskets. To sell from baskets or to spread the goods on the pavement for sale on the big markets leads to problems though. Firstly "strongmen" request a rent which might be quite substantial and secondly, the police drive the people away. Finally, to open a

---

The participant who is willing to pay the highest interest to the others is given the pool. The danger involved is that either members cannot continue paying into the pool and that those who have received the share already leave the group. Accordingly, share games are only played with good friends.

[80]The augmentation of income sources is discussed by McGee (1979) and Eames and Goode (1973). For a discussion of these strategies in Klong Thoey slum, see Korff (1986).

[81]Buying a rent contract (saeng) is the most common way of gaining access to space, as the landowners are hardly willing to sell the land they own.

shop or stall depends on investment in goods and equipment. Only the activities with the least returns are comparatively free.

Pattern of traders in a slum area

The vendors in the slum area have to be differentiated into two main groups: Firstly, those using trade as main[82] and/or only income source, which are predominantly those owning shops and stalls, which generate a sufficiently high income, but demand the labour power of the whole household. Secondly, those using vending as additional income source, which are mainly those using stalls and walking around selling from baskets. This group has to be differentiated furthermore into those regularly engaged as vendors and those taking up vending occasionally in case of unemployment.

The shop owners in the slum area usually earn a sufficient amount of money for the household to live on (about 300 to 400 Baht daily). To use fixed installed stalls demands less labour power, but the income is lower (seldom above 150 Baht). In the case of the shops, most household members are involved in vending and related activities like buying goods at the markets etc. In the case of the stalls, it is predominantly an activity of one or two household members; while the others engage in wage labour. The keepers of smaller stalls and those walking around, carrying their goods, engage in this activity mainly as a sideline in case of unemployment, as the income is usually insufficient.

Looking at biographies of vendors, one notices that those using stalls or walking around with their goods started vending after losing their job, or when unable to work in a job due to age, illness etc. In this case, they usually start with a stall set up in front of the hut. This allows a combination between vending and subsistence production, as the place of residence and the place of vending is the same. Migrants coming to Bangkok, who find it difficult to get work, often engage in vending. As access to better paying activities and places is limited, the income can only function as an addition to other income sources. The shop owners, and those owning installed stalls at central locations are in a much better position as the income is much higher. They don't need additional jobs. However, to get a shop, high initial investments have to be made. The money to get a shop comes from savings, winning in the lottery and from work in the Middle East.[83]

---

[82]Main income source is defined such that more than 50 % of the income of the household is derived through the activity.

[83]Recently several new shops opened in the slum area, run by persons who had worked in the Middle East and used their savings for purchasing a shop.

Some examples will indicate the differences:

1. A woman selling fruit at a fixed stall

The fruitstall is located adjacent to a shop. From this shop she is supplied with electricity. The owner is a friend of hers and often both sit together for a chat. In the morning between six and seven she takes a mini-taxi (so-called Subaru "Four-wheel") to Klong Thoey market. There, at a stall, she purchases the fruit for sale. She has known the trader for a long time, and gets good prices from the trader, partly because they know each other, partly because she buys bigger quantities. Her daily investment is between 200 to 400 Baht, depending on which fruit are in season and popular for sale. With another mini-taxi she goes back and prepares her stall with the fruit. She stays at the stall until all of it is sold, which might take until the night. She started selling fruit because she had no other work to do and likes fruit. Her income depends very much on the seasons and the fruit she can sell. During the hot season, when popular fruit like Mangooes or durians are available and cheap, her income is high, while in the cold season it is much lower.

2. A woman selling dried fish

Beside the fruit stall is a place where an older woman sells dried fish. She buys the fish at Klong Thoey market in the early afternoon, and sells it in the afternoon to those preparing the evening meal. Her investments are small, seldom more than 200 Baht. Nevertheless, she earns up to 50 Baht per day, which is an additional income. Her working time is much shorter, compared to the other woman. After five to six p. m. the fish has to be sold, as later nobody is interested in buying it any more (The usual time for preparing the supper is between six and eight). While the woman selling fruit can keep it overnight, or make it into sweets, this woman has to sell all the fish, as it would get spoilt if kept for too long. She was able to buy the stall when a neighbour who was the previous owner left the slum area.

3. A woman and her daughter selling grilled squid

In the morning they use the public bus to go to the harbour at Samut Prakan. The squid is cheaper there than at Klong Thoey market, and transportation with the public buses is cheap. At noon they are back again and prepare the squid (the squid is cut into pieces and put on sticks). In the afternoon they go to their stall and start grilling the squid. Business ends when all of it is sold. Grilled squid is popular as a snack. Workers going home buy it as a snack before supper, friends sitting together and sharing drinks like it, so that until late at night, people still pass by and purchase squid. Their income is between 70 to 90 Baht per day, an amount insufficient for a household to live on. The husband and the son work as daily labourers at the harbour. Their income from wage labour, although higher, is insufficient for the household as well.

4. A shop in the slum area

At a crossing of walkways a shop selling all kind of merchandise, ranging from toilet paper to tinned food, soft drinks, chilled fruit and sweets, is located. A small restaurant and coffee shop belongs to the shop. Two tables and several chairs stand in a corner and food is prepared on a stove close by. The shop is supplied partly directly from the factories or merchants (ice, soft drinks), and the owner drives with his own pick-up to the markets in Bangkok to buy other goods. He uses the pick-up as a bus service between the slum area and the market close by as well. The income from the shop is at least 300 Baht per day. The woman is known as a money lender.

5. A couple selling sugar cane juice

Two years ago they came to Bangkok. As they found it difficult to get work at the harbour or in construction, they thought of engaging in trade. As they lacked social relations, they had no chance of getting a stall. After trying to sell several different goods, they finally ended up selling sugar cane juice as the best choice. From some savings they bought tin cans. One is filled with crushed ice, another with sugar cane juice, prepared at home from sugar cane bought at the market. The cans are carried with a stick on the shoulder and they walk through the slum trying to sell the juice, which is quite popular as a drink with a snack from a stall or food taken at some of the food stalls or restaurants. Together they earn up to 100 Baht per day, on which they can live.

6. A young woman selling a pig skin salad

She works as an employee in an office. From time to time (about once a week), if she needs money for some purchases, she prepares a bowl of a spicy pig skin salad at home. In the evening (she works during the daytime) she goes through the slum area with the bowl, selling the salad especially to people sitting around in the huts enjoying their evening drinks. From the sale she earns some 80 to 100 Baht. She does not engage in this activity as her main occupation for two reasons. Firstly she prefers her job as an employee which has a higher status, and secondly, she regards the demand for her - albeit very tasty - salad as rather limited.

To engage in trade within the slum area is relatively easy. However, the returns are low. For the stalls they are hardly more than 150 Baht per day. Even the shops seldom make more money than 300 to 400 Baht daily. This amount is very small if compared to the returns from vending at the markets. At the markets, however, the initial investment is much higher and access much more difficult.

Trade and Commerce on Klong Thoey Market in Bangkok: A Brief Description

When Klong Thoey market developed some thirty years ago, its location was at the fringe of Bangkok, along the road and railway track leading to the harbour. The demand for workers at the harbour led to a rapid settlement of the area, and soon one of the biggest slums in Bangkok emerged there, a squatter slum on land belonging to the Port Authority of Thailand. Today, parts of this slum have been cleared to make space for the extension of the port. To provide shelter for the people, a large housing project was set up in the area by the National Housing Authority. Through the rapid development of Bangkok, Klong Thoey market is now part of the inner city area.[84] Recently, a new road was built cutting through the main market. Although this hinders commerce, it has integrated the market even into the more strongly city. A newly constructed super highway provides easy access to most parts of the city and the hinterland.

What is commonly referred to as Klong Thoey market consists of several different but connected markets and numerous shops and stalls.[85] Kiat (1982) counted in a survey 1500 stalls and shops inside and alongside the five main market halls. Klong Thoey market is well known as a place to purchase cheap imported consumer goods. Competition on the market is very high although the price level is rather fixed. This is partly due to the price mechanism on other markets and the prices demanded by the merchants and factories, partly it results from observations of the prices among the vendors themselves. Klong Thoey has a reputation as a cheap market, where wares of good quality are sold.

Klong Thoey market is a twenty-four hour market. In the morning, that is between four and seven o'clock, it is predominantly a wholesale market for food (vegetables, meat from the nearby slaughterhouse, fish from the harbour at Samut Prakan 20 kilometers southeast of the market, etc.). The vendors buying at Klong Thoey market use the goods either in restaurants and stalls for further

---

[84]In Bangkok it is impossible to speak of a "central business district". Instead of a compact inner city, the commercial areas are spread along the major roads and streets. Even in the inner city one still today finds free space, away from the main roads. The size of Bangkok and the integration of formerly outlying sub-centres leads to the emergence of several centres and to shifts of these centres. What can be regarded at present as the major commercial area, where the biggest shopping centres and department stores are located and the land prices are highest, used to be swamp thirty years ago.

[85]Besides the main food market inside the five halls, there are numerous shops around and several other markets, in which consumer goods are sold, like Dalad Penang, Dalad Penang Gao, Dalad Singapore I, Dalad Singapore II. An additional new commercial area is currently planned.

preparation or buy the goods to be sold on other, smaller markets and in commercial areas. The streets and lanes are filled with pick-up trucks and small lorries delivering goods and sending them away. At about seven o'clock in the morning, other stalls and shops open. They sell predominantly for retail. In the afternoon another rush takes place on the market. Traders come and buy goods to sell on other markets and in commercial areas in the evening, and people pass through, buying their food for the evening meal. After eight p. m., many food stalls and restaurants open, and the market becomes an eating place. After nine pm, lorries arrive from the surrounding areas, goods are unpacked, partly sold and everything is prepared for the morning sales.

Besides the shops and stalls in the market halls, people walk by and sell their goods from baskets or from blankets spread on the sidewalk. Others sit behind their baskets, sheltered from the sun by umbrellas and resting on benches. Umbrellas and benches are rented out by the shop owners. While the first use public space, the latter group pays a rent to the owner of the shops in front of which they sell their goods.

Klong Thoey market, as a very busy market drawing many customers, is an attractive location for vendors. However, it is very difficult to find a stall there. The houses were built by a construction agency on land belonging to the Port Authority. After thirty years of lease, now houses and land belong to the Port Authority again. The official rent is comparatively low. However, to get a rent contract, high sums have to be paid to the former renter or sub-renter (the minimum is more than 500,000 Baht for a four to five year rent contract). The same pattern exists for setting up a stall. As all space is occupied already, one has to know persons who intend to sell their rent contract. In other words, one has to have social contacts with the traders on the market. High initial payments are necessary nevertheless. Even those without a stall, selling the goods from baskets or from blankets on the sidewalk, have to pay money to "local strongmen" and the police, to avoid being driven away. Although the prices are high, there is no difficulty in selling or renting out a stall on this market. The demand is much higher than the availability of stalls or shops for sale or rent. Access to Klong Thoey market is definitely not free at all.

The traders at Klong Thoey purchase their goods at several different places. Many go between two and three a. m. to Phakklong Dalad, which is by far the biggest market in Bangkok, with more than 3,000 stalls and shops in the market area alone, and buy their goods there. Phakklong Dalad, located at the river, is one of the oldest markets in Bangkok and predominantly a wholesale market for vegetables, fruit and flowers. Besides those going to this market, other traders are directly supplied by merchants with their commodities. In addition two other patterns exist.

1. Traders from the provinces:

At one location at the back of the market, traders from Phetchburi province sell their goods. In the morning or at night, they buy the goods (mainly vegetables) at the local markets. Jointly they rent a lorry. On the floor of the lorry the baskets filled with the goods are heaped. On an intermediate level, planks are put in, on which the traders sit during the 200 km journey to Bangkok. They reach Klong Thoey market in the early afternoon. The goods are unloaded and put in space now made vacant by other traders from that area, who came to the market the day before. When everything is unloaded, these traders get on the lorry and drive home, to return the next day, packed with vegetables.

The baskets with the merchandise are set up in front of shops, for which a small rent has to be paid. The traders are mainly wholesale traders. By reaching the market in the early afternoon, they can participate in the rush hour during the afternoon (when other vendors come to buy vegetables for their stalls, and people pass through, purchasing the food for supper), and the early morning wholesale rush.

2. Klong Thoey traders buying at provincial markets:

Traders from Klong Thoey market go to markets of the cities in the vicinity of Bangkok to purchase goods themselves. At Nakorn Pathom (a city eighty km west of Bangkok), in the middle of the night, a market starts. Producers from the surrounding areas of Nakorn Pathom go there to sell their produce, mainly vegetables, fish, fresh water crabs etc. For the producers, the prices they receive on this market are slightly higher than the money they would receive from selling to traders or to Phakklong Dalad, the big wholesale market. For the vendors in Klong Thoey market, the goods in Nakorn Pathom are cheaper than in Phakklong Dalad. In that respect, both can increase the returns through setting up a new market in Nakorn Pathom. The inhabitants of this city participate in the market only as providers of services (restaurants, coffee stalls etc.). On this market, one hardly finds any traders from Nakorn Pathom.

The households in Bangkok are integrated into the trade in the city. On the one hand, they themselves are engaged in trade, either as full time or as part time traders. On the other hand, they are consumers. Firstly such an elaborate trading network, in which many are involved, but most only have small returns, integrates all households in the city and keeps the expenses for consumer goods low.[86] Secondly, trade as an additional income source allows wages to remain

---

[86]It is astonishing that the overall price level for consumer goods in Bangkok is lower than the price level in the provinces. Soft drinks cost 4 Baht in Bangkok, in the provinces 5. A brand of popular liquor costs 70 Baht in Bangkok, upcountry 75 to 80 or even 100. Even

low. Thirdly, the small vendors and hawkers buy their goods from bigger traders, through which the demand is focused. Fourthly, the traders are connected with landowners, construction firms and banks. Especially the landowners and construction agencies are able to demand high rents and payments for rent contracts, as the demand for space is high, allowing for land speculation. Because access to space for trade is expensive, the banks become important as sources of credits.

The notion of "free entry" to informal sector activities tends to ignore the importance of access to land as a precondition for engagement in any kinds of activities in a city. To be sure, "mini" land speculation, that is the selling of rent contracts, the renting of small plots in front of a shop or in a commercial area, etc., may in comparison with the amounts gained by big land speculation seem small. However, in its sum the amount is quite considerable and through engagement in mini speculation, a chance for accumulation for the better-off groups (upper middle classes) is opened. Needless to say, the urban poor often suffer more from mini speculation than from the big speculators.

The heterogeneity of trading relations and their interdependency cannot be grasped by a concept like "informal sector". The reproduction of the eight million inhabitants of Bangkok is based on the heterogeneity of interdependent relations, which is expressed by the term "market economy" as Braudel (1986b, 1986c) uses it. Trading relations of this pattern make it possible that the people in Bangkok can survive without direct intervention from the state or public institutions. Interventions usually result in a destruction of the trading network, leading to urban conflicts.[87] Obviously, a public agency is unable to organize such a complex affair as supplying a metropolis. In addition, the big enterprises find it more profitable to participate only in those spheres of the trading network where profits are high and secure, leaving niches for others to engage in. The result is that the trading relations are strongly based upon the creativity of the people themselves in their endeavour to survive in a big city.

Gender Division of Labour and Subsistence Production

World-wide, women perform the biggest part of domestic subsistence production, in which the most original and basic form of subsistence production, the reproduction of human life, plays a dominant role. Also within wage-labour

---

fruit and vegetables are cheaper in Bangkok than in the provinces. One reason is that quite often, the produce is first sold to merchants in Bangkok, predominantly at Phakklong Dalad, and these merchants in turn supply traders upcountry.

[87]An example from Bangkok is the struggle against the vendors at the roadsides by the Bangkok Municipality.

relations women are doubly burdened by the involvement in subsistence production, which is on the one hand conditioned by the hierarchical and virifocal structure of most family and kinship systems, and on the other hand intensified by the increase of domestic subsistence labour. Although the employment figure for women in West Germany has hardly changed during the last century - in 1880 it amounted to 53 % and in 1984 to 56 % - there has been, however, a substantial sectoral shift. Thus, there has been a decrease of female employees in private households from 18 to 1 % during this period (Heinze, Schedl and Vogler-Ludwig 1986:32-33). That means, however, that subsistence production has increasingly become unpaid domestic labour. It might be considered an irony of history that the world-wide process of "housewife-ization" has also involved men, and that the social stratum of the unpaid housewife is now shared by unemployed men. Also in developing countries, the double burden of women is being aggravated by the revival of subsistence production, the increase of the modern nuclear family and consequently by the process of "housewife-ization" (Werlhof, Mies and Bennholdt-Thomsen 1983; Werlhof 1985).

Light and Shadow

It should have become clear in connection with the question of women's labour that subsistence production and labour in the informal sector are not just peripheral phenomena in economy and society, as has been implied by the titles of some newer publications.[88] For every society, it is rather the direct survival production, which begins with the "production" of human life, that is fundamental. The continued existence or even the expansion of alternative forms of economic action within the informal sector points to the limitations of rational goals, in spite of an economic system steered by exchange and power processes. From the point of view of the subsistence producer, respectively the producer within the informal sector, the shadow economy consists rather of the official and formal economy of large organizations and state bureaucracies should be planned and towards what goals they should be directed is a problem which cannot be solved by means of "profit-maximization" or similarly simplifying variables of "rational choice" theories.

---

[88]Like, for example, the title of the Info-Institute for economic research, in which "growing domains at the margins of the official economy" is spoken of.

Survival Strategies in Southeast Asian Cities

Survival Strategies in Bangkok

There is hardly any city in the Third World which does not have large areas of squatter settlements, slums, shantytowns or rundown housing estates. City planners have failed by and large to reconstruct these areas or to restrict their growth. But it would be quite mistaken to assume that these urban quarters are "unplanned". The difference between the neatly zoned business district or upper-class suburb and the rest of the city is that the former is planned by architects, city-planners and other government agencies, whereas life in the slum is based on the planning and strategic action of the slum-dwellers themselves.

In recent years a number of studies have used the term "informal sector" to draw attention to any productive activities that are going on in Third World cities without the regulation, approval or even knowledge of government authorities. Attention has also been drawn to the many self-help activities of individual households and voluntary groups in low-income areas. But in most of these studies another, not less productive sector has been overlooked, namely the production of goods and service for own consumption. We have used the term "urban subsistence production" to designate this sector (Ever and Schiel 1979; Evers 1981a).

In fact, among the poor in Third World countries the growing of food and its processing for own use, education, construction of housing, health care etc., take place largely outside the market economy. Most activities in this primary reproduction sphere are carried out by unpaid labour, mostly female, and do not enter government statistics. This direct production-consumption-pattern is usually referred to as a subsistence economy. In rural areas the subsistence economy is often regarded as an important though vanishing form of production. Peasants produce their own food and perhaps their own clothing, their own tools and other household utensils. Less recognized is the fact that production for own consumption also takes place in urban areas on a large scale. Of particular importance is the construction by people of their own houses and the creation of a habitat that allows survival in a difficult urban environment. If we use the term "urban subsistence production" rather than "urban subsistence economy" we wish to draw attention to the fact that the social economy of the poor urban masses is neither a market nor a subsistence economy, nor does it neatly fall into the formal or informal sector.

Different types of labour in the form of wage labour in the formal or informal sector, in the form of unrenumerated labour, especially of women and children used, nevertheless, for market-oriented production and used to produce goods and services for the own consumption of the immediate family or household, are combined into an intricate pattern of socio-economic organization to ensure survival in an urban environment. The self-organization of work and production, the combination of different sources of income, and various forms of mutual help are highly sophisticated and ingenious devices in an economy no less complex than industrial production in the formal sector.

Before a worker can perform his or her task in a factory or office his or her labour power has to be produced and sustained. The reproduction of labour power is a fairly complex process which includes not only the buying of the necessary food, clothes etc. but also the growing of foodstuffs and their processing, education, running a household, the building up of a rudimentary infrastructure of the organization of people to demand this infrastructure from the government, and last but not least, the building of houses and organization of festivals. It is important however that a large part of this reproduction takes place as directly linked production and consumption outside the market economy. This "subsistence production" is often seen as an important though vanishing form of production in the rural sector. Less recognized is the fact that a similar process takes place in the urban economy. Though most foodstuffs consumed in a city are, of course, "imported" from rural areas, some of them are nevertheless grown by the urban consumers themselves. But before rice, potatoes or noodles which have been purchased in the market can be consumed, considerable labour has to go into their preparation to make them fit for consumption. Obviously, in the urban setting a great part of subsistence production is replaced by commercial products, but still, the condition of a low irregular income makes subsistence production a necessary basis for reproduction (Evers, Wong and Clauss 1984).

This subsistence production can be distinguished on two levels. On the one hand we have the everyday reproduction within the household, including all the household activities like washing, cooking, housekeeping, bringing up of children etc. One the other hand, subsistence production is organized on a more extensive scale as work like house building, organization of festivals etc. done by several households or parts of households in cooperation,

Case studies

1. How Lop extended his house

In the fast growing city of Bangkok, the capital of Thailand, production of housing or a "habitat" by the people themselves is on the one hand an important form of subsistence production and on the other the only means for poor families to find shelter. To buy a house or apartment in a condominium is too expensive even for middle-class families. Most of these houses are used by rich Thai or foreigners, experts, embassy staff, or they are empty. Flats built by the National Housing Authority of Thailand are insufficient and the people living in slum areas do not want to live there as these flats are too expensive for most of them, although rent may be as low as 300 Baht per month.

The following case study might serve as an example how a family in Klong Thoey, a Bangkok slum, solves its housing needs. Lop is 26 years old and currently has a regular job as a driver for a Japanese construction firm. During the night he works as watchman for the firm as well. His wife Phen is 25 and works irregularly in a nearby garment factory. If she has time, she embroiders socks that are distributed by a firm to several households in the slum at home. They have a little boy of three. While Lop and Phen are working, their son Mong stays in the house of Lop's mother, who lives next door. They give her about 400 Baht per month for taking care of the child.

Lop earns about 2,000 Baht per month from his two jobs. Phen earns about 1,000 Baht from her work in the factory. For the socks she gets 5 Baht per dozen. Usually she finishes only two to five dozen per day, sometimes none at all. In general she earns 200 Baht per month for this work. With an income of almost 5,200 Baht per month the family is not regarded as poor by their neighbours; Lop considers his household poor but not very poor. Every day they have to spend between 100 to 150 Baht on the necessary basic goods.

Three years ago, after his marriage, Lop built a house himself with the help of his friends near his mother's place. Klong Thoey slum is a squatter slum, which means the people live on land belonging to the Port Authority of Thailand which is illegally occupied. Therefore Lop did not need to buy any land or pay rent for it. This is the regular pattern in Klong Thoey slum, 90 % of the houses belong to the users and were built by them. Lop's house was very small (6 m²) at that time because he had very little money to buy timber. After they had saved some money they decided to extend the house.

Some days before the work started Lop spoke with some friends and told them that he would work on his house the next Saturday. He directly asked only one of them, a carpenter, for help. On that Saturday, Phon, the carpenter and Od and Rydi, two other friends, showed up at his place. He had bought wood, drinks and food for the day. Not much was done on this day because the carpenter fell from the roof at noon. So they all stayed at Lop's place, enjoyed food and drinks and had fun together. The next day, three friends showed up again to continue the work. Again, work stopped at noon. The wood Lop had bought had been used up and he had no money to buy timber. The third day, when again several friends came, the house was finished. The people helping Lop were all his friends, not his relatives or relatives of his wife. The food and drinks during the days were all paid for by Lop himself.

The friends came to help Lop voluntarily. Lop would not have been angry if they had not come and they will not be angry if he does not come when they work on their houses. The reason for asking friends for help instead of using hired labour is twofold: for a carpenter he would have had to pay 100 to 120 Baht per day and person. Although he does not have to invite them for food and drinks he would be regarded as stingy if he did not. On the other hand, working together with friends is more fun and, if his money was all spent, they would buy drinks and food instead. In total, Lop spent 1,800 Baht on timber bought at the nearby markets, harbour etc. and 600 Baht on food and drinks.

Lop used two methods of contacting his friends. The friends with special qualification as carpenters (Phon and Thaeng) were asked directly, the others either heard that he was working on the house and came to see him or saw him working and joined in. For Lop it was easy to find persons who would help him. He has a lot of friends in the slum area. Except for Rydi and Surin, they had all known each other for nearly twenty years. In this case it is obvious that Lop could extend his house without using hired labour only because he had friends. What is friendship in the perception of Lop and the others?

Three different categories of friendship are differentiated by Lop and his friends. A negative friend is the "puan kin" or friend for eating. He will come only if he can get something for free. Puan si and puan tay are similar in their meanings. Both terms are used to indicate close friendship. Puan tay, a friend till death, will help his friend even if this would be disadvantageous for him. A puan si will help a friend, but not to such a degree. "The idea of puan tay (friend to the death) itself connotes a man who never leaves his friend even in times of greatest danger. He will face death together with his friend rather than to leave him in order to survive alone" (Akin 1975:246f.). In his study of a slum area in Bangkok, Akin notes the instrumental nature of friendship. According to Akin, a friend is described "as the one who first sees his friend is out of work, and thirdly, lends his friend money when he needs it." Akin 1978:58). In some ways, the description of friendship by Lop and his friends focuses on the first aspect of friendship much more than on the other two. For Lop it is important to be seen, to drink together, to eat together and to have fun together. These mechanisms are also the mechanisms by which persons are identified with a group. But, obviously, friendship has an instrumental character. For example, Lop helped a friend to find a job with the Japanese firm and they all help each other in case of need. We think that the instrumental character of friendship is not a primary one. Friendship as an instrument results from the closeness of the social relation which connotes friendship. Friendship is always more than a mere instrument. For example, there are moneylenders or persons who give jobs who will never be regarded as friends. On the other hand a lot of friends are unable to give either money or jobs to their friends.

In this way it makes sense that friends are important for finding a job, for getting help etc. but that friendship would never be defined by these aspects. Nobody would say, this is my friend, because he found a job for me, but this is my friend, we eat and drink together.

To summarize: The extension of Lop's house was a task that he could not perform alone. He needed the help of his friends because he did not want to hire labour and could not afford it. The user of the house, or the unit of consumption of subsistence production in this case, is the household of Lop. The building of the house can be regarded as subsistence production because producer(s) and consumer(s) do not enter into a monetary relation. The production is for direct consumption, not for market exchange (but social exchange!). Money was, however, used for buying the necessary inputs, for the market and subsistence production tend to be closely related in the urban economy. As the main principle to define the unit of production, friendship between equals can be identified. The mechanism to define the unit of consumption is entirely different. Here family relations serve as principles of social organization.

2. Housework in Somshid's family

Five persons live in Somshid's house. Since her husband died one year ago, she sells life-insurances, which takes from morning till evening and sometimes continues at night. Her daughter Maeu (16) was born up-country and used to live at her grandmother's place until one year ago when she came to Bangkok to live with her mother and finish her education at a trade school. She takes care of the household. Since Maeu goes to trade school, Somshid sells noodles at a central place in the slum at night to have enough money for the tuition fees. Her selling the noodles used to be the main source of income for the household when her husband was still alive. Now this is only an irregular sideline with little importance in comparison to the selling of insurances. Three other children live in the house, one is retarded due to malnutrition in his early life.

The income of the family is mainly made up by the commission Somshid gets from the insurance company; about 4,000 to 5,000 Bath per month. The average income from the noodles is 50 Baht per night. On average, the household has a monthly income of about 5,000 Baht, which is comparatively high. There is only one unit of consumption and only one person works for a monetary income.

In this case, the unit of consumption is Somshid's family. The main producer of subsistence goods and service is Maeu, the oldest daughter. Somshid only does a little bit of housework because she has no time. Her two jobs are necessary to have sufficient money for everyday consumption and overall expenditures like school fees, etc. The other three children do not work in the house at all as they are too small.

3. Housework in Da's family

Only one incomplete nuclear family lives in Somshid's house. In Da's family the situation is different. Currently, 16 persons, all related, share one two-storey wooden house. The house was built by Da's father ten years ago. Since then some household-members have married and raised children.

If the kitchen is used as indicator for the existence of a household, only one household occupies the house, Everybody uses the kitchen of the parents. If eating together is considered, three distinct households can be separated:

1) the household of the parents: mother, father, grandmother, Shamu, Thum and her daughter;

2) the household of Da: Da, his wife Oy, their daughter and the two nieces of Oy's;

3) the household of Doi: Doi, her husband and their three children.

The picture becomes even more complex if who washes whose clothes is considered the unit of consumption of another subsistence service. In this case, five units can be found. The mother washes for herself, Da, the daughter and the two nieces. Doi washes for herself, her husband and the children. Shamu and Thum, who eat with their parents, wash their own clothes.

In this case the housework is mainly done by women. Only Shamu washes his own clothes. On the other hand, only the men leave the slum to go to work. Da works at the harbour as a coolie and sometimes as a singer. Doi's husband works at the harbour as well but with a different group than Da. Shamu drives a taxi and goes to school in the evening. The parents earn money by selling fruit and sweets at a little stall in front of the house. Doi and Thum used to work in a garment factory nearby but stopped working after they married or gave birth. Doi is taking care of the three children, and the small daughter of Thum is still being breast-fed. Thum intends to go back to work when the child is older. Then her mother will take care of the little child while she is working. Thun will give her 600 Baht for this. This is the regular price for a person who takes care of little children in Klong Thoey slum. Da and Doi's husband mainly go out to work if they are unemployed; they help in the household as well, mainly with the cooking, taking care of the children, etc. This indicates that subsistence production will be extended if wage labour is reduced.

In other words, the labour power not used for earning money is used for subsistence production. This is clearly indicated by the fact that the men engage in subsistence production if unemployed as well. On the basis of these three cases we are now able to draw some general conclusions.

Household and Networks of Reproduction

The cases show that subsistence production is closely related to the availability of labour power in the household and the allocation of this labour power. The latter depends heavily on access to wage labour or informal sector income and on the amount of necessary goods that have to be bought: in other words, the interconnection between reproduction, production and consumption. In Somshid's case, her income is sufficient for the household, therefore the children do not need to earn any money. Somshid's work demands nearly all of her labour power, for this reason her daughter Maeu's labour power has to be used for subsistence production. On the basis of this allocation of labour power in the household, Meau can go to school and Somshid can earn the money. This allocation would have to be different if her income were reduced.

The case in Da's home is more complex because of the interwoven nuclear families. Da and Doi's husbands are earning the money for their families. Shamu is working for himself and gives some money to his parents because he eats with them. The parents depend on their stall to earn some income. Provided that the income of the men is sufficient, the women engage entirely in subsistence production. If the income is reduced and this reduction is related to unemployment so that they have sufficient time, the men start engaging in subsistence production as well.

If the income is reduced for other reasons, or the expenditures increase so that more money is needed without more available labour power, the women engage in earning money as well. Their main activity then is to cut bamboo sticks. This shows the necessity of a flexible utilization of all household resources (mainly labour power). The constantly changing situation in which urban households find themselves requires frequent readjustments, changes in location (i. e. internal migration) and changing sources of income. We therefore found it useful to use the term "floating mass" to describe the urban masses in Southeast Asian cities (Evers 1981b).

Generally, the income of one person is not sufficient for the necessary expenditures. The household has to use several income sources which is only possible if sufficient labour power is available. Households regarded as very poor are usually households which lack sufficient labour power and find it difficult to combine different types of work. In these households nearly all labour power has to be used for earning a monetary income. As this is very time-consuming because of the need to look around for work, there is simply no more time left for subsistence production. The households find themselves in the dilemma of having a low income and high expenditures because some services and goods provided through subsistence production in larger households have to be purchased by households with little available labour power.

Survival Strategies in Jakarta

Income and expenditure surveys are beset by many problems and the resulting data have to be interpreted with caution because of the many sources of error. In addition to the usual problems of survey research such as sampling errors or inaccuracies in responses, some major systematic under- and over-estimations are vaguely known but hardly ever accounted for. In general, it can be said that incomes and expenditures of both the highest and the lowest incomes groups tend to be under-estimated. The category of "own consumption" or "income in kind" is included, but usually insufficiently, in most income and expenditure surveys. The importance of these items as a major contribution to household income, particularly in developing countries, is recognized by some authors (e. g. Fisk 1975a, 1975b), but they are usually quick to admit that the conceptual problems and the technical problems involved in these matters are formidable and largely unresolved (McGranahan 1979:37).

This is true also in the case of Indonesian income and expenditure data. The contribution of goods and services provided by the consumers themselves, or received free of charge outside the market economy, remains unclear. The major source of expenditure data, the National Socio-Economic Surveys (Susenas), include some goods produced or received by the consumer for own consumption, but no services. Other surveys such as the Inter-Censual Population Survey (Supas) exclude even this limited enumeration.[89] Differences become apparent when one compares the two 1976 surveys conduced by the Central Bureau of Statistics. The average household expenditure figures for the Supas are 37 per cent lower for urban households and 27 per cent lower for rural households than the figures from the 1976 Susenas. In addition to other possible sources of error, the apparent exclusion of own consumption in the Supas may well be a major reason for this difference in expenditure estimates.

There are further indications pointing to a systematic undercount of own consumption. As has often been observed, expenditure figures tend to be higher than income figures (McGranahan 1979:17). This also holds true for the Susenas data and some other surveys. Thus, as long ago as 1937 the Coolie Budget Survey of the Batavia Municipality stated that "in all wage groups, except the highest, the households spent more than they earned. It is not possible to give a satisfactory explanation for these deficits."[90] It is well known to field researchers that respondents find it difficult to recall expenditures over long periods of time and are reluctant to give accurate income figures. This might partly account for these discrepancies, but the omission of production for own consumption and services rendered by members of the household is likely to be a major source of

---

[89]The Supas data are derived from a single question which does not expressly ask for own consumption items. The data thus derived must be treated with considerable caution.

[90]"The Living Conditions of Municipally Employed Coolies in Batavia in 1937", in: W. F. Wertheim (1958: 124).

error as well. This is not necessarily the fault of respondents, however, since adequate questions are often not provided.

Another indication of under-estimation of goods and services received outside the market economy may be gained from an analysis of income distribution in urban Java as provided by Sundrum (1977), based on data from the 1970 and 1976 Susenas. The following calculations are rough estimates and should be taken as an illustration of general trends rather than as accurate figures. As shown by Sundrum (1977:106), 11 per cent of urban households (some 1.7 million persons) in Java had a monthly income of less than Rp 10,000 (or Rp 1,883 per person, assuming the Susenas average of 5.5 persons per household) in 1976. The lowest income category, with a monthly income of less than Rp 5,000 per household (or Rp 942 per person) accounts for 2 per cent of urban households, or more than 300,000 persons. The Susenas data imply that the daily expenditure per person on food was about Rp 25 for the lowest, and Rp 50 for the second lowest income group. Both these figures are upper limits, not averages, which means that there should still be 300,000 persons in urban Java who were able to subsist on an expenditure of less than Rp 25 per day per person. If they lived solely on cassava, they would just approach a daily intake of 2,150 calories.[91] As the income of Rp 25 is the upper limit and as it is hardly possible to live on cassava alone, some doubt is in order as to whether the Susenas income figures are not under-estimates.

The point here is not primarily to suggest that the urban poor of Java are better off than the statistics suggest, but rather to stress that they are more productive, more "gainfully" active for their own benefit than is evident from the official statistics. In order to draw attention to this area of productivity, perhaps a new and more comprehensive concept is needed. This paper reports on the results of a survey designed as a first attempt to provide data on what may be called urban subsistence production in Jakarta.[92]

The 1979 PLPIIS Survey in Jakarta

Between June and August 1979, a sample household survey was carried out within the training programme of the Jakarta Social Science and Research

[91]This figure is based on WHO/FAO calculations for Java. Sayogya found an average food intake of 1528 calories per day per person in a sample survey of 30 Javanese villages (Sayogyo, Usaha Perbaikab Gizi Keluarga, LPSP, Bogor 1975, reviewed by Anne Booth in BIES XIII, No. 2, July 1977:117-119).

[92]Theoretical issues concerning subsistence production are discussed in Arbeitsgruppe Bielefelder Entwicklungssoziologen (1979). Some background material in preparation for this survey has been published in Sumardi and Evers (1979) and in Sumardi and Evers (1980). See also Evers (1980b:27-35).

Training Station (Pusat Latihan Penelitian Ilmu-Ilmu Sosial). The survey was divided into ten sub-surveys. Each used questionnaires with a common part and a special schedule focusing on one particular "basic need". The researchers, all of whom were staff members of Indonesian Universities, spent four months conducting the interviews.[93] Three areas within the township of East Jakarta which were thought to represent typical segments of Jakarta's kampong population were selected: the old established area of Jatinegara with many "informal sector" activities; the Perumnas housing project at Klender, settled almost exclusively by lower income government employees; and Pulo Gadung, known as one of Jakarta's new industrial areas with a large migrant population. Within these predefined areas, neighbourhood wards (RT) and households were randomly selected.[94] The sample of 1,083 households which forms the basis of the following analysis is not representative of the Jakartan population in a statistical sense, though the distribution of a number of important population parameters resembles those of the total Jakartan population. But it can be regarded as fairly "typical" of the kampong dwellers of the Indonesian capital, who account for some 80 per cent of total Jakartan population. The 1976 Susenas indicated an average household size of 5.37; the average in our Survey was 5.34. Tables 1 and 2 show that age distribution and monthly per capita expenditure as found in our Survey did not diverge greatly from 1971 Census age distribution or 1976 Susenas income distribution.

The main purpose of our Survey was to determine what Jakarta's low-income population regard as their own basic needs and how far they are being satisfied. As it turned out, subsistence production was a major factor in the household economy, particularly of the poor, and, in a large number of cases, crucial to their survival within a metropolitan habitat.

Urban Subsistence Production in Jakarta

Own consumption of agricultural production in rural areas is, of course, a common feature throughout rural Indonesia and extends into agricultural areas within city limits.[95]

---

[93]The surveys were closely supervised and directed by Dr. Mulyanto Sumardi and the author. Detailed findings are reported in a series of papers which are to be published in Mulyanto Sumardi and H. - D. Evers (n. d.).

[94]In some cases, selected RT had to be replaced for administrative reason. Random selection could not always be maintained. The present analysis is based on 9 out of the 10 sub-surveys.

[95]10.8 per cent of the urban labour force of Indonesia and 3.7 per cent of the Jakartan labour force were engaged in agriculture in 1981. See Walter Mertens and Secha Alatas

But even a superficial tour through the completely urbanized areas of Jakarta indicates that agricultural production is still carried on small house plots, in vegetable gardens along canals, railway lines and roads, and that chickens, ducks and other animals are kept. Though some of these products may be sold on local markets, most appear to be consumed by the producers themselves. But subsistence production does not stop at this type of urban subsistence agriculture. The construction and maintenance of houses, collection of firewood and water, and the processing of food, sewing of own clothes, health care, recreation and transport are other areas of household production which were entered into in the household expenditure schedules of our sample survey and calculated at current local market prices.[96]

(1978). There were still 11,602 ha of rice land (sawah) within the city limits of Jakarta in 1976 according to the Central Statistical Bureau's Statistik Pertanian 1976.

[96]According to one of our sub-samples of 120 households, 16.7 per cent of food derived from subsistence production. Coverage of all subsistence goods and services was by no means complete. Valuation of subsistence production, particularly of services, presents special problems since the products and service derived from the subsistence production sector are not sold on the market. We have attempted to estimate current local market prices for services and goods consumed. Some sociologists would argue that subsistence production is not directly determined by market forces but by social demand for the satisfaction of basic needs (c. f. Georg Elwert and Diana Wong 1980).

Table 8: Percentage Distribution of Population by Monthly Household Per Capita Expenditure Classes, Urban Java 1976 and Jakarta 1979

Urban Java 1979		Jakarta 1979	
% of households	Expenditure per capita	% of households	Expenditure per capita
	RP/mo		RP/mo
2.6	1,000 - 1,999	3.0	2,000 - 3,999
11.7	2,000 - 2,999	10.1	4,000 - 5,999
14.3	3,000 - 3,999	17.4	6,000 - 7,999
15.5	4,000 - 4,999	16.3	8,000 - 9,999
10.1	5,000 - 5,999	12.7	10,000 -11,999
18.1	3,000 - 7,999	17.5	12,000 -15,999
10.1	8,000 - 9,999	10.3	16,000 -19,999
11.2	10,000 - 14,999	8.7	20,000 - 29,999
6.4	15,000+	4.0	30,000+

Source: 1976: Susenas May-August 1976 (N=6,375 households for urban areas throughout Indonesia); Jakarta: PLPIIS Survey, June-August 1979; (N = 1083 households with 5,790 persons)

The Jakarta price index roughly doubled between 1976 and 1979. As no conclusions concerning change of income distribution are intended, this rough estimate may suffice.

Unfortunately, data on "own consumption" as part of household expenditure was not separately available from Susenas or from the 1978/79 Cost of Living Survey, though self-produced or received food items were included in the schedules. But we believe that our data cover a somewhat larger proportion of total household consumption since we used the above extended definition of subsistence production and paid special attention to full coverage of all subsistence items. According to our survey data, subsistence production contributed about 18 per cent to the total consumption expenditure of households in East Jakarta. This figure is considerably higher than the 5 per cent found to be the contribution of own consumption to household expenditure in Bangkok in 1975/76.[97] The Bangkok figure is certainly an under-estimate since housing is

---

[97]Calculated from Oey Astra Meesok, Income, Consumption and Poverty in Thailand, 1962/3 to 1975/6, (World Bank Staff Working Paper 1979: Tabel D1).

expressly excluded. If, as we suggest, the Indonesian Susenas data under-estimate subsistence production as well, a certain proportion of income may be missed in national accounting.

More relevant is the strategic importance of subsistence production for low-income households. For about one-third of the Survey household, subsistence production contributed more than 20 per cent of monthly household expenditure. Among these subsistence producers, poor households were over-represented. In fact, the subsistence production index correlated negatively with monthly household money expenditures ($r = -0.38$).[98]

From this we can draw the conclusion that subsistence production plays a major role in the household economy of the urban poor. The relation between subsistence production and household resembles an Engel's curve except that in this case it is not expenditure on food, but subsistence production that declines with rising incomes. The same relationship emerges from a comparison between income classes. The systematic under-estimation of household expenditure is therefore relatively more severe for lower income groups.

Table 9: Subsistence Production as a Percentage of Total Household Consumption

Household		Subsistence Production as % of Total Consumption
No.	%	
54	5.0	0
231	21.3	0.1 - 10
435	40.2	10.1 - 20
220	20.3	20.1 - 30
143	13.2	30 +

Although our data are still inadequate and prone to sampling and other errors, they at least point to the importance of subsistence production as a third sector in the urban economy next to the formal and the recently "discovered" informal sector producing for the market. The maintenance of subsistence production

[98]The subsistence production index measures subsistence production as a percentage of total household consumption.

may, indeed, be of strategic importance for the satisfaction of basic needs and the survival of low-income groups in a metropolitan environment.

Stepping out of the Shadow

Reproduction of labour power turns the slum into a unit of consumption but into a productive unit as well. The labour power within the slum is used to quite some extent for the reproduction of the slum itself. In calculating the quantitative amount of subsistence production for the reproduction of a household, two different approaches appear to be useful. On the one hand, the time budget of household members can be calculated and the percentage of time spent for activities like cooking, washing, housekeeping etc. reflects the amount of subsistence production. This approach was used in the Bangkok study. On the other hand, subsistence production is reflected in the consumption pattern of the household as "own consumption". Our Jakarta study used this approach and calculated the value of subsistence production in terms of local market prices (Evers 1981a). Although the approaches differ, the results may be compared.

In Jakarta an average of 18 % of the total household consumption was derived from subsistence production. In Bangkok 24 % of the total working time of the household members was used for subsistence production. Another share of labour power is used for goods and services in the slum area itself like small-scale trader, hawking and handicraft (or like carpentry, foodstalls etc. in the case studies). Another, although lesser part of labour power is used for petty commodity production like cutting of bamboo sticks for sale outside the slum. Subsistence production and labour employed in the so-called "informal sector" within the slum account together for approximately 50 % of the demand for labour.

This "invisible economy" or "shadow economy" is usually underestimated or ignored in previous studies of urban areas, especially slums. For example, Meesok (1978:79) calculated the percentage of "own consumption" in Bangkok Metropolis in 1975/76 as being only 5 % (excluding housing) of total income. This figure appears much too low compared to our field data.

Although the share of labour power used productively in the slum is higher than usually expected, this does not mean that the slum is an isolated area. On the contrary, by defining a slum as a spatial unit for the reproduction of labour power, all these productive activities, be it subsistence production, petty trade or services etc., have the function of supplying the urban labour market with cheap labour power. This urban labour market is one of the necessary connections between slum and city because the reproduction of labour power and subsistence production depend on monetary inputs either for consumer goods, starting with the radio and ending with rice, or "means of reproduction" like timber, land, household utensils, etc., as a basis for subsistence production. The amount of necessary expenditures per household and day is low, but a slum is a densely populated area and the sum of the expenditures of all households is unexpectedly high. In Klong Thoey, for example, the approximately 6,000 households spend about 1 million Baht every day! Keeping this in mind, it is not astonishing at all that one of the biggest markets of Bangkok - Klong Thoey Dalad - emerged on the land which used to be part of the slum in the sixties.

To meet the individual demand for necessary consumer goods the households have to employ strategies to use the available labour power in the most efficient way. The difficulty for them is the low wage they receive for their labour and the irregularity of employment.

One strategy can be described as specialization. As in Somshid's case, one household member specializes in one activity if this income is sufficient for the household. If it works, the rest of the family labour power can be used for further education of the children or directly as subsistence production. Although the incomes of persons in specialized jobs are higher, the employment is usually very irregular. In Da's family, nobody has yet been able to specialize to an extent that one individual income is sufficient to maintain the household.

The members of this family have to use all possibilities that are available to earn a little money, starting with working in the harbour and ending with cutting of bamboo sticks. This family has to be extremely flexible in using every income source to satisfy its basic needs. A third strategy

Table: Distribution of Subsistence Production in Bangkok and Jakarta

Subsistence production in percent of time or expenditure	Jakarta	Bangkok
< 10 %	26 %	19 %
10.1 - 20 %	40 %	25 %
20.1 - 30 %	20 %	19 %
> 30 %	14 %	37 %

is followed by Lop and his wife. He himself has rather specialized, works as a driver and she works occasionally in a garment factory. Hereby they combine flexibility with specialization. In Lop's case this strategy is possible only through a great reduction in subsistence production. This means increased monetary expenditures, like the 400 Baht he gives his mother for taking care of the child. Most of his and his wife's labour power is used to earn a monetary income.

In general, the strategy used is related directly to the amount of labour power available, or in other words, household members of working age. In this Lop's case is an exception because the strategy aiming at the combination of specialization and flexibility has the highest demand for labour power.

The strategy of combining specialization with flexibility seems the most successful, but it has a weak basis. Illness or other disasters by which the labour power of the household is reduced make it impossible to continue with this strategy.

The trend towards extended families in the slum area indicates the importance of utilizing several different sources of monetary income to compensate for the worsening conditions of the urban labour market and extend subsistence production to compensate for higher consumer prices.

Households are thus labour-pooling units rather than income-pooling units (Wallerstein 1982).

Urban subsistence production obviously is here to stay as an important feature of the urban economy. It provides cheap labour power and creates a vast market for consumer goods as inputs into subsistence production. The possible reduction of subsistence production over time is not a result of "modernization", but a result of the destruction of the means of production or the access to them for the people. Slum eviction has to be seen as a step in this direction. The agencies who plan slum eviction see an alternative for the people in cheap high-rise flats; the people in the slums know that eviction and life in these flats would reduce their means of reproduction and the possibilities for subsistence production. Furthermore access to work is more difficult due to the location of these flats. This is the simple reason why the slum-dwellers prefer to stay in the slum and are starting to fight against eviction. For them the slum is the place where production under deteriorating circumstances is still possible. For the urban planner it is a mere cancer in the city.

5. Access to Urban Space

Urban Land Tenure, Ethnicity and Space

Despite the importance of the topic, data on urban land-ownership are extremely rare.[99] This contrasts sharply with research on land tenure in rural areas. Theories and studies on landlords and peasants abound and very sophisticated schemes have been developed to deal with land tenure systems and with conflicts arising out of land concentration. Whereas writings, especially by French Marxist structuralists on the "question urbaine" (Castells 1979), have somewhat neglected ownership of land, studies of "peasants" have used land tenure, absentee landlordism, and landlessness among peasants to explain rural class conflict and peasant revolution. But in the cities of the Third World, landlordism and landlessness are equally common and even more pronounced than in rural areas. Absentee landlords after all tend to live in cities and invest in city property as well. Conflict between landlords and squatters is frequent but also rural urban migrants compete among themselves for urban land to be able to take part in the higher income opportunities that, in their perception, exist in Third World cities. Internal migration tends to be high or, to put it in other words, the poor in cities are pushed around and relocated through the dynamics of urban property development. Urban conflict, urban unrest, race conflicts, strikes and riots are expressions of the tensions among the city population, and the struggle for control over the means of reproduction - that is, urban land.

There is certainly no lack of studies on urbanization and urban life in developing countries. Many aspects have been discussed, but one is curiously missing: urban land-ownership. A perusal of readers and summary works quickly shows that urban land tenure is not among the often discussed topics. Terry McGee's standard text on the Southeast Asian city, so far the only comprehensive study on Southeast Asia urbanism, excludes urban land tenure despite some occasional references to land speculation. Recent French and German studies concerned

---

[99]Even in the recent study of Rüland (1996) land-ownership patterns are not touched upon in the respective analysis of urban management of the capital cities in Southeast Asia. Obviously "who owns the Southeast Asian city" still is a very hot iron that hardly anyone dares to touch upon.

with the housing question and urban property in European cities have not been extended to the Third World, but even these European studies usually contain no primary data on land-ownership, so that Lipietz (1974:94) can claim with some justification that no detailed survey on land-ownership exists: "La propriété foncière s'entrouve d'un voile de secret."

Perhaps the extreme difficulty in collecting data on thousands of parcels of land in the city explains the lack of hard data, but notwithstanding the methodological difficulties, there is certainly no lack of political and social problems all connected with urban land tenure. Urban unrest has often been a landlord-tenant conflict, as in the late 1970s and early 1980s in Europe, but all along in Southeast Asian cities. Attempts at urban planning have been obstructed by powerful landowners. Rampant corruption has been widespread in this connection. Land-use patterns have been changed by accumulations of land in the hands of a few and through land speculation. As Cornelius (1976) points out, a formidable array of political, economic and demographic forces have combined in recent decades to restrict housing opportunities for the poor while creating unprecedented opportunities for profit-making and capital accumulation among a limited sector of the city's population.

In studies on urbanization and urban life many aspects have been discussed, and considerable progress has been made in understanding the process of urbanization and the change of urban social structure over time. One aspect has, however, been curiously neglected, namely urban land-ownership and urban land tenure. This is even more surprising as there is an abundance of studies on rural land tenure. Neither classic sociological studies like Max Weber's "The City" nor the far-reaching ecological studies of the Chicago School in the 1920s and 1930s have placed any great emphasis on the ownership and transmission of land in urban areas. Whereas the questions of how urban land is used, who occupies it, and what price it fetches on the urban land market have been discussed in great detail, the question of who owns the land has hardly ever been touched upon since an early interest in the late nineteenth century has quickly lapsed.

Modern studies of the Shevky-Bell-type social area analysis have introduced many variables and factor-analyzed them. But neither the earlier studies of Shevky and Bell nor studies like Berry and Spodek's (1971) factoral ecology of large Indian cities have introduced land-ownership as one of their main variables. A brief survey of summary works and readers on urbanization and urban society in Africa, Asia and Latin America shows that patterns of land-ownership and related problems of concentration of ownership and its dispersion are hardly mentioned.

General works surveying a field of urbanization in newly developing countries like Breese (1969) or McGee (1967) neglect the problem of land-ownership altogether. This neglect is difficult to explain. There is certainly no lack of political or social problems connected with urban land-ownership. To mention just a few: Urban unrest is often based on landlord-tenant conflicts; urban planning is frequently obstructed by powerful landowners; there is frequently rampant corruption in relation to urban land questions and urban planning (Janssen and Ratz 1973); there is increasing land speculation and, resulting from all these problems a growing discussion on the need to nationalize city land in Europe and the United States (Hofstee 1972; Barras et al. 1973). But even in socialist countries where radical land reform programmes had been instituted, a change of urban land-ownership was difficult. Thus, even in the People's Republic of China, urban land had not, by the middle of 1966, been nationalized, and many landlords still drew rent from their property, although at controlled rates (Wheelwright and McFarlane 1970:104).

Urban ecologists have found it useful to distinguish between two major aspects of the urbanization process - "expansion" and "aggregation" (Quinn 1971). The first refers primarily to the spatial growth of the urban complex and the latter to the increasing population concentration in urban areas. We will devote attention to the first aspect of spatial urban growth, or "expansion", only.

A few studies address themselves to the question of what happens to the ownership of urban land when urban expansion takes place. All these studies conclude that urban expansion is accompanied by land subdivision and fragmentation of land-ownership. McTaggart (1966) provides us with a detailed study of the development of land-ownership in Noumea, the capital of French Caledonia, covering the period from 1880 to 1960. He concludes that "as a rule, in the conversion of land from rural to urban there is fragmentation of ownership" and "once achieved, patterns of land fragmentation in urban areas are remarkably persistent" (1966:189). In this process, the percentage of large-scale landowners in Naumea has declined and that of small-scale owners has increased (1966:191). Several earlier studies on urbanization in the United States show that this process of subdivision in the suburban areas produces a concentration of owner occupancy on the city fringe, whereas the city core has higher tenancy rates (Quinn 1971:468).

Wolfe's study (1967) of a Seattle, Washington, suburban area also shows these processes of subdivision but adds some further refinements. As the city moves out into the suburbs, subdivision of large estates takes place at first. But then a short period of reassembly occurs wherein urban developers buy up land for housing estates. "Consequently a myriad of small ownerships now exists even though a 'momentary' reassembly did occur," concludes Wolfe (1967:280).

A somewhat similar pattern emerges from our study of Upper Orchard Road, Singapore, an area which developed recently into a subsidiary town centre (Lim 1972). In the wake of urban expansion, subdivision took place. Eventually big developers bought up land and assembled lots for large-scale commercial enterprises and hotels. The Upper Orchard Road study covers only a minute section of the city of Singapore. The results of the study do, however, help to explain the land fragmentation profiles of another study area, a small town on the east coast of West Malaysia. Land fragmentation is highest in the city centre and in several fast-developing suburban areas. Subdivision is lower in the area surrounding the centre. This area is partly used for government offices, schools, graveyards, and hotels and parties as a village-type residential quarter (kampung). This process of leaving areas of almost rural land use and land-ownership patterns within the urban area has been described as "leap-frog development," as urban growth "jumps" across these areas and leaves them at least temporarily intact.

It can also be learned from these studies that subdivision usually precedes urban development, though on some occasions the expected urban development might not take place at once, as the studies by Parson (1972) on Northern California, and by Fellmann (1957) show.

A concentration on the process of subdivision of land and fragmentation of land-ownership seems to be somewhat limited in scope. A host of more important problems can be posed. If urban expansion and subdivision occur, what impact has the existing land tenure system of the surrounding rural areas on the emerging patterns of urban land-ownership? It surely makes a difference whether urban expansion takes place in an already highly fragmented and densely populated rural area or in almost open space such as in the Middle West of the United States during the past century. Does subdivision of land into smaller plots really mean a deconcentration of land-ownership, as suggested by McTaggart (1966)? As land values rise, the ownership of a fairly small plot of land can be far more significant than owning a large tract of low-value property. Who are the owners of land before and after urbanization, or, more generally, what is the link between urban social structure and changing patterns of land-ownership?

Urban Expansion, Land Speculation and Land Tenure

Differences in urbanization between developed and underdeveloped countries have frequently been pointed out. In order to stress these differences, the somewhat unfortunate terms "pseudo-urbanization" (McGee 1967:17) or "over-urbanization" (Sovani 1969) have been used. These terms refer to the fact that, in many underdeveloped areas, urbanization takes place without industrialization and exceeds the rate that might normally be warranted by the internal economic and social structure of the respective countries. The social and economic structure of Third World cities tends to be determined by the preponderance of government administration and by the commercial links with the world-capitalist system. Relations with the peasant sector of the hinterland are very often primarily extractive or exploitative. Cities attract resources from rural areas in the form of migrants or deliveries of victuals. Very little returns to rural areas in form of private investment or government subsidies. Quite often, cities tend to be inhabited by foreign or local ethnic minorities, adding a further dimension to urban-rural differences (Kimani 1972).

All this has serious consequences for urban land-ownership patterns. The local urban bourgeoisie that profits from commercial transaction with the word-capitalist system finds it difficult to invest profits from commerce and corruption as there are few industrial enterprises in the country itself and open investments abroad are normally restricted by currency regulations and tax considerations. There is also inflation, a lack of expertise and a general mental block against seeking investment in industrial enterprises or in areas far away from the city of origin. The result is conspicuous consumption, the use of land as a status symbol, and investment in property. The pressure on urban land is thus increased not only by the growing urban population but also through the lack of alternative investment opportunities. Land prices spiral, and Third World cities are hit by waves of land speculation as soon as some economic development takes place. This is pointed out in a United Nations report as follows: "Speculation in land in the very largest Asian metropolitan centres has indeed risen to such an extent that urban land prices are higher in the developing countries in Asia than even in the most developed countries" (United Nations 1968:52).

The existence of rampant land speculation in the cities of the ASEAN countries is well known although it has not been analyzed in any consistent fashion. Studies on the urban land market carried out by economists provide interesting overall data, but the buyers and sellers themselves are left in the dark. The stress tends to be on the "blind" market forces. The genesis of land speculation or its social consequences are hardly discussed at all.

Land speculation appears to be connected with high growth rates of the GNP, an unequal distribution of income, particularly in the urban areas, and the accumulation of wealth in an urban upper class. As the slowly emerging industrial sector is dominated by foreign capital, investment in land becomes one of the major avenues of economic success. Land has always been one of the safest forms of investment in politically unstable situation. Furthermore, profits can be made with a minimum of management and business skills.[100]

---

[100]The boom years in Southeast Asia during the last decade and the "Crash of 97" (Biers 1998) are closely linked with land speculation. During the boom the land prices appreciated

It appears that land speculation started in the mid-1960s in Malaysia, Singapore and Thailand though the number of speculators was apparently limited at the beginning.

In the wake of increasing speculation, land transactions tend to become largely "institutional", that is between speculators, rather than "terminal", that is between the speculator and ultimate resident. This became apparent in the study of Georgetown, Penang, Malaysia, an area that was hit by a wave of land speculation in the early 1970s (Goh 1975). Detailed data on this process are also provided by Sargent (1972) on Buenos Aires. The institutionalization of land speculation reduced the ability of poor migrants to buy land for residential purposes in the rural-urban fringe as these areas tended to become the object of land speculation rather than urban expansion and urban development. This led among other things to an overcrowding of the city centre and the formation of working-class slums (Sargent 1972:368). Another outcome of land speculation and increase in land prices may be an extension of squatter areas (that is, a breakdown of the norms of land-ownership) and "leap-frog" development.

A general housing shortage and the formation of slums in city centres seem to have been connected with this type of land speculation. When with rising incomes through increased employment opportunities the middle class in Southeast Asian cities tried to improve their housing conditions, they found that land on the immediate outskirts of cities had been bought up by speculators and land prices were rising fast. In Bangkok, chain speculation has provoked a considerable increase in the price of urban and suburban land. On the one hand, this has speeded up the decomposition of peri-urban rural communities, and on the other hand, has prohibited the major part of the urban population from owning urban land, in a context where no public housing aid was available (Durand-Lasserve 1980:10).

This process, however, does not stop at the lower classes, but eventually reaches the middle class. Singapore provides a good example. Despite largely foreign-induced industrialization, land speculation became rampant at the end of the 1960s and beginning of 1970s. According to a report in a Singapore trade journal in 1969/70, "middle-income earners woke up with a jolt to find that they had been priced out of the housing market" (Singapore Trade and Industry 1973:21), whereas advertisements lure millionaires to upper-class areas with a promise to "pamper them with a palatial home priced at $ 1 Million and over" (1973:11). Prospective homeowners are thus reduced to tenants or seek

---

rapidly giving rise to the "bubble" which finally burst in 1997. The role of rentiers in this context is indicated by Yomo K. S . (1997).

investment in land elsewhere. As a consequence, small-scale investors join large speculators to increase the pressure on prospective urban land, and speculation is directed to new areas. Though exact data are difficult to obtain at present, there are nevertheless indications that waves of speculation extend from major urban centres to secondary towns and rural areas, sometimes even transcending national boundaries.

This process is documented in the study of Upper Orchard Road, Singapore. This area is now one of Singapore's major shopping and hotel centres. In the 1950s it connected the central business district with the upper-class area of Tanglin and was lined by Chinese shophouses, hawker centres and middle-class residences. In our study, we coded the land sales from the records of the land registry. Between 1950 and 1960 the turnover rate was low. Some subdivision took place when new shophouses were built. Thus, the number of lots increased from 107 to 114 in this ten-year period. In the following five years from 1962 to 1966 land sales increased and 66 % of the lots changed their owners. The number of lots almost doubled through subdivision, a sure sign of rapid urban development. After 1967, it turned out that land had been systematically acquired by some large companies rather than by individual owners as before. Land was amalgamated to larger plots suitable for the building of large shopping centres and hotels. Land sales were still high (about half the land was sold again between 1967 and 1971) but this time were primarily sold by land development companies to hotel and business concerns. A new wave of speculation, but now mainly in apartments, hit Singapore in 1978 - 80, followed by a decline in 1981/82. But in Kuala Lumpur, the capital of Malaysia, property prices were still rising by about 50 % in 1980 (Far Eastern Economic Review, February 13. 1981:52). In the wake of the currency crisis of 1998 property prices fell sharply in all urban centres of Malaysia, Thailand, Indonesia and Singapore, but showed signs of recovery first in Kuala Lumpur and Singapore by the end of 1999.

Similar data on land-ownership in the other ASEAN capitals, like Bangkok, Manila and Jakarta, as well as other major towns, could be marshaled to show what amounts to a similar pattern of land speculation and urban land-ownership. In very general terms the following picture emerges: The first wave of land speculation takes place in the inner suburbs where new subsidiary town centres and new middle and upper-class housing develops. A second wave of speculation then engulfs the city centre and creates a new and dense central business district with offices of local and multinational corporations. The resulting population movements create a severe urban crisis. Inhabitants of the former inner-city slums are pressed to move to the suburbs, where they compete with land speculators and housing developers. At the same time rural-urban migrants move into the suburban ring, further intensifying the struggle for urban land. This latter process is strengthened by the land speculation that has started in the rural areas surrounding the big cities of Southeast Asia.

This process is well documented, also for the capitals of those ASEAN countries in which, unlike in the Philippines, large-scale absentee landlordism was, until now, the exception rather than the rule. When Prime Minister Sarit died in December 1963 after five years in office, it was disclosed that he and his wife (or wives) owned vast tracts of land, especially along the highways leading out of Bangkok. While in 1971 the US Department of Agriculture still thought fit to state that "problems of land tenure are not acute in Thailand... nearly 82 % of the Thai farmers own all or part of the land they cultivate" (1972:17), the report introduced a note of caution in 1972. Based on information supplied by international organizations and the Bangkok Bank, it disclosed that "tenancy in the central plain is spreading largely because of land speculation (generally by urban residents) and mortgage foreclosures". Although the Thai nobility already owned land in irrigation schemes introduced in the 1930s, absentee land-ownership, particularly in the central plain surrounding Bangkok, has become widespread only recently and now poses a serious threat to Thai peasants.

Absentee landlordism is in fact largely an urban phenomenon. This applies also to Indonesia. Whereas rural unrest in the 1960s and the rural conflict and large-scale killings following the 1965 coup might still partly be explained in terms of a rural class conflict between landless labourers and small peasants (Wertheim 1969), the situation appears to have changed considerably. Land speculation in Jakarta, connected with the Indonesian oil boom and the influx of expatriates in the 1970s, has meanwhile been extended to the rural areas surrounding Jakarta as well as other larger Indonesian towns. Though there are no survey data of land-ownership in Jakarta or its surrounding areas, spot checks have revealed that vast tracts of land, especially in the hill country of the Priangan, have changed hands and now belong to Indonesian generals and their families, higher government officials and other members of the Indonesian upper class. "Officials are moving into rice-land-ownership on a considerable scale, significantly changing the power structure in rural Indonesia" (Robinson 1978:33). The so-called "crony capitalism" of Indonesia, which included land on a vast scale owned by the children of General Suharto, was common knowledge but became officially apparent after his demise.

As alternative investment opportunities were expanding in most Southeast Asian countries during the 1980s a decline in urban land speculation may be envisaged. The rather spectacular collapse of the land market in Hong Kong and, to a lesser degree, in Singapore and Kuala Lumpur during the early 1980s and late 1990s, appear to point in this direction.

We might thus summarize the general picture as follows: land speculation on a large scale started in the ASEAN cities at different times but has taken similar forms. Speculation normally started with an upswing of the national economy (GNP growth rates of more than 5 %), and the concentration of wealth in an urban upper class. In the beginning, land speculation took place primarily in the inner-city suburbs, and then extended both to the city centre and the rural urban fringe, and then into the rural areas surrounding the cities. Land speculation and change in the ownership of urban and rural land has certainly contributed to redistribution of the urban population: high population densities in the inner suburbs, mixing of ethnic groups, urban conflict between squatters and landowners, and race riots.

Though absentee landlordism is, of course, a long-established feature of most predominantly agrarian societies, the chances are that more and more land in the immediate vicinity of large towns is going to be owned by an urban élite as soon as economic development takes place. In Southeast Asia, both Burma and South Vietnam provide us with early examples of a growing loss of land to absentee landlords. In colonial Burma, large tracts of farmland had been acquired by Chettiars living in Rangoon and early Burmese nationalism focused very much on this issue of land tenure (Mahajani 1960:68). In South Vietnam, an estimated 70 % of all farmers no longer owned any land in the 1950s. A study of a fairly representative village some thirty miles from Saigon showed more than one-third of all rice land was owned by only one absentee landlord (Hendry 1964:34). Some paddy land was also held by nonresident teachers or minor government officials as a "supplemental source of income" (Hendry 1964:38). The impact of land speculation by an urban-based élite on the rural areas surrounding the cities can also be demonstrated by more recent examples taken from Thailand and Indonesia.

An earlier report of the Thai Ministry of National Development (1964) states that in the central plain area surrounding Bangkok 19 % of the paddy farmers owning no land at all had sold their land only recently. In the early 1960s, when the data were collected, about one-third of all peasants were already landless. This figure is much higher than the national average. Problems of land tenure were not acute in Thailand until recently, and tenancy and absentee ownership were not widespread, except perhaps here and there in the Northeast (Luther 1970b) and in the Bangkok area. Nationwide, nearly 82 % of the Thai farmers owned all or part of the land they cultivated (U. S. Department of Agriculture 1972:17). This demonstrates very clearly that absentee landlordism is here primarily an urban-induced phenomenon. A discussion of rural land tenure without taking urbanization and urban social structure into consideration would thus be misleading. For Java, Indonesia, exact information is even more difficult to obtain. Data from an agricultural survey and the 1971 census at least give some rough indication. They show, that the higher the urban population in a province is, the higher is the percentage of land under rent or sharecropping.

This gives at least some indication that urbanization and the growth of urban élites may result in an increase in absentee landlordism or landlessness (Evers 1984a).[101]

It is also an open secret that land speculation is rampant in Jakarta and its vicinity. It appears that higher civil servants and military officers are now engaged in buying up agricultural land in villages. This is aided by the 1960 Land Reform Laws which state that only members of the Armed Forces and government officials are allowed to own land outside the district of their residence. Also here absentee landlordism appears to be on the increase as a result of urban development and the growing relative affluence of an urban upper class (Evers 1973a). There are also several cases where urban residents tried to regain control of their former rural landholding, which had been confiscated under the 1960 land reform laws prior to the coup of 1965.

Despite increasing pressure on rural land throughout Southeast Asia, in most villages the housing plots are at least owned by the occupants. Among some ethnic groups, e. g. the Malays, land within settlements was deemed to be ownership of houses - a valuable asset - and the right to put up a house, according to the advice of the village head. In urban areas the situation is, of course, quite different. Despite the fact that in some towns like in Padang, West Sumatra, traditional forms of communal land-ownership are still found, private property rights are firmly established. Urban land has become very scarce indeed, and has been extended into a vertical dimension piling up floor after floor in multistoried buildings which may be owned separately in the form of condominiums or apartments. In some documented cases individual occupancy or even property rights to very small spaces have developed while land prices have soared.

Whereas rural land has become the major means of production in the countryside, urban land is now the most important means of reproduction of the urban population. With increasing commercialization of the peasant sector agricultural products are used less for own consumption and more and more for cash crop production. In urban areas, however, a relatively small proportion of urban land is used for market-oriented productive purposes. Most urban land is utilized as living space for the reproduction of the urban population. The typical Chinese shophouse in Southeast Asian cities shows a combination of both. The ground floor is used for commerce or manufacturing, the upper floor for living.

---

[101]We are, of course, aware of the fact that many other variables should be considered to prove the point. Populations density, land use, and nonagricultural employment are some of the factors that would have to be considered. In any case, the data in Table 1 do not contradict my hypothesis.

The ownership of urban land, i. e. the ownership of the means of reproduction, has become, I would submit, a major criterion in defining class relations in Southeast Asian cities. Perhaps it is even justified to venture that the contradiction between urban landlords and tenants is still more decisive than the contradiction between employers and wage labourers. This may be due to the relatively small size of the wage labour force in the so-called formal sector and the preponderance of commerce and informal sector occupations.

Who then owns urban land in the Southeast Asian city? There are four major categories: individual landlords, companies and corporations, religious and other institutions, and the Government. If we exclude land for "collective consumption" like roads, squares and thoroughfares, urban land in a sample of 16 Malaysian towns was owned as follows (Evers 1982:217):

Table: Categories of landowners in 16 Malaysian towns

Individual landlords	55 %
Companies	14 %
Religious and other institutions	9 %
Government	22 %

Individual land-ownership should further be divided among owner/occupants and small or large landlords who rent land and houses to others. If we add the class of non-owners we can draw the following figure:

Table: Urban property classes:

Big Landlords	Companies	Institutions	Government
Muslim Owners		Religious/others	
Owner occupants			
Tenants			
Subtenants			
Boarders			Squatters
Homeless			Subsquatters

The upper section of the landowning class is very marked in Southeast Asian cities. Though, for instance, the Indonesian upper class has invested in all sorts of companies, the focus of capital investment in fully-owned companies has been primarily in real estate. This tendency is logical enough. Fall from office will not affect ownership of real property since retention of such property is now dependent on continuing control over allocation of concessions, nor does it involve reinvestment or production. The big families have moved into urban property in hotels in a substantial way just as they have on a smaller scale also moved into the purchase of private luxury homes, of resort housing, and of riceland in rural Indonesia (Robinson 1978:33).

What Robinson has outlined on the basis of a detailed study of the ownership of Indonesian companies could probably also be said about the investment strategies of the bourgeoisie in other Southeast Asian cities. The rising cost of land and houses leads to a considerable strengthening of an urban landowning class that comes into the possession of a huge and constantly growing "urban capital stock" consisting of urban land and buildings. The concentration of land-ownership is very high indeed. Thus, our survey revealed that 5 % of the landowners owned 52.8 % of the urban land in the 16 towns. That concentration is high is shown by comparison with a middle-sized German town. In Göttingen the top 5 % of the landowners owned only 17 % of the urban land in the central area in 1970 (Städtebauliche Forschung 1972:114-17). In comparison 5 % of landowners owned 44 % of the land in Taiping, and more than 50 % in Georgetown, Penang. if we were to use land prices and the consolidated value of the land, this would probably show an even greater concentration, as big landowners and speculators alike tend to accumulate the most valuable property. But even without these figures based on land prices, it is obvious that an urban landowning class owns a large proportion of Malaysia's fixed urban capital, that is, urban housing and land.

Data on the long-term development of land-ownership would, indeed, be useful in answering the question whether economic and industrial development and the urbanization process in general lead to a concentration of urban land in the hands of an urban upper class. As these data have not been processed so far a comparison of Malaysian towns at various stages of urban development might at least give some indication. If we compare Penang, a highly developed commercial town, with Kota Bahru, the old capital of the sultanate of Kelantan with a largely Malay urban population, little commerce and even less industry, and Jeli, a still largely rural area, earmarked for urban development, with the completion of the east-west highway linking Kota Bahru and Penang, a fairly clear picture emerges. In the peri-urban area of Jeli, land is almost equally distributed. In Kota Bahru, some land concentration, particularly in the city centre, has taken place. In Penang, concentration has already reached a high level.

The question remains whether the comparison of towns could be interpreted to represent an evolutionary sequence. This is, indeed, highly questionable. On the other hand, data on land speculation seem to suggest that economic growth and an increasing income differentiation are linked with land and consequently the concentration of land in the hands of a small urban upper class becomes greater.

This, again, is in line with the findings of studies on the effects of the Green Revolution and agricultural intensification on rural land tenure. Also here a differentiation of the peasantry and an increase in absentee landlordism seems to have occurred at least initially.

There is, however, no doubt that in the ASEAN countries the accumulation of capital has taken place largely in terms of land speculation and concentration of urban land in a few hands. This process has often been hidden by an increasing subdivision of land, while owners own many small parcels in different locations. I would, therefore, be hesitant to call this concentration of land "urban latifundismo", a term used by Cornelius (1976:249-70). That the large urban landowners constitute an upper class, accumulating surplus from the urban tenants, is shown in the severe overcrowding in the large cities, where houses are often sublet, even rooms subdivided. A "trickle-up" of rent is accumulated by landowners, and the living quarters of low-income groups are further compressed by urban development, slum clearance and construction of housing estates for middle-income groups. Administrative and political control over the "means of reproduction" through the establishment of very small administrative units and vigilante groups, both in Malaysia and Indonesia, and countermoves by the lower classes which take land as squatters, should, therefore, be seen as complementary in the process of urban growth and underdevelopment.

The economic policy of the Malaysian government promises the eradication of poverty. President Suharto of Indonesia has even gone so far as to proclaim in 1979 the so-called "eight ways of increasing equality" (delapan jalur pemerataan). These are promises, but the degree of concentration of ownership of urban land has not been mentioned expressively in any of these policy statements. It may not be without importance that the politicians and civil servants proclaiming these policies of eradication of poverty and equal distribution of income are heavily involved in urban land-ownership and land speculation, as shown by our analysis.

Another aspect may be of importance. As we know from household budget surveys (including our own survey in Jakarta in 1979, see Evers 1981a), a very large proportion of the income of lower-income groups in urban areas is spent on rent which in turn is acquired by property owners. If the ownership of large tracts of urban land is concentrated in the hands of a few persons, families or companies, the majority of the population has no chance of owning the land on which they live. So far, strangely enough, there is no "land to the urban tenants" movement comparable to a "land to the tiller" movement in rural areas. Concentration of land-ownership tends to lead to overcrowding and high population density in some urban areas and under-utilization of space in others, if land is held for speculation ("leap-frog development"). Property taxes so far do not help to alleviate the situation, as quit-rents and property taxes do not follow the principle of progressive taxation introduced in income taxation a long time ago and used as a major measure to achieve a more equal distribution of income. Without accurate data on the degree of concentration of urban land-ownership appropriate measures cannot be taken to effect a more equal distribution of urban land, should this be desired by benevolent governments.

The most consistent land policy has been followed by the Singapore government. Urban land has been acquired, public housing has been constructed and the subdivided flats have been rented or sold to the poorer sections of the Singapore population. The government thus maintains a high degree of control over the means of reproduction of the Singapore working class by controlling not only access to urban space but also by regulating the conditions of urban living.

We may thus tentatively conclude that the specific type of "development" taking place in the urban centres of Third World countries leads to increased land speculation, the enrichment of a land-owning urban élite, increased absentee land-ownership in rural areas surrounding the city and thus a growing social and economic dependence of rural areas on the dominant city. Urban expansion thus reaches much further than the immediate suburban fringe, where subdivision and urban development might take place, as discussed earlier.

Changing Concepts of Land-ownership

In the process of land speculation, a landed urban élite attempts to reach out to the rural urban fringe and beyond. But there is not only an increase in absentee land-ownership and growing control of the city over the countryside, but also a cultural change in legal norms governing land-ownership. The process of urban expansion and the physical extension of built-up areas has so far been analyzed in terms of an increasing subdivision of land on the rural urban fringe and the spatial extension of the power of a land-owning urban élite. We now have to add the third aspect of urban "cultural expansion". The diffusion of urban cultural patterns into the countryside can take many forms. In the context of this paper, we shall refer only to norms of ownership as an important aspect of this cultural pattern.

The concept of "ownership" of land as incorporated in most legal codes today is of relatively recent origin. During the European Middle Ages and still in many parts of Asia and Africa today, land is held for use rather than "owned" (Vance 1971:107). Right to the use of land were either an integral part of citizenship or of membership in a kinship group. It was only with the development of mercantilism and capitalism that pieces of territory came to be viewed as commodities capable of being bought, sold, or exchanged at the marketplace (Soja 1971:9). Ownership of land, in fact, was the basis from which the dominant position of private property in modern capitalism developed (Marx

1955:91). The city, however, was the centre of this development (Weber 1958:97). Urbanization and the development of the concept of private property are thus intrinsically linked.

Wherever colonial cities were founded, this European concept of private property was implanted and expanded with urbanization. One of the first tasks a colonial government tended to undertake was the measurement and registration of urban land. The outcome of the introduction of a Western concept of property was usually a dual system of land rights differentiating between Western individual property rights in the city and "native land rights" in the rural areas.[102]

Conflict between the two systems was and is frequent and becomes particularly pressing in the rural urban fringe where land developers and land speculators expand the capitalist concept of individual property rights against a peasantry that still maintains a socially bounded concept of customary land rights. The outcome of this struggle depends very much on the political situation, but frequently the urban speculators, aided by professional lawyers. courts, and police, remain victorious. Gananath Obeyesekere (1967), e. g., describes how lawyers use Roman-Dutch law to overrule intestate succession to land according to Kandyan customary law. In this way, they manage to reap monetary profits or bring agricultural land under their control.

Indonesia provides us with another well-documented example of a dual legal system. In the Dutch East Indies, a sort of "apartheid order" of land rights was developed. The urban centres were usually governed by Dutch law, while the areas inhabited by the local population was governed by a multitude of customary land rights (adat). Non-natives were not allowed to exercise any native land rights (Wertheim 1958:56). Though Indonesians were allowed to make use of Dutch private property laws and register their lands, this right was rarely exercised expect perhaps by the Chinese minority (Pieters 1951:124). Nevertheless, the measurement and registration of land under Western law has increased slowly either in terms of registered area or in its impact or "undermining" of customary land rights (van Vollenhoven 1925:29).

On the other hand, customary land rights have, in some areas of Indonesia, been more powerful than originally expected and have adapted to the new conditions of urbanization and urban crowding (Evers 1974).

With the increasing social and economic power of the urban upper class and its speculative endeavours, pre-capitalist land rights are reduced and consequently the social and economic condition of the peasantry in the rural urban fringe is weakened. A frequent outcome of this development is a mixed urban land tenure

---

[102]The situation in plantation areas was different but should not concern us here.

system that has no real legal basis:[103] Land is owned by urban absentee landlords, whereas houses are built and "owned" by tenants who pay a nominal land rent to the landowners. This system is described by Clifford Geertz (1965:31) for Javanese towns. In the kampong areas of these towns, a whole block is owned by one or two people, quite commonly but not necessarily one of the people in the stone houses facing the street.

Ethnicity and urban land-ownership

The ownership of urban land, one of the most scarce and valuable assets in any country, has indeed hardly ever been subjugated to research and analysis in Southeast Asia. There are no statistics available so far on who owns Manila, Jakarta, Singapore or Kuala Lumpur. Major legal and administrative measures like the Malaysian National Land Code (Act No. 56 of 1965), or the Indonesian Land Law (hukum agraria 1965) take little note, if any, of the special conditions of urban land-ownership. The anti-land-speculation legislation of Malaysia has been enforced without any prior knowledge of the structure of urban land-ownership and consequently with little chance of estimating the likely results. Urban master plans now available for all ASEAN capitals are worked out and zoning is attempted without studying the effects on the redistribution of urban land.

Overall national planning also touches on urban land problems without being able to refer to an adequate data base. The Third Malaysia Plan, 1976 - 80, stipulates that the percentage of Malays in urban areas of 10,000 population and above will have to increase from 18 % in 1975 to 21.3 % in 1980 (Third Malaysia Plan 1976:149). Will these urban Malays be tenants or landowners? Will they share in the ownership of strategically located and valuable city centres, allowing them to participate in trade or commerce? Or will they dwell on the semi-rural fringe, owning the remnants of rural land left by the Chinese urban settlers? The bloody urban riots in May 1969 in Kuala Lumpur promised Malaysia a greater share in the Chinese-dominated economy. Policy measures are largely seen in a racial framework, either directly by fixing targets for the proportion of capital, market shares etc. to be held by Malays or, indirectly, by giving the Malay-dominated Civil Service a share in the economy by founding government corporations and enterprises. MARA, a trading organization, and UDA, an urban development authority, have been used to acquire urban property to give Malays a greater chance to participate in urban life and urban commerce. In this respect the ethnic distribution of land-ownership became extremely

---

[103] In Western law, property usually encompassed both land and buildings thereon. Thus, paragraph 94 of the German "Buergerliches Gesetzbuch" stipulates that buildings are an essential part of a plot of land.

important. Also in Indonesia, the domination of shopping centres and business districts by Chinese has been the cause of urban riots and disturbances (Jakarta, January 1974; Ujung Pandang, 1981 and many more). Ownership of urban land and, therefore, access to business opportunities have, indeed, become a major issue in Southeast Asia's plural societies, but again little is known about the distribution of urban land by race, not to be confused with occupancy, which can be studied from census reports.

In Malaysia, more than in any other 'Southeast Asian country, there has been a tendency towards rural/urban residential segregation and occupational specialization by ethnicity. Whereas Malays have been concentrated in rural or administrative occupations, a disproportionately large number of commercial and industrial jobs have been filled by Chinese. The policy under the Malaysia Plans to reduce the imbalance by restructuring society is, however, made difficult by the pattern of urban land-ownership. Access to the urban commercial market and access to participation in commercial activities is conditional upon access to urban areas, particularly the central business district of Malaysian cities. Conflict over urban land has arisen on various occasions and seems to have been a major factor in the riots and killings of 13 May 1969, which led to the proclamation of a state of emergency and the virtual abolition of the democratic political system in Malaysia from 1969 - 74. Indeed, access to urban areas and the use of urban land is, to a large extent, determined by the property owner. Without ownership or urban land, participation in the urban economy is extremely difficult. Some relevant data are provided by our survey of urban land-ownership in Peninsular Malaysia.[104]

Contrary to popular perception Chinese do not necessarily own more urban land than should be due to them according to their share in the urban population. Overall there is a slight imbalance in favour of Chinese owners; however, the

---

[104]One of the few studies on urban land-ownership (the only comprehensive study in Asia) was conducted in 1975 - 79 in a sample of 16 Malaysia cities. This study was conducted under the auspices of the Centre of Policy Research, Universiti Sains Malaysia, Penang. It was directed by Hans-Dieter Evers and Goh Ban Lee with the assistance of the Urban Development Authority of Malaysia. These towns have been selected to represent major types of urban areas in terms of population size, location in different economic zones of Peninsular Malaysia, and in terms of the racial composition of its population. Though we cannot claim that the selected towns and cities comprise a statistically representative sample of all Malaysian urban areas, at least our sample coincides with some of the major parameters of the Malaysian urban population. In a rather labourious process the parcels of land were listed from data contained in the State Survey Offices. These lots were then sought in the Legal Land Records and coded according to size, land use, ownership by type, ethnicity of owner, frequencies of sales, or inheritance, mortgages, subdivision and other variables.

distribution of urban land by ethnic group varies considerably from town to town. In Kota Bahru, on the east coast, and in Alor Setar, on the west coast, Malays own the largest proportion of urban property. This may partly be due to the fact that a large proportion of the land owned by Malays is, in fact, tanah wakaf, i. e. Muslim religious endowments, or Malay reservations, which cannot be alienated to members of other ethnic groups.[105] In some cases, rural Malay kampongs have recently been included in the town boundary, thus increasing the share of Malay-owned land.

Of all the urban areas in our sample of 16 Malaysian towns, which to a certain extent might be thought of as representing the overall situation in Peninsular Malaysia as a whole, 29 % of urban land is owned by Malays, 61 % by Chinese, 9 % by Indians and 1 % by others. In comparison, the population distribution by ethnic groups in these towns is 30 % Malays, 58 % Chinese, 11 % Indians and 1 % others.

This almost equal ethnic distribution of urban property might, however, give a wrong impression. Even in those towns in which the majority of the land is owned by Malays, the city centre or the commercial district tends to be more or less completely owned by Chinese. In fact, land owned by Malays is less subdivided than land owned by the other ethnic groups, indicating a lower state of urban development or a predominance of multiple or communal ownership. More than one third of urban land of lots of more than 5,000 sq ft (i. e. larger than normal housing lots) is owned by Malays. This also indicated that Malay land is often rural land on the city fringe recently incorporated into the town limits. With further urban expansion this land might be taken over by development corporations which later subdivide, build houses and sell them to more affluent, mostly Chinese, urbanites. Malays migrating to urban areas are then faced either with overcrowded slums in Malay-owned areas or are faced with paying rent to Chinese landlords. The government has therefore stepped in recently and started to support the building of low-cost housing estates in which preference is given to Malay tenants. These government measures should also be seen as a strategy to reduce the likelihood of urban conflict.

In general, there was up to 1975/76 still a tendency for an increase in the ethnic imbalance of urban land-ownership. In 1975/76 most urban land that changed ethnic ownership was sold by Indians to Chinese, showing both the general decline of the economic importance and the wealth of Indians in Malaysia. On

---

[105]Malay reservations were introduced by the British in the 1930s after the great economic crisis to protect Malay peasant from losing agricultural land to other ethnic groups, particularly Indian moneylenders. Though urban areas were largely excluded from Malay reservations (Ali 1983).

the other hand, this might also reflect the last stage of earlier patterns in which Indian Chettiar moneylenders bought up Malay land due to foreclosures and sold it at a later date to Chinese, indicating that all government policies to the contrary have not yet had the desired effect.

On the basis of the available data we might thus conclude that the balance between urban land-ownership and urban population is only slightly tilted in favour of Chinese if we consider the overall situation. There is, however, increasing pressure on Malays and Indians, the two urban minority groups, to sell land to the Chinese. This may be due to the expansion of urban areas into the urban fringe and the building of housing estates for middle-income groups as indicated above. Lower income groups, to which a large section of the urban Malay population belongs, are forced to sell and to move either beyond the city limits to squatter areas, or as tenants into low-cost housing projects.

The ethnic ownership of land in other Southeast Asian countries is not known, but it can be assumed that there are considerable differences between occupancy and ownership. Conflicts have certainly arisen out of this situation, particularly in connection with migration and the internal redistribution of the urban population. In fact, changes in the ownership of urban land giving access both to urban production and commerce and also to the means of urban living reflect perhaps more than any other economic feature the most basic social processes in any given society.

Conclusion

In this survey of studies of urban land-ownership, we found that there is a general lack of empirical research in this area. During the process of urban expansion into rural areas first of all subdivision and land fragmentation take place with possibly short periods of reassembly by land speculators or developers. In this change of the ownership structure, land is eventually developed and its use changes from rural to residential. We have also noted that this trend might be interrupted by land division without development or by a "leap-frog" development, whereby large areas remain unused because of land speculation.

With economic development in a market economy, the urban upper class tends to engage in land speculation due to lack of other investment opportunities. This speculation may become institutional - that is, speculation between speculators- and eventually extend beyond the rural-urban fringe into rural areas. Some of the consequences of this process have been pointed out.

Urban expansion does not, however, only take the form of a physical expansion and a change of land-ownership, but also of an extension of legal concepts that originate from the city centre and are historically connected with urbanism and capitalism.

Changing Property Rights in Padang

The Minangkabau of West Sumatra are widely acclaimed as the world's largest matrilineal society and a fair number of ethnographic studies have appeared describing the basic features of their tightly structured social organization (Joustra 1923; Schrieke 1928; Willinck 1909; de Josselin de Jong 1960. Bachtiar 1967; Naim 1973; etc.). In the most general terms it can be said that Minangkabau society is divided into two basic adat groups. These are made up of a large number of named clans (suku). From there, there are sub-clans, matrilineages and minor lineages held together by an ascriptive leadership and various degrees of communal land-ownership.

Despite the strict traditional adat prescriptions that appear to a large extent to still be maintained, the Minangkabaus have played a major role in the modernization of Indonesia (Swift 1972). The first Indonesian novels were written by Minangkabaus in the 1920s; "progress" (kemajuan) was a major topic of discussion in Padang during the 1930s (Taufik Abdullah 1971); Islamic modernism found its staunchest supporters in West Sumatra (Hamka 1967); and the ideology of Indonesian independence was to no small part created and actively pursued by political leaders of Minangkabau origin, spanning the political spectrum from Vice-President Mohammad Hatta to one-time communist leader Tan Malaka.

If major forces of modernization evolved from Minang society what then accounts for the considerable persistence of traditional Minangkabau social organization? From an early date commentators on the social situation of West Sumatra have predicted drastic changes and a breakdown of the Minang matrilineal system. As early as 1909 Willinck reported that Minang social structure was changing (Willinck 1909:622), Joustra followed suit in 1920 by pointing out that closer father-child ties had partly replaced the traditional mother's brother-sister's children (mamak-kemanakan) relationship, thus upsetting the core of matrilineal organization (Joustra 1920:132). Schrieke in his famous Westkust Rapport of 1928 speaks of an "agrarian revolution" (vol. Ia:102-104) and a breakdown of communal land-ownership (Schrieke 1960:118-119); Mohammed Yamin (1952) even proclaims a "revolution" of inheritance cases: "the communal matrilineal system of inheritance is fading away".

Despite all these claims Minang adat and Minang social organization are still going strong and appear to be far from a breakdown. Two aspects of life in West Sumatra have been discussed frequently to explain both the changes in and the stability of Minang society: the conflict between adat and Islam (Prins 1953/54;

Abdullah 1966; Hamka 1968), and merantau, the system of voluntary migration (Swift 1972; Naim 1971, 1972, 1973; Evers 1972b). I wish to add another aspect here, namely the communal ownership of land. The importance of the system of land tenure in the maintenance of corporate groups (in lineal societies) has long been recognized by anthropologists. It is the purpose of this paper to study the forces of change and tradition as they impinge on the keystone of Minang social organization, namely communal land-ownership. My data are primarily derived from fieldwork in Padang, the provincial capital, where in an urban environment with a long colonial history, the forces of change and modernization are likely to have been the strongest. It is felt that in the rantau town of Padang, far from the darat stronghold of traditional Minang adat, whatever is available in terms of defense mechanisms to maintain the system of communal land-ownership will become apparent[106].

The Importance of Land-ownership in Minangkabau Society

It is not necessary to engage in a detailed discussion of the intricacies of Minang adat and its regional variations, as there is an extensive literature on the subject culminating in Professor de Josselin de Jong's sophisticated analysis (de Josselin de Jong 1960). It will suffice simply to discuss certain features of customary law as they relate to land tenure.

There are three basic types of land tenure:

(1) land held by individuals under individual ownership rights, (2) land held by descent groups of varying size and generational depth (de Josselin de Jong 1960:21-22, 56) under communal ownership rights and (3) land held by local groups, namely village communities. Traditional adat prescriptions stress the distinction between self-earned property (harta percaharian) and ancestral property (harta pustaka), and regulate the inheritance and disposal of both types of property. Ancestral property is always owned under communal property rights, so that ancestral land (tanah pusaka) is also communal land (tanah kaum). According to adat, self-earned property is turned into "low ancestral property" as soon as it is inherited and becomes "high ancestral property" after several generations. Communal property rights (hak ulayat) can be vested in a matrilineage (kaum) or minor lineage (perut), in a clan (suku) or in a village (nagari) (Sihombing 1972:73). The following tabulation of terms gives a somewhat simplified version of the Minangkabau land tenure system and defines the terminology as it is used in the city of Padang as well as in this paper:

---

[106]The following is based on field research in Padang as reported in Evers 1997.

Ownership rights are held by	Property rights:	Type property
(1) an individual	hak milik	Harta pencaharian
	(private, individual property rights)	(self-earned property)
(2) a descent group	hak kaum	Harta pusaka
a) minor lineage (perut)	(communal property rights)	(ancestral Property
b) matrilineage kaum		
c) clan (suku)	hak suku	
	(clan rights)	
(3) a local group	hak ulayat	
a) village (nagari)	(community property rights)	e. g. virgin land
b) several villages		e. g. market place

Communal landrights give the highest possible claim to land-ownership (Saleh 1972:10; Joustra 1923:103, 119), and communal land cannot be sold except for explicitly stated, specific reasons. In any case the consent of all adult members of the extended family and of its head, the mother's brother (mamak kepala waris) is required. Communal land should not be divided until when after five generations a fission of the original lineage into new autonomous units takes place. In fact lineage segmentation is common and disputes on the subsequent division of land rights occur frequently (Tanner 1969:22). On the other hand communal land can be mortgaged (Guyt 1936) and the right of occupancy transferred more or less permanently.

The fundamental importance of rights in land is widely recognized in West Sumatra. The extensive literature on Minang adat that is still produced by clan chiefs (datuk) never fails to refer to the intricacies of land-ownership and inheritance. Since the turn of the century Minangkabau intellectuals and adat specialists have fervently discussed the compatibility of patrilineal Islamic law of inheritance and matrilineal customary law, and several seminars and meetings have been convened focusing on this issue. The conference of adat chiefs and Muslim scholars convened in Bukittinggi in 1952, the 1968 seminar on adat law whose proceedings were published by the Centre for Minangkabau Studies (Naim 1968) and the 1971 symposium on "Communal Land and Development" of Andalas University (Sa'danoer 1971; Boerhan and Salim 1972) are examples of the importance attached to this issue by the local intelligentsia. The maintenance of communal property is, in a way, the keystone of Minangkabau adat as a functioning, living system. It is widely recognized that matrilineal inheritance and group coherence depend on common property and that individual ownership of land will lead to a demise of Minangkabau social structure. The migrant areas elsewhere in Sumatra and in Java provide an example of what might happen to the heartland, to the "Realm of Minangkabau" ("alam Minangkabau"), if property rights change from a communal to an individual basis and inheritance follows the patriline rather than the matriline. In these areas matrilineal Minangkabau social organization has, indeed, more or less disappeared (Naim 1973). If traditional matrilineal organization broke down even in West Sumatra, the Minangkabau heartland, then the basis for the current system of communal land-ownership would disappear too. Informants in West Sumatra were quick to point out that in this event foreigners or other ethnic groups tend to invade the territory and take over land. A frequent example which they offered was North Sumatra, where Bataks allegedly gave up their adat-based patrilineal organization and lost their land in consequence.

Adat, matrilineal social organization, communal property rights and land-ownership are therefore closely interwoven aspects of Minangkabau life. We shall now delve into this complex matrix and, on the basis of some case studies, try to unravel basic patterns and sequences of change in an urban context.

Communal Land Tenure in Padang

In this study we are concerned with urban land located within the city limits of Padang, the provincial capital of West Sumatra.

Most of the land is used for residential purposes, but on the outskirts, incorporated into the town limits in the 1950s, there were still about 800 ha of rice paddies and gardens featuring spices, coconut palms and vegetables. The links between urban and rural areas are, in fact, quite strong as a large proportion of the population (more than one third in 1970) are migrants from other, predominantly rural, areas in West Sumatra (Evers 1972b, Colombijn 1994). Both migrants and locally born inhabitants (orang Padang asli) frequently retain property rights in communal land outside the city and periodically visit their "home villages". About 80 per cent of the population is Minangkabau, and there is a sizable minority of Chinese (about 8 per cent, concentrated in one area of the town) and of Javanese (5 per cent), most of whom serve in the armed forces or the civil service.

Land owned by Chinese, land that was formerly owned by the Dutch and government lands are all measured and registered and titles are issued. According to officials from the Land Registry these lands account for most of the approximately 40 per cent of the city area which is held under individual property rights (eigendom, hak milik). The remaining 60 per cent are not registered and are owned under Minangkabau customary law. It is likely that most of this land is communal land owned by matrilineages as ancestral property. From a cursory examination of the land records in the Sub Direktorat Agraria Kota it appears that this proportion of communal to private land has not changed much for a considerable period of time. We are thus faced with the same question posed at the beginning of this paper, now, however, specifically related to land tenure: How is it possible that communal land-ownership can be maintained to such an extent in a fast growing city of almost a quarter of a million inhabitants?

Scores of authors have proclaimed the city as the centre of modernization (Lerner 1958; Goh 1973; Sternstein 1972, to name but a few) and the individualizing impact of urban life has been stressed by authors from Toennies and Louis Wirth to Alex Inkeles. Why does the city of Padang not exhibit this feature and allow instead the maintenance of communal ownership of land?.

An examination of four basic types of urban land tenure which we found in Padang will provide some empirical data with which we attempt to find an answer to the question posed.

Types of Urban Land Tenure

The urban land tenure system of Padang, the capital of the province of West Sumatra, is rather complex and exhibits a wide variety of land tenure arrangements. It was, however, possible to group the cases collected during the field study into a simple typology of four major types of urban land tenure[107]. This typology is not theoretically consistent - it does not cover all theoretically possible cases - nor is it, as yet, a model or a theory explaining the dynamics of Minangkabau land-ownership. It is just a classification of empirical cases into a descriptive typology.

The unit of analysis in each type is the lot of land over which ownership rights are exercised and which is occupied by a particular grouping of people.

TYPE A consists of a piece of land which is owned and occupied by the members of one lineage (kaum). The lineage is divided into several minor lineages (perut) which own, and dwell in, a house or a cluster of houses. The

---

[107]See Evers 1975 and Colombijn 1994:182ff, Colombijn 1992.

whole area, including agricultural land is, however, owned more or less according to the traditional organization as also found in villages consonant with adat prescriptions.

TYPE B represents a lot owned by a lineage whose core or senior sublineage lives in a large house on the land. In most cases the lineage members would be descendants of early settlers of Padang. Some of them would claim aristocratic status and trace their origin back to the royal houses of Pagarruyung and Indrapura or to a former governor (panglima or regent). On the same plot there also are several smaller houses that are occupied by descendants of workers, possibly slaves, of the original kaum and by rural urban migrants. From their long residence the people in the smaller houses develop claims to parts of the original lot, assume a sort of "permanent resident status" and, normally, do not pay rent. This is recognized in traditional Minang adat where newcomers (orang datang) can attach themselves to early settlers (orang asli) lineages (Tanner 1969:22).

In TYPE C the lot is owned again by a lineage or sub-lineage but none of the members live on the land. The land is occupied by rural-urban migrants who "own" the houses but pay land rent to the head of the landowning lineage. This type can thus be described as a form of "absentee communal landlordism".

TYPE D represents the most individualistic case. Here rights to a plot of land are held by a single person who lives in a house on the land together with his spouse and children, or who rents the house to whomever he sees fit on a monthly or yearly contract.

We shall now illustrate each type with a case study.

TYPE A. The plot of land in our case study is situated on the urban-rural fringe of Padang. It extends over about 2 ha, including 0.8 rice fields (sawah). The whole area is owned and occupied by the members of one matrilineage, which in turn is divided into four minor lineages. At present there are 22 houses of varying sizes and of varying types of construction, depending on the wealth of the inhabitants, but there are still two old wooden houses that are said to be the ancestral homes from which the minor lineages branched off. The lineage head does not live on the land but, according to the rule of uxorilocal residence, in his wife's house in nearby Kampung. He receives one third of the harvest or the sawah, which he is supposed to spend on funeral expenses or other rituals for members of the lineage. But as he is not well off himself he usually consumes the anyhow rather limited amount of paddy himself. As the sawah is very small, the use of the land is rotated between the four minor lineages in such a way that a nuclear family from each one works the land every four years and receives the balance of the harvest after the lineage head has taken his share.

As agriculture provides only a very minor part of income, most males of working age are daily-rated workers engaged primarily in the construction industry. According to our household sample census of 1970 this kampung is indeed the most typically "working class area" in so far as a fairly large percentage of the workforce is employed as labourers. There are no migrant families in Kampung Mas though a few husbands hail from villages elsewhere in West Sumatra. There has been, however, considerable outmigration of males, primarily to Pekan Baru, a booming oil town in Riau, and to Jakarta.

My principal informant was relatively well off. He had recently retired from the army and opened a shop in the Central Market of Padang. His house is owned by his wife and her younger sister, who had inherited it from their father. The father had built the house from his own earnings (harta pencaharian), and the house is therefore now regarded as "low ancestral property". The land on which the house is built is, however, regarded as "high ancestral property" and is part of the communally owned lineage land. The other members of his wife's minor lineage live in a cluster of four houses close to her own house.

TYPE B. The lot of more than 2 ha in this case study is located in the old Minangkabau centre of Padang, which is so vividly described by Marah Rusli in the by now classic Indonesian novel "Siti Nurbaya". The land is owned communally by a lineage which traces its origin back to families from whom during Dutch times governors emanated. Members of the lineage there still lay claim to aristocratic titles like Sutan and Marah (male) or Putri and Siti (female). The land is dominated by a huge wooden mansion, the ancestral home (rumah pusaka) of the lineage. It is surrounded by another old house and a cluster of twelve smaller houses and huts that are, in contrast to the ancestral house, termed rumah gedang. Some of them are owned and inhabited by members of the landowning lineage and their husbands, others by descendants of former servants; still others are rented by recent rural urban migrants. According to our household sample survey more than half, in some streets over 70 per cent, of the inhabitants in this Kampung are migrants and population density is the highest in Padang (about 15,000 per square km). This high density may explain why informants tended to stress the unity of the original lineage and sometimes even referred to it as one perut despite the genealogical distance between the minor lineages. Members of the lineage also claimed that the land under discussion is actually part of a much more extensive area owned by their clan. About ten ha of it is sawah and located just outside the city limits. This land is worked by other minor lineages of the same clan. Theoretically they ought to surrender a share of the harvest but the head of the urban lineage "does not ask for it any more".

TYPE C. The lot of land (1 ha in extent) concerning us here is part of a densely settled kampung traversed by narrow muddy footpaths. It is situated at the fringe of the old, pre-independence town. There are by now about 25 wooden houses on the land, which was probably settled in the 1930s. The occupants own the houses themselves, but pay rent to the head of the landowning lineage. They maintain occupancy rights as long as their houses are inhabited and they pay a fee to the landlord if they repair their houses, as this prolongs the possible occupancy. Most of the inhabitants have moved into the area only recently either from other crowded areas of Padang or from rural areas. Almost all of the adult males are small traders or hawkers with only a marginal income. It is these traders rather than industrial workers who make up the bulk of the urban proletariat. The lineage head, who collects the rent and administers the land, lives, contrary to adat prescriptions, in his mother's house, although he is married.

The proceeds of the urban land go to his mother, his sister and her children (his kemanakan) though he admits that he keeps some of it for his trouble in looking after the land. His minor lineage also owns some 4 ha of rice paddies and coconut gardens outside the city, which are rented out on a sharecropping basis. Half the produce is kept by the tenants, the other half goes to his mother who distributes it to other members of the lineage as she sees fit. Some of the ancestral land is already sold, as his lineage is small and found it difficult to look after the land, let alone cultivate it. The lineage represented by its head thus functions as an absentee landlord of both urban and rural land.

TYPE D. The lot in this case study is situated near the central market and is registered as the individual property of our informant's wife's mother. He migrated to Padang from a coastal village, married and took up residence in his wife's mother's house. He expects that the land and the house will be inherited jointly by his own and his sister-in-law's children, which is in line with Minangkabau adat. This arrangement is very common in Padang. In a survey of 345 government employees it was found that 31 per cent lived in houses owned by their wives or wives' mothers.

Another case illustrates a similar trend. Our informant this time was a successful trader who migrated to Padang penniless as a young man. From the proceeds of his business he bought a house which, however, he registered in the name of his children. This he did to forestall any claims of his sisters' children (his kemanakan) to inherit his land and house according to adat law, leaving his own children without property.[108]

Another case does not require any detailed study. A plot of land and a house is owned by the male head of the household who has provided in his will that his

---

[108]His children might, however, inherit property from their mother's brother. As their mother hailed from a distant village, their chances to use his property were minimal.

property will be inherited by his children. When interviewed, the owner stated quite clearly that he did.not believe in Minangkabau adat any more. This case then represents a fully individualized type of urban land tenure.

Dynamics of Urban Land Tenure

The description of types of urban land tenure and the illustration of these types by case studies immediately raises the image of a fixed unchangeable pattern. Nothing is further from the truth. Despite the fact that the proportion of urban land held under communal land right has not dwindled rapidly but remained fairly stable, the internal dynamics are considerable. The observations of scholars who described a trend towards individual land-ownership and towards a bilateral inheritance pattern are basically correct (Schrieke 1928; Joustra 1920; Sa'danoer 1971 and others). They missed, however, the almost equally strong trend towards the re-establishment of communal land-ownership and somewhat modified "neo-traditional" inheritance patterns. We shall therefore briefly analyze these processes and attempt to explain the long-term maintenance of communal forms of land tenure in an urban setting.

The precondition for these processes is the relative strength of adat in West Sumatra. A constant stream of publications on adat is pouring forth with undiminishing strength; an interest group of lineage chiefs (datuk, penghulu) preserves adat customs; a government-sanctioned organization, LKAAM (Lembaga Kerapatan Adat Alam Minangkabau), provides an effectively organized pressure group to keep adat low and frequent meetings and the overlong speeches in which Minangkabau like to indulge spread knowledge of adat. At the same time a convenient confusion of ideal adat and reality takes place. The social world is interpreted in adat terms and contradictory evidence is distorted to match the adat "facts". This makes fieldwork extremely difficult as questions pertaining to social facts tend to be answered by referring to normative adat prescriptions (Evers 1969). Blatant inconsistencies are often explained by regional variation of adat. In fact the flexibility in the use of terms is as annoying to the sociologist (see e. g. de Josselin de Jong 1960:10, 50ff.) as it is convenient to the Minangkabauadat specialist.

The continuance of adat as a normative system that is widely known and regarded as legitimate is thus an important social fact in itself. As communal land-ownership is an important feature of Minangkabau adat, its various safeguards to maintain the system still exert their influence. As mentioned earlier, there are strict prescriptions against the sale of land. If land is sold nevertheless, there is yet very strong pressure to sell it only to other Minangkabaus, or, if possible, pawn it more or less permanently to distant lineal kin in preference to others (Tanner 1969:49). Outsiders have therefore found it difficult to purchase land and former communal land, even, if sold, is still owned by other Minangkabaus who are bound by the same adat prescriptions. These may eventually pressure them into converting individual land into lineage land again, as will be described below. Another safeguard is the maintenance of fictional communal property rights. Even if land has been mortgaged permanently, which amounts to a de facto sale, the clan, lineage or minor lineage members often claim that the land is actually theirs though they do not demand a share of the proceeds from the land "at present". If conflict over the ownership of the land arises, an energetic lineage head can exert his influence and cause land to revert to communal tenure.

Customary inheritance law is another feature safeguarding communal property. Individually earned and owned property becomes "low" ancestral property (harta pusaka rendah) after inheritance. According to adat individual property held by a man is inherited by his sister's children and is added to their father's property. In order to avoid this, a father could dispose of his self-earned property by giving it directly to his children during his lifetime or by giving it to his wife to ensure eventually matrilineal inheritance by his children. Amilijoes Sa'danoer's study of a random sample of 1,401 inheritance cases provides us with detailed data on the actual practice in West Sumatra (Sa'danoer 1971). On the basis of data presented in Table 1 it can be shown that in 25 per cent of all cases the father's sister's children still inherited self-earned property (mostly land and houses) in line with traditional adat prescriptions.

Unfortunately Sa'danoer does not distinguish between male and female testators and, therefore, it must be assumed that a larger number of cases than indicated was actually in line with adat, as children inherited their mothers' property.

Ancestral communal property, according to Sa'danoer (1971:14), is still inherited by corporate kinship groups as prescribed by Minangkabau adat.

Table 6: Inheritance of self-earned property in West Sumatra

Inherited by	Intestate Succession	Gift	Total
		(Warisan)	(nibah)
Children	399 (64 %)	522 (68 %)	921 (64 %)
Sisters' Children	202 (32 %)	149 (19 %)	351 (25 %)
Other	27 (4 %)	102 (13 %)	129 (11 %)
	628	773	1401

Note: The sample is drawn from Padang (n=272) and selected villages (n=1,129).

We may therefore conclude that a lively adat tradition provides various safeguards against the individualization of property rights. There is even a tendency, especially in rural area, for a minor part of the individually owned property to revert to communally owned property. These forces are pitched against the pressures of urbanization in the growing city of Padang. In order to analyze how communal land-ownership changes and survives in an urban setting we shall again start with a typology which describes sequential patterns of changing land tenure. This will then be followed by case studies and a conclusion.

In traditional Minang village society a minor lineage occupies a large house (rumah adat), which provides one of a series of rooms along a verandah for each adult female and her visiting husband. A large number of these "long houses" are still found today in villages and even in towns in the Minangkabau highlands. When the minor lineage occupying the rumah adat became too large a new house was built on the lineage land. In most cases these houses would be "ordinary" ones without the elaborate carvings and without the huge sloping roof. In the coastal lowlands and in Padang there have never been any long houses, but the principles of home occupancy and residential segmentation are still the same. The sequential pattern of urban land tenure would thus start with a rumah adat (lowland style), occupied by members of a minor lineage and the husbands of married females. In the following generation a new house would be put up to accommodate nuclear families or new minor lineages (type A1). This process might proceed faster or slower, depending on the number of female siblings and on the rate of outmigration. Now the pressures of urbanization are starting to impinge on the system. As has been shown in another context (Evers 1973b), urban residents tend to move out to other areas and rural-urban migrants tend to move in. These migrants now intermingle with the original members of the lineage from whom they rent land to build their own houses (type B1). With increasing population density and pressure on urban land the city limits are pushed outwards to include former agricultural land or unused land. As this land is of necessity part of the communally owned lineage land, we might find the development of "absentee communal landlordism" (type C1). Tenants on such lands may eventually buy the land on which they already own their houses (type D1). Individual ownership of houses (type D1) may also come about in a "short circuit process" when agricultural land is bought or mortgaged directly from a lineage (type A2). Since, according to adat, land can only be sold under strictly prescribed circumstances and with consent of all adult lineage members, this short circuit is only likely to occur in the event of lineage segmentation when conflict about the distribution of agricultural land arises and/or there is pressure to reduce the number of lineage members to a "manageable" size.

The change of land-ownership patterns from type A to type B, C and D has thus been brought about by the following urban processes: the expansion of the urban area into former agricultural land; rural-urban migration; the differentiation of land-ownership and occupancy; increasing population density and crowding; and selling and mortgaging of land. But the sequential pattern does not stop here, as there is a tendency for type D1 to change into type A2 and a new cycle of changing land tenure and occupancy patterns then starts.[109]

The new cycle starts when the plot of land of type D1 is inherited from its original owner. In this case the land reverts back to the original lineage, since according to the principles of matrilineal inheritance the land will go to the male owner's sisters' children and will be added to their communal property. If the owner is a woman, the land is inherited jointly by her children who thus form a new property-owning minor lineage.[110]

---

[109]If one considers the "short circuits" and deviations from this sequential pattern one might, of course, argue that the term "sequential pattern" is no longer justified. As this model however illustrates the general directions of change and consequently yields hypotheses on the dynamics of urban land tenure it is proposed to retain the sequential pattern model as a heuristic device.

[110]Sa'danoer (1971:23-25) found that in villages in 176 out of 1052 known cases individual property became communal property on inheritance, in Padang he found only 3 out of 189 known cases. There are, however, 83 additional cases for which information is not available. I see no reason to assume that in all these 83 cases individual ownership was the result of inheritance, particularly as individual ownership is much more clear-cut and "uncertainty" is more likely to occur in cases of communal ownership where the precise definition of who belongs to the owning lineage or who does not is often not quite clear and leads to disputes (Tanner 1969). In any case the principle is decisive: There are cases in which individual ownership reverts to communal ownership.

This reversion to full communal ownership can be circumvented if the owner uses Islamic law rather than adat law to regulate inheritance. In this case the land is divided among children and males receive a double share. However, despite the strength of Islam in West Sumatra Islamic law is used only in very few instances to regulate transfer of land (Sa'danoer 1971). The owner can also register the land and dispose of it as laid down in a will. In this case the land may eventually drop out of the cycle of changing land-ownership patterns. The most frequent type of inheritance seems to be, however, a transfer of land from female to females and thus the formation of a property-owning minimal matrilineage. Each new generation also signifies an increasing population density. New houses are then constructed on the land or further rooms added. We are then back to types B and C, with the possibility of a development again into type D.

There is, of course, a limit to this process which could better be described as a spiral whose turns become narrower and narrower. Whereas our cycle might have begun with a rather large plot including residential as well as agricultural land, the new case A2 in the second cycle is likely to have lost the agricultural land in the urbanization process. In fact the agricultural land of A1 at least in our model has been turned into type C. With increasing lineage segmentation there occurs increasing land fragmentation, which in turn is accompanied by higher population density and crowding. Though some high density slums are being formed on communal land, the spiral process does not appear to have progressed further in Padang.

We shall now relate some case studies to illustrate the changing patterns of land tenure in West Sumatra's capital city.

CASE 1. Our informant, a government employee, lives uxorilocally in his wife's ancestral house. He claims that the house and the land on which it is built is "high ancestral property" because it was inherited from his wife's mother's brother, i. e. his wife's mamak. The early history of the lineage is not clear but it appears that it had its origin in a village close to Padang. On lineage segmentation the ancestral rice land may have been divided while the new minor lineage moved to Padang. It could not be established how the minor lineage came to own the land in Padang, but the land is now regarded as ancestral property. The mother's brother (Generation III) of our respondent's wife earned money as a trader and purchased a plot of land on the outskirts of Padang and built a house on it. This house land, originally his private property (harta pencaharian) was not inherited by his children but by his sisters (our informant's wife's mother) and her children. This, of course, was in line with adat prescriptions that the sister's children (kemanakan) inherit self-earned property. The land was thus transformed from individual to communal land and added to the ancestral property of the lineage. The original house was then vacated and the mother with her children moved to the newly inherited house. While her children grew up and married two more houses were built on the new land. Only recently a small shop, whose owner pays rent to the lineage, was constructed on a corner of the property. He sometimes sleeps in his shop and we may expect that sooner or later he will attempt to enlarge his shop into living quarters and bring his family to live there. Meanwhile a few huts have been constructed on the by now vacant plot of land that was occupied by the lineage a generation ago. The agricultural land is worked by tenants, who are distant lineal kin and give half the harvest to our informant's wife's mother, who distributes the proceeds as she sees fit; a share also goes to the new lineage head M2, who happens to be her eldest son, as she no longer has a living brother.

Case 2. In this case the land is situated in a fast-growing area close to one of the major roads leading out of Padang. The area was until the late 1960s the private property of a Chinese who had rented it out. Tenants built and owned their houses on this land. In the wake of anti-Chinese feelings the tenants, aided by the government, brought pressure on the Chinese landowner who "sold" the land to the tenants. No new titles have been issued so far, but the individual plots were recently measured by the Land Registry. The general area is becoming crowded by migrants and our household sample census shows that more than 60 per cent of the inhabitants were not born in the city of Padang. The pressures of urbanization and the transitional character and uncertainty of land-ownership and occupancy is also evident in our case study. The whole plot of land covers not more than 300 square meters. It is occupied by an old, relatively large, wooden house on stilts (1 in figure 8), a newly built bungalow (no. 2) which is still under construction, a wooden shack (3 - 4) and a low adat house (5 - 7), recently attached to the back of the old house.

The land and the houses (except for the wooden shack) are owned by an older woman who occupies the old house with her children and her husband HH1). Her eldest daughter's husband (HH2) has meanwhile constructed a small modern bungalow-type house, but so far both nuclear families still form one household. The old woman, her daughters and her daughters' children regard themselves as one minor lineage. It is understood that they will own the property jointly; in fact the proceeds from the land, i. e. the rent paid by the tenants (households 3 to 7), are shared by all lineage members. Furthermore, the woman's brother tends to be consulted in conflict situations. The tenants (HH 5 - 7) at the back of the old house are all from a village some 20 km along the road that passes by the property. All three women were only recently married and are related as shown in figure 8. While these rural-urban migrants (as well as those of household 4) have moved in, several earlier residents have moved out and left Padang for other towns. This case, which is illustrated in figure 8, shows the evolution of a pattern in which a woman and her daughter(s) are the joint owners of urban land

and of houses. This system often becomes combined with landlordism and house ownership. Frequently the tenants form incomplete families because of migration, but may eventually develop into minor lineages.

We are now in a position to summarize and discuss some of our findings. Any attempt to generalize is severely hampered by the lack of comparative data on urban land tenure, particularly on communal land-ownership (Evers 1975a). Brunner's studies on Bataks in Medan (North Sumatra) give some useful insights into the maintenance of lineages in an urban setting but do not provide us with information on the land questions (Brunner 1963). Urban lineage land was prevalent in Yoruba towns in Nigeria, but unfortunately Mabogunje's recent comprehensive work on urbanization neglects this aspect.[111] (Mabogunje 1968).

Even our own findings that communal land-ownership did not break down in the process of urbanization are difficult to generalize and should be treated with caution. The city of Padang grew only relatively slowly, it did not experience much industrialization and it is not yet differentiated into clearly defined social areas (except for a Chinese one). In fact the city has "involuted" (Evers 1972a) and its basic social structure has not changed radically.

With these cautions in mind we may suggest the following basic processes of urban land tenure that may prove to be useful as hypotheses for studies of similar cases.

(1) In the process of urbanization, rural land is constantly incorporated into the city limits. As rural land is held communally by large corporate descent groups, the fund of urban communally based land is regularly replenished.

(2) Growing population density and intra-city migration lead to early and frequent lineage segmentation and consequently land fragmentation. This trend towards individualization of land-ownership is, however, counteracted by "crowding". In the course of the growth of lineages it becomes impracticable to subdivide land further. The result is a kind of "forced" communal land-ownership as the number of lineage members living on one plot of land increases.

(3) Rural-urban migrants find it difficult to purchase land because of lack of funds and because of the restrictions placed on the sale of land to outsiders. The result is a differentiation of land- ownership and house ownership, which is now

---

[111]This is pointed out by Paul Wheatley in his review of Mabogunje's book in *Economic Geography* 46 (1970:102-104). In traditional Yoruba towns land was owned by corporate descent groups (*ilu*). We could not ascertain whether communal land-ownership is still found in modern Nigerian towns.

very common. Houses may come to be communally owned by minor lineages in the same way as land.

(4) Urban occupations are predominantly carried out by men, in contrast to the situation in traditional rice agriculture. Men thus have a chance to earn cash and purchase or mortgage land from lineage members or others, which then becomes individually owned property. There is, however, a strong trend for this land to revert back to communal ownership as it is given to the wife and is eventually owned by the wife and her daughters. This has led to a new type of communal land-ownership by a minimal lineage consisting of mother, and children or mother, a married daughter, unmarried daughter and children.

It is probable that with progressing urbanization communal land-ownership is maintained for a long time, as indicated above. I would expect, however, an increase of individual land-ownership under two conditions, namely a rapid decline in birth rates and the formation of a landowning upper-class élite.[112] Fertility decline would produce smaller families and would retard the above-mentioned process of the re-establishment of minor lineages and communal ownership. The formation of an urban landowning élite would probably introduce land speculation (Evers 1973a, 1975a), the intrusion of outsiders not bound by traditional customary law, and small households without lineal relatives or tenants. This would eventually lead to an increase in the urban area owned individually but hardly to an abolition of communal urban land-ownership altogether.

Access to Land in Bangkok

It is astonishing that although all research on urban problems in Bangkok notes that land speculation plays a role, no detailed study on urban land-ownership exists. This is even more surprising because the property rights to land and the land prices define the usability of the land and thereby access to the city for the people. One conflict is implicit to urban land. On the one hand urban land has an exchange value, particularly for those who find it hard to invest in industries and try to make quick profits through land speculation (Evers 1976:71). On the other hand, urban land has a use-value for those who live on it, for whom it is their home. The increased usage of urban land as an investment for speculation

---

[112]The Agrarian reform laws of 1960 have not uniformly been applied to West Sumatra. They require that all land is registered and private titles are issued (Swift 1972:261; Harsono 1971). These laws also limit the extent of land to be owned by one owner but this regulation, even if imposed, would have little impact on urban land-ownership patterns as the upper limit on landholdings is geared to agricultural land and therefore relatively high.

reduces the possibilities of using the land as a means of reproduction for the mass of the population. Durand-Lasserve (1982) notes: "One could say that from the middle of the 1960s the poor have been virtually excluded from the town. Only the existence of temporary tenure settlements (Slum areas, H.D.E./R. K.) on a very large scale has countered to any degree exclusion of the poor towards the outer rural urban fringe of Bangkok and has ensured that they can be established near their place of work" (Durand-Lasserve 1982:9f.).

Pattern of Land-ownership and Access to Land in Bangkok

The pattern of land-ownership in Bangkok has historical roots. Firstly, huge amounts of land were given by the king to nobles to build their palaces and houses. Secondly, when Bangkok was founded, a community of traders was resettled in the area of Wat Sampheng where they built their own houses. Thirdly, land was allocated to people resettled to Bangkok, following warfare in the eighteenth and early nineteenth century, people like Malays and Southern Thais, Khmer, Mon, Laotians etc. These people could buy the land for a small token amount of money. Through resettlement quarters with a particular ethnic characteristic initially emerged. Fourthly, when the public agencies were founded at the end of the nineteenth and early twentieth centuries, land was allocated to these by the king. As an effect, in some areas of Bangkok, even the inner city areas, land-ownership is very fragmented (predominantly those areas where land was allocated to groups of settlers), while in other parts of the city land-ownership is concentrated. Initially, the public agencies and the nobles were the biggest landowners in Bangkok. When Bangkok's territorial growth started on a rapid scale after the fifties, even more land speculation took place leading to the increased concentration of land-ownership at the fringe areas as well.

In the Sukhumvit and Dusit area, for example, land was allocated by the king to nobles, when the residence of the monarch was moved from the old royal palace to the new location at Chitrlada. Many nobles moved in this direction or to the Sukhumvit area, which was well connected to the city centre via a canal. The land in these areas either belonged to the king or to farmers and was cheap. Thus the plots owned by individuals were quite large. The plots allocated to those resettled were much smaller. At Khingphetch, where Khmer Chom were resettled, they could buy the plot for 2 Baht. In this region land-ownership is fragmented among numerous smallholders, owning just the land on which their house is built. An example of land donation is Chulalongkorn University. When founded in 1913 it was a campus university, quite far away from the city proper. To accommodate the students in this far away place, hostels were provided. Through the extension of Bangkok the land donated to the university, which had no real value in 1913, is now one of the prime locations in Bangkok.

As Bangkok was located on an alluvial river plain, the city proper was surrounded by fertile rice fields and orchards. The rice fields were irrigated by numerous canals crossing the area, of which the bigger ones were once used for transportation and commuting. The houses used to be located on higher ground on the banks of the bigger canals. After the fifties these canals were filled up and transformed into streets. The major thoroughfares of today's Bangkok used to be formerly canals. The settlement pattern remained. The houses were built alongside the roads. When space became scarce the areas left inside were built up. Increased density of the areas induced an increase of commercial activities. Shops replaced the residences alongside the streets. Still today this pattern prevails: the main roads and bigger streets are lined by shophouses, while the residences are further away from the streets and roads. This gave rise to a pattern of mixed land use, making it impossible to differentiate between residential and commercial areas. As recently as the eighties clearer differentiations evolved with the construction of huge apartment houses, office towers and shopping centres, covering large plots of land in between roads and streets.

The pattern of settlement is related to the land prices in Bangkok, which depend on the distance of the plot from the respective city centres, and the distance from a major road or smaller lane. Within the same area, land located 50 meters away from the main road is 20 to 40 % cheaper than land located directly at the road. Land located in a lane is more expensive than land not directly connected to the street network. In consequence, within one area the differences between land prices are more than 60 %. The building of an infrastructure in the form of small lanes connecting the plot with the street by the landowner himself, is a possibility to considerably increase the land price. The building of lanes by the landowners poses problems for the planning of streets within Bangkok though. As the landowner is only concerned to connect his plot with the lane or street, a network of small winding dead-end lanes emerges in which two cars can hardly pass. The extension of the lane network through developing land increases traffic congestion on those lanes, by which the others are connected with the main streets, as the lanes are unable to handle a higher traffic load. The traffic jams from the lanes spill over into the streets and lead to a regular collapse of traffic in Bangkok.

While up to the twentieth century quarters characterized by ethnicity could be differentiated - namely the European quarter along the river and Silom and Sathorn Road, the Chinese quarter at Sampheng and Yaowarat, the Indian quarter at Phahurat Road and the quarters of those peoples resettled in the eighteenth and nineteenth century like the Khmer at Khingphetch, the Malay at Phya Thai and Klong Dan etc. - this differentiation more or less completely dissolved after the fifties through in-migration and internal migration in

Bangkok. Through the development of a land and real estate market a process of differentiation of areas in Bangkok along social variables is currently taking place. Where land-ownership is fragmented, it is more difficult to set up larger structures as before real estate development can take place a land title has to be purchased from several smallholders, of which some might be unwilling to sell their land. The common land use in these areas, like Khingphetch or Vithayalai Khru, are small shops, three or four floors high, used for commerce, as the owner's residence or as rooms for rent, and smaller and cheaper apartment houses. Where land-ownership is concentrated, as in the Sukhumvit area, it is possible to set up bigger structures like hotels and high-rise apartment buildings. This in turn has an impact on commercial activities within the quarter. In the middle-income areas there are services like cheap shops, restaurants, hairdressers etc. which are needed and frequented only by those from within the area. With the construction of apartment houses, hotels etc. used predominantly by rich people and expatriates, who tend to use the car for shopping at department stores and going to restaurants anywhere in Bangkok, former shops and services disappear, partly because the higher rents cannot be paid any more, partly because the demand is small, and are replaced by those shops, restaurants etc., catering for the rich like fancy pubs, boutiques etc. The food stalls and small shops, common in all middle- income streets, are few in number in these areas and frequented only by the maids.

A special case is land-ownership by public agencies and temples. Firstly, these own huge plots of land at central locations, and secondly, they hardly ever sell the land, but rent it out on thirty-year lease contracts. Most of the big office towers and large shopping centres are established on public land, which thereby reinforce the centrality of the location.

How do the people gain access to urban space? At present, three main options can be distinguished:

1. Gaining access to urban land through social and political relations:

The easiest way to gain or keep access to urban land is through inheritance and thus ownership of the land. 16 % of the population residing in the city and 28 % of those living at the fringe and 40 % of those in the suburbs do own the land and the house on the land. This distribution is rapidly changing through the integration of the fringe and the periphery into the city proper. Land-ownership, which until now has been fragmented among smallholders at the periphery, is concentrating with urbanization. Those who own land in Bangkok are in a favourable position, as there land is rapidly increasing in price in most areas. The land title guarantees (at least to a certain degree) that the title holder can physically be in the city and cannot be removed from his land, and is able to generate profits through the control of access to that particular urban space.

Migrants gain access to urban space either through relatives and friends, or their employer, or they stay in the temple. As Textor notes: "Many a Northeastern driver residing in a Bangkok temple does so under the sponsorship of a monk in that temple, who hails from the same home area. ... Loose as it is, this temple connection serves to fill a number of the driver's needs, such as the need for a secure and safe place to live" (Textor 1961:23). A study on migrants from the northeast by Meinkoth (1962) shows that one forth intended to stay with relatives and/or friends in Bangkok, and about the same number intended to stay in temples in which some of the monks came from the same village they came from. Of those who were recruited by labour contractors, (mostly those working in construction) nearly all stayed at the place of work.

Especially in slum areas or in areas where small plots were allocated to households, one pattern is that relatives or children build a new house adjacent to the former one, or the existing house is extended, as is common practice in the rural areas. The pattern is described by Vinyu Vichit-Vadakan (1975): "A family comes to settle in the area. If this family is successful in any particular kind of trade, ..., his friends and relatives will learn of it, and come to join this family. At first, they will live in the house of the successful family. They may even be seasonal migrants and come to Bangkok only for a certain period in a year. Later however, they will build their houses adjacent to the house of the successful family, and the same pattern of settlement will be repeated for each successful family" (Vinyu Vichit-Vadakan 1975:130).

Another means to gain access to urban space is the occupation of empty land, thus giving rise to squatter areas. There are still quite a lot of slums on public land which can be defined as squatter slums, because the people occupy the land without any contract of tenure. Formerly empty land could quite easily be occupied by people. The agencies which owned the land usually took a neutral stand, as the land was not needed. Recently, the policy has changed and attempts at occupation are made impossible. One of the last successful cases was the emergence of a squatter slum along Ratshadhaphisek Road. Immediately after the road, a major thoroughfare, was finished in 1982, alongside some parts the land was occupied by people who set up their huts. Immediately police came to destroy the huts. During the night, the huts were rebuilt, and again dismantled during the day by the police. This went on for a few days until the people were allowed to settle in the area for a fixed period. This slum was finally on the way to being evicted in 1989.

2. Gaining access to urban land through administrative means:

The public sector, namely the National Housing Authority, provides shelter for low-income families through high-rise flats and by providing plots for people to build their own houses at the urban fringe. For many employees of public agencies, like the Port Authority, The Bangkok Municipality, the Military etc.

housing is provided by the agency itself. The National Housing Authority acts in these cases as a land developer, building high-rise flats on land belonging to the public agency. One problem is inherent in the low-income housing schemes: The poor cannot use the new opportunities and sell their right to low-income housing to middle-income groups.

A second means of gaining access to urban space through the administration are so-called land-sharing schemes. Land-sharing schemes are set up if a slum area faces eviction but is organizing a struggle to stay on the land. The conventional strategy used to be to re-house the slumdwellers at alternative locations possibly in low-income housing schemes of the National Housing Authority. As these are rather costly, and as most people prefer to stay in the slum rather than move into the flats or into housing schemes at the periphery of Bangkok, a new solution was sought. Land-sharing arrangements divide the slum area into two parts. One is for the landowner to develop to his best commercial advantage, the other is leased to the residents, who have to organize themselves into a cooperative to build new homes. For the residents it means smaller, but secure plots of land, for the landowner, it means fast financial gains instead of prolonged and often costly confrontations with those living on the land. Land-sharing schemes are accompanied by slum-upgrading projects of the National Housing Authority or the Bangkok Municipality. Land-sharing is the attempt to formalize and legalize a previously illegal situation. The people live on the land without any legal tenure agreement, but have been doing this already for several decades. The long-term lease contracts bargained out between landowner and slum dwellers by the National Housing Authority or other agencies as intermediary provide a security of tenure for those living on the land. One pattern however often emerges after long-term tenure contracts have been issued and slum-upgrading has taken place: middle-income people buy the tenure agreement.

The housing schemes of public agencies are for their employees, who are mainly middle-income groups, and even the housing schemes and land-sharing schemes aiming at solving the housing needs of the poor are used by middle-income groups who purchase the rent contract from the low-income households. For the poor two main options are open: occupation of empty land (the main pattern of emergence of slums on public land) and occupation of marginal land, paying a token amount of rent to the landowner (the main pattern of emergence of slums on privately owned land). The poor form into a "mass" floating through the slum areas of the city (Evers 1980b).

3. Gaining access to urban land through the market:

Gaining access to urban land through the real estate market is the way most inhabitants of Bangkok find housing. Gaining access to land through the market is the purchase of land, long-term tenure arrangements and renting of constructions (rooms, houses etc.). The market regulates access to urban land in determining the price levels for rents, long-term tenure agreements, and land titles.

The market serves those who can afford expensive luxury apartments and fancy housing estates, like multinational personnel (employees of multinational corporations, employees of the international development business), rich Thais, but also middle-income groups demanding cheaper apartments, houses in housing estates at the periphery, etc. Even the poor are involved in this market, either through paying small amounts of rent, or, which is more common, through renting a room in a shophouse or even in the slum, through sharing rooms in apartments, and indirectly, through eviction from the land which is to be transformed into apartment houses, tennis courts or shopping centres. For many, especially younger people, the sharing of a room is a common means to save on the rent. If several share the room, even the apartments catering for the middle-income groups are rentable. The market also provides expensive offices with "good addresses", shops in fancy shopping centres, etc., and shophouses in middle-class neighbourhoods; not only this, but even the setting up of a stall alongside a road or in front of a house is regulated through the market.

In general the market is quite transparent. It is known which are expensive places, where moderately priced housing is available and where cheap accommodation can be found. The same transparency exists when space for commerce is sought for. This transparency concerns principally the "consumers" of real estate, and less the developer of real estate. The developers try to keep their projects secret until land purchases have been secured to avoid land speculation.

The different agents involved in the real estate market in Bangkok can be differentiated on the basis of the scope of the activity, economic and other resources. The mechanisms are rather similar on all levels though. There is no "informal sector" of real estate development. Land speculation does not only occur with big projects, involving several hundred million Baht, but can be detected on a smaller level as the selling of tenure contracts in slum areas.

It could be expected that the upper part of the real estate market, that is, projects of several hundred million Baht like condominiums, office towers, shopping centres, hotels, luxury housing estates at attractive locations on the urban fringe etc., would be rather cartelized. Although the degree of monopolization in the industries producing goods needed for construction, like cement, iron etc., are strongly cartelized by three enterprises owned by the major shareholders of the biggest banks in Thailand, and the number of big construction firms is limited, the real estate market cannot be regarded as cartelized. One reason is that landowners, who own large plots of land in a high-priced area like Sukhumvit are themselves engaged in real estate development projects. A second reason is the investment in real estate development by enterprises which have their main base in other endeavours. Although in 1988 and 1989 the estimation of how much the market could bear was ambiguous, investment in real estate was regarded as a long-term investment for the future. The expectation of some developers and owners of units is that in the near future the prices will increase from 40 to 50 %. Thirdly, extra market mechanisms play a role in the real estate market. As much land in attractive locations is owned by public agencies, access to decision makers within these agencies is a potential resource for developers. The high potential profits which can be generated if information about planned constructions is available allows those who have access to this information to involve themselves in the market, without having the economic resources normally needed. This speculation makes the market unpredictable and is one reason why the big banks do not involve themselves directly in this business. As the case of the Emerald Tower and the Mahbunkrong shopping centre indicates though, the banks have a powerful background position in the business, as the necessary funds for financing have to be provided by the banks, and as most of the industries related to construction are owned by the major shareholders of the banks. The big construction firms, national like Ital-Thai and multinationals like Sumitomo, are predominantly engaged in the construction of infrastructure projects like airports, harbours, expressways etc. For them, the construction of high-rises or housing estates is not the main activity. Thus, any attempt by them to monopolize the real estate market remains limited. However, while the real estate market is competitive, the construction material market is strongly cartelized.

Housing for middle-income groups is provided primarily by real estate developers acting on a smaller scale than their counterparts involved in the high-rises. Some of the landowners, particularly those who do not belong to the "rich", are themselves involved in real estate development in this segment of the market. In general, the scope of the projects is much smaller than the projects mentioned above. Competition is comparatively high, and the economic resources of the developers are limited. Due to the limited capital available, constructions on a modest scale are initiated on land which still is comparatively cheap, usually land in areas where land-ownership is fragmented. This market serves particularly those who can afford decent housing in Bangkok or on the urban fringe, and smaller businessmen setting up shops in middle-class neighbourhoods. Although the profits are far below what is expected in the upper market, speculation takes place. This speculation concerns less the purchase of land, than the purchase and sale of long-term tenure agreements.

Although the dividing line between land developer and speculator is thin, as both have in common using the land or the unit for high and possibly rapid profits, the developer usually has a good reputation and the support of leading banks. The speculator, who often lacks sufficient capital and particularly the support from the banks, has to follow a different strategy. Usually the speculator acts as a broker who buys pieces of land which are becoming popular for real estate development. One tactic is to get acquainted with the landowners (businessmen, high ranking civil servants and politicians) in the areas and either get hold of a land title from these or gain support to get land titles from other landowners in the area. With a letter of intent, experienced speculators will make an installment payment to the landowners, while expecting that, in a short time, they will be able to resell the land at a considerable profit to other brokers or developers.

It is crucial for successful speculation to have information on those areas which are going to be used for development. Then, the land needed for access routes to housing estates or central pieces of bigger plots are bought by the speculators. As construction can only start if this land has been bought by the developer, high profits can be made with little initial capital. Examples for constructions delayed or made impossible due to speculation are given by Somchit (1978). The construction of a new international airport at Nong Nguhao has been made impossible due to land speculation. When the project was in the initial planning stage, "influential investors" (other sources mention at that time high ranking civil servants) bought land from the owners for low prices. When the government tried to buy the land, the price rose up to more than 1,000 %. Something similar happened when a road parallel to the Chao Phya river was to be built. It was delayed for a long time due to land speculation by some "influential persons" (Somchit 1978:149). This kind of speculation is an obstacle for the developers, as the speculator controlling access to land which is crucial for the project (the connection between housing estate and road, a central piece of a plot to be developed etc.) can demand large sums of money, which increases the costs of the project, and thus reduces the profits of the real estate developers.

Another form of speculation concerns the sale of long-term rent contracts, the so-called "saeng". The selling of long-term tenure contracts is common in Bangkok because it is nearly impossible to purchase land in the city any more. "Saeng" is the purchase of the right to rent something for a given period. Especially the public agencies hardly ever sold their land but rent it out on the base of long-term lease agreements (usually thirty years). When the lease contract terminates, the land and the buildings on it become the property of the landowner. The lease contract can be sold to "sub-renters". Sometimes a pattern emerges in which a tenant makes a lease contract with a sub-renter and demands an additional rent. The sub-renter in turn may sell the rent contract etc. The prices for these rent contracts and the monthly rent of buildings or units can reach quite large amounts, reflecting the overall development of real estate prices. During the thirty-year leasing period the contract itself changes hands quite often. Because after termination the renter has no more legal claim to the land, during the last years the buildings tend to deteriorate rapidly. The prices for rent contracts indicate whether a new land use is profitable or not. After termination either the buildings are demolished to make space for new land use, or the people stay on paying a monthly rent without any long-term security of tenure.

The possibilities to control the market and the constructions by the administration are limited, as many of those engaged in real estate development, particularly on the upper scale, belong to those who usually have good connections to influential persons in the government and administration. In addition, the sheer number of sites distributed all over Bangkok makes it impossible for the administration to control constructions. The difficulty of enforcing the construction regulations in Bangkok by the administration became obvious when a not yet finished building collapsed and killed 13 workers living on the site. It was found that the construction had already started before the plans were approved. In the Bangkok Post (September 13, 1988) it was estimated that hundreds of these illegal structures have been built in Bangkok or are under construction. In the case of the collapsed building plans for a two-storey building used for accommodation had been submitted. When a check by the city officials revealed that it was a three-storey structure, district officials withheld construction permission. Construction continued, however, not only without permission, but also without a qualified engineer.

The difficulties of the administration to even control buildings with several floors alongside the main roads became obvious, with the "Golden Building" at Sukhumvit. Construction started in 1984 but was halted when the owners ran into financial problems. Since then the raw structure of ten storeys has adjoined Sukhumvit Road. When an inspection took place in 1988, several weaknesses due to corrosion were detected. When the owners were to be asked to either demolish the building or recondition some parts, they could not be found. It was mentioned by officials at Phrakhanong that within one month, more than 120 charges were filed against people constructing or modifying buildings without permission.

The difficulty the municipal administration has enforcing the control of constructions implies that the real estate market will become the major force in shaping the development of urban land, if not kept under control by the state through urban planning.

Limits to Urban Planning

During the last three decades the population of Bangkok tripled, and the extension of the city increased 20 times over. This urban growth followed the major roads (a pattern referred to as "ribbon development") and was an unplanned and uncoordinated growth of scattered developments in some places, leaving out other places and making it impossible for the Bangkok Municipality to provide any infrastructure. In a statement, the city planning office pointed out, "Scattered and unorganized development of communities has not enabled the government to expand infrastructure facilities and public utilities along with demand. In addition, some residential communities have been built in unsuitable areas such as low places causing subsequent flooding problems. Other communities have expanded into areas with canals and fertile land suitable for agricultural purposes" (City Planning Office 1989).

Public agencies, particularly the military (especially the army), the Bureau of the Crown Property, and the railway authority, are the biggest landowners in Bangkok. Most other public agencies own huge plots of land in Bangkok as well, which was given to them when they were founded. This state of affairs appears at first view an excellent opportunity for successful urban planning, as the need to reach an agreement with private landowners are small. The fact, however, is that an implementation of urban development plans, which have been prepared since the late fifties, hardly ever took place. The existing plans are referred to if they fit projects, but they are ignored if the project does not fit the plan.

One reason for this is the involvement of numerous agencies in Bangkok, not only in terms of land-ownership but of influencing the development of the city. Damrong (1973) lists eleven agencies, on a local and national level, which are more or less directly dealing with the development of Bangkok.

The first is the National Economic and Social Development Board, which prepares the overall development plans for Thailand. In these, Bangkok of course plays an important role. To finance development projects in Bangkok, the Budget Bureau has to allocate funds, and thus has a stake in what is planned in the city. The Department of Town and Country Planning in the Ministry of Interior prepares development plans for the towns in the different provinces for the first time. In 1989 this department prepared a development plan of Bangkok and the surrounding provinces. Most directly involved is the Bangkok Municipality and its City Planning Office. In addition, the Department of Municipal and Public works of the Ministry of the Interior is involved in preparing the designs for infrastructure work. The Treasury Department is involved with land transactions and the land titles held by the state. The Land Department provides the official land titles. The Highway Department of the Ministry of Communication is involved with the construction and maintenance of the main thoroughfares in Bangkok, while the Harbour Department is responsible for the water traffic. Even the Ministry of Agriculture is involved in Bangkok, as the canals in the city fall under the Department for Irrigation. In addition, the Expressway and Rapid Transit Authority is responsible for the expressways passing through Bangkok, or those scheduled to by-pass Bangkok. The Ministry of Education has an influence through locating schools in Bangkok. Finally, the following state enterprises are concerned with the development of Bangkok: the Metropolitan Water Works, the Telephone Organization, the Electricity Authority of Thailand (EGAT), the Government Housing Bank, the Bureau of the Crown Property, the State Railway and the Port Authority of Thailand (Damrong 1973:27ff).

The involvement of these numerous agencies is a problem because no central agency exists which co-ordinates and enforces the implementation of projects within the realm of the different agencies. Phisit Phakasem (1987) makes it clear that the co-ordination of the planning of Bangkok has to be by an agency on the national level, as Bangkok is of highest importance for the country as a whole. The existing Department for Town and Country Planning has so far hardly ever had any influence on the co-ordination and implementation of the different projects by the different agencies in Bangkok. The planning divisions of the Bangkok Municipality is, as a local body, unable to devise an urbanization strategy concerned with provinces beyond the authority of the Bangkok Municipality, as Bangkok now is already spreading into other provinces (Phisit 1987:7f). The sixth Development Plan of Thailand takes these problems of co-ordination into consideration. "The management of Bangkok Metropolis suffers from many problems and weaknesses, including overlapping responsibilities and insufficient programme co-ordination among governmental agencies, local authorities and state enterprises. The problem is particularly noticeable when it comes to finding solutions for problems such as traffic and public transport, where the role of the private sector is limited" (Office of the Prime Minister: Sixth National Development Plan 1987 - 1991 p, 292). A solution of these problems is seen in the establishment of a "national urbanization development institution" and a "Bangkok Metropolitan Regional Development Fund". This central organization will be established to lay down and co-ordinate policies, plans and programmes, and allocate investment funds for these programmes and projects.

So far, this organization does not exist. However, in 1988, after three years of preparation, a development plan for the Bangkok Metropolitan Region was presented by the Department for Town and Country Planning. This plan, which is above all a land use plan, incorporates an area of nearly 8,000 square kilometers. Beside covering the Bangkok Municipal area, the provinces of Nakorn Pathom, Samut Sakhon, Phathum Thani, and Samut Prakan are included. Already prior to its public reading the plan was severely criticized. Notably the zoning of differential land use came under critique, as it implied a ceiling for land prices. The legal means to enforce implementation appear quite bearable. Violators are subject to a maximum fine of 10,000 Baht or six months' imprisonment. Considering the costs for real estate development, these fines are small. In fact, when a department store with more than ten floors was built in Banglamphu, where no house with more than five storeys can officially be erected, a daily fine of 500 Baht had to be paid to the Bangkok Municipality. The additional monthly expense of 15,000 Baht is about the same as the monthly rent for a small cubicle stall at Siam Square. When the plan was prepared, which took more than three years, many new housing estates and high-rise buildings were under construction or planned. As the President of the Association of Siamese Architects argued, developers were speeding up projects to finish them before the new laws were enacted or enforced. The question is whether this latest development plan will have the same fate as its predecessors.

The problem in implementing a development plan of Bangkok is the involvement of several different groups in the real estate business. For the public agencies land is a source of revenue and a source to compensate shortfalls in the budget allocated to them. Several persons who have higher positions within the administration and the government are themselves involved in the real estate business, particularly as landowners. For these, the assignment of their land for agricultural use would not be appreciated. Finally, the implementation of the development plan would require the different agencies to cooperate and thereby lose autonomy to another organization. Namely the Bangkok Municipality would lose much of its influence to the Ministry of the Interior, which, besides the Ministry of Defense, is the biggest and most influential ministry. The conflicts between the Governor of Bangkok and the Minister of the Interior in 1988 and 1989 do not suggest that the Bangkok Municipality will easily let go of its competencies.

The sphere in which public agencies have a direct influence on the development of Bangkok, and which could be used as ramification for urban growth, is infrastructure, especially streets and public transportation. Only where access to land is established through street construction, especially for middle and higher-income groups, does it make sense to be established. The building of streets is, however, not only done by the public sector. On the one hand the private sector is interested in projects on a grand scale "ranging from elevated roads, expressways and elevated train tracks to the skytrain" (Preyaluk 1989:161), on the other, many of the smaller streets connecting housing estates with main roads are built by the developer of the housing estate. The public agencies in turn often face problems when new roads are projected and built. Firstly, construction might be delayed and get more expensive due to land speculation. Secondly, the purchase of private land is difficult in some cases. An example is Soi Thong Lor at Sukhumvit.

To distribute traffic better between Sukhumvit and Phetchburi Road and to ease traffic congestion of the streets connecting these two roads (Soi Asoke, Soi

Ekamai, Soi 71), it was planned to reconstruct Soi Thonglor into a major six-lane thoroughfare. Construction got underway and was finished up to a canal. On the other side, between the canal and Phetchburi Road, a private landowner was unwilling to sell his property, a massage parlour. The consequence is that Soi Thonglor can now be regarded as one of the best built cul de sacs in Bangkok.

Another example is the development of the "one-way traffic system" in Bangkok. To improve traffic flow on the main roads in Bangkok (Sukhumvit, Phetchburi, Phya Thai), a one-way system was worked out in which one street leads into the city, while the other leads out of the city. Obviously, the selection of what streets were to lead in which direction created some difficulties. Sukhumvit Road and Phetchburi Road are connected with the expressway. However, those leaving the expressway block the road to those who want to enter the expressway due to the arrangement of the one-way traffic system. The system would work smoothly if the direction of the two streets had been different. One reason for this state of affairs is said to be that the owners of apartment houses alongside Sukhumvit strongly objected to the plan to make Sukhumvit Road the street leading out of Bangkok. As the one-way system did not halt traffic congestion, a mixed type was established. In some streets, at some times, some lanes lead in one direction, at other times in different directions. This tends to change irregularly so that nobody really knows where which street and which lane is supposed to lead to.

In conclusion, the ability to determine urban development in Bangkok by public agencies is rather limited, and the possibilities to overcome the problem of co-ordination of the different agencies involved is restricted. Efficient co-ordination implies a loss of autonomy and therefore also a loss of influence and power for those who have high positions within these agencies. Thus, the development of urban land in Bangkok is left to the market. Changes in land use result from changes in the pattern of land-ownership, land prices, and expected returns for constructions. Capital is invested where the returns are expected to be highest and most rapid, regardless of what the land means to those who live on it, and what it implies for the overall development of Bangkok. The floating of capital investment into attractive spots in the city finds a counterpart in the floating of people, especially the poor, through the slum areas of the city.

Pattern of Development of Urban Land

The expected profits from the use of land is the main mechanism of urban change in Bangkok. This concerns most strongly slum areas, as areas which initially integrate space into the city through the integration of the inhabitants into the urban labour and consumer goods market, and which, when this integration has reached a certain degree, are evicted from the land, as a profitable use is possible. As long as the costs for upgrading the plot and connecting it to the street were high, no profitable use could be made of the land. An often recognizable pattern was that the house of the landowner was surrounded on three sides by houses and huts of those to whom the land was rented out. As the landowner normally had a higher social status than the others, this pattern is often interpreted as featuring patron client relations. In fact, the stability of the tenure agreement depended considerably on social aspects associated with patron client relations (Akin 1975; Cohen 1985). Eviction from private land often occurs after the death of the former owner, if the heirs want to sell the land or use it for a different purpose. With the death of the former "patron", the moral obligations cease to exist, and the heirs are free to evict the people from the land. The land use after eviction clearly indicates that the land is transformed into urban space to which only the middle and higher-income groups have access, like shopping centres, apartment houses, etc. Thus the poor have to make way for the better off and move to another location.

As since the seventies, the slumdwellers have tended to resist eviction, and make their fate a public affair, forms of compromises have to be found. Firstly, housing for those affected by eviction are supposed to be provided by the National Housing Authority. The supply of low-income housing by the National Housing Authority is insufficient though, and many people do not want to move to the housing schemes on the fringe, far away from their places of work. Slum development and slum upgrading combined with negotiating long-term lease agreements between the owners of the land and the inhabitants is a strategy instigated by the Municipality of Bangkok and the National Housing Authority to solve some of the most urgent problems related to housing. Slum upgrading certainly makes sense if it is to improve the living conditions of the slumdwellers. One problem, however, often arises after slum upgrading has taken place: Middle-income groups are interested in purchasing the tenure contract. The result is that those who are poor tend to sell their contract and leave the area for another slum, while those who are better off either move into the upgraded quarter or are able to stay. Thus slum upgrading and security of tenure destroys the possibilities for the poor to remain in the area and induces the transformation of the former slum into a middle-class living area. The case of Klong Thoey Slum serves as an example for this kind of development.

From slum to middle-income residential area

Klong Thoey slum:

Not until the mid-fifties did significant numbers of people begin to settle in the Klong Thoey area. The movement of people into the Amphoe Klong Thoey, then located on the fringe of Bangkok, and the building of houses on the swampy land of the Port Authority was related to the development of the port of Bangkok. Klong Thoey port was developed into the major port of Thailand with the establishment of the Port Authority of Thailand in 1951. The Thai Waters Act required all imports, except military cargo and petroleum, to be unloaded through Klong Thoey port. In total 904 ha were given to the Port Authority for the construction of the harbour facilities.

The first people who came to settle in the area were employees of the Port Authority, construction workers, and workers at the harbour. Employment opportunities at the harbour and related to the harbour, like customs clearing, brokerage etc. led to a further influx of people into the area. Soon Klong Thoey was well known to people in the provinces seeking employment in Bangkok during the period when agricultural work was low. One respondent argued,

"At first people from up-country came and wanted to earn some money for marriage or something else. When enough money was earned they returned home. The people there were astonished at the amount of money he had earned and soon Klong Thoey became for them the only known destination in Bangkok. There was no need to build good houses, because anyway, people wanted to stay temporarily only. A simple, small hut was sufficient. Later on, they stayed in Bangkok, but still the houses were only slightly improved as then no money was available for improving the houses. Since then Klong Thoey really became a slum."

The first slum developed on land close to Rama IV Road and the railway line, what is today Klong Thoey market. When slums in the city burned down, or people were evicted from other slums, many found their way to Klong Thoey, as there housing was available (unoccupied land was still plentiful) and employment opportunities existed. In 1964, people in the slum close to the slaughterhouse in Klong Thoey were evicted and resettled in the slum at the railway track, called Lok 1 to Lok 12, which was on land belonging to the Port Authority. In 1972, people from the slum at Phrakhanong canal were evicted and also resettled in the area of Lok 1 to Lok 12. This area became what was commonly referred to as Klong Thoey Slum, with 6,000 households the biggest slum in Thailand.

In 1980 the inhabitants of the major part of this slum area, which until then had acted as a retreat for those affected by eviction from other slums in the district of Klong Thoey, were informed that the land was to be used by the Port Authority to build a new container terminal. The National Housing Authority offered a new location for most of the inhabitants at a housing scheme in Ladkrabang, a suburb of Bangkok, about 30 km away from the port. As many people worked at the port or in the vicinity of the slum area, they fought against eviction and demanded a long-term lease agreement on different plots of land belonging to the Port Authority in the vicinity. As this slum was well organized and could use relations to politicians to strengthen its position, a final settlement was reached.

The Asian Development Bank provided funds for the development of unused land at the harbour on which the people could build new huts and houses.

The rents for the plots differ in regard to closeness to the streets and lanes passing through the area. Those plots adjacent to the main road cost about 2,000 B per month, while those away from the lanes, accessible only through walkways, cost 120 to 160 B. Rents, however, have until yet hardly been paid. In 1989 the cases were brought to court and a decision is still pending. It is obvious though, that nobody is able to pay the debt of an unpaid rent for the last three years. The question is whether those unable and unwilling to pay the rent will be forced out, as they do not fulfill the contract obligations.

Walking through the area, it can hardly be regarded as a "slum" area. Particularly along the main streets, well-built houses have been established, and even in the inner area quite a lot of nice houses can be seen. As explained to me, many of these houses do actually not belong to those who received the tenure agreement, but to people who moved into the area recently, who had bought these tenure agreements. Already when eviction and resettlement started, some people sold their tenure contract. At that time the price was about 20,000 Baht. Since then many have followed. At present the going rate for a plot at the main street runs higher than 150,000 B. It is estimated that at least 30 % of those currently living in the area are newcomers, mainly middle-class people who had difficulties finding accommodation in Bangkok. It is expected that the sales to outsiders are going to increase when a new commercial centre currently under construction close to the residential area will be finished.

Muban 70 rai, as the area is referred to now, is in fact an attractive spot within Bangkok. Although located in the inner city area, pollution is low, because on the opposite side of the river is the green belt of Bangkok: Prapradaeng. Through the construction of a new super highway through Bangkok, which has its main crossing in Klong Thoey, any place in Bangkok can be reached quite easily from Klong Thoey. The rents and even the prices for rent contracts are still low compared to other parts of Bangkok. Thus it is understandable that middle-class people move into the area through purchasing the tenure contracts.

As an earlier study of Klong Thoey slum indicated (Korff 1986), the slum area was socio-economically differentiated, with really poor people and middle-class people living side by side. The demand for tenure contracts generated by middle-income groups outside of the former slum is satisfied by the poor people, who have no opportunity to improve their lot. For these the money gained is more important than a long-term guarantee of tenure. The middle-income groups of the former slum, however, stay in the new environment. The former slum has turned into a middle-class living area. What happened to those who sold their contracts? Following the information given to us, many moved into Makkasan slum and other slums in Bangkok.

Until the late 1970s people could be evicted quite easily through offering token sums of money and force. Since the eighties, slum eviction is accompanied by protests. One result of these protests is that those who are to be evicted are provided with alternative housing (a new plot of land or a flat in the housing schemes) by the National Housing Authority, and a compensation is paid by the land developer using the land for the huts built by the families. The people have the right to a new plot only once though. If they sold a long-term lease contract after slum upgrading, or their admittance to the low-income housing schemes, this right is relinquished. Many people take the money and sell their new lease contract, and again have to move into another slum area. This strata of the urban population in fact is a real "floating mass", floating from slum area to slum area.

In Klong Thoey slum the integration of the slumdwellers into the urban labour and consumer goods market integrated the slum as a residential quarter of urban workers into the city and thus made it an object of processes of change in the city. In a second step, on the fringe of the slum and close to the roads and lanes, middle-class housing in the form of shophouses evolved. One reason, besides others, why the businessmen moved into the area was the concentrated demand by the people in the slum. With middle-class people residing there the demand for land by people able to pay higher sums of money led, little by little, to the shrinking of the slum and the extension of middle-class housing. When an even more profitable use of the land in form of office houses, villas and condominiums is possible a third phase of transformation takes place in which the slum is further reduced or completely dissolved in favour of middle and upper-class housing or economic activities.

Pattern of change in middle-income residential areas

While the poor have to invade land and occupy it, the middle-income groups have access to urban land which is unattractive (due to its location away from major centres, and due to fragmented land-ownership) to the big real estate developers as regards transforming it into a fancy housing scheme or high-rise building. Real estate development for middle-income households takes place predominantly at the urban periphery. Depending on the scope of the project, it is conducted by smaller developers, or by those who are engaged in the construction of high-rise buildings and high-income housing estates. The prices for houses in these housing schemes are between 200,000 to 400,000 Baht per unit, which is below the price for a middle-range Japanese car. For civil servants another option is open: As the public agencies usually have huge plots of land in Bangkok, this is partly used for housing schemes for employees of the agency. The staff of Chulalongkorn University for example can reside in flats located on the campus. Other housing schemes exist for military personnel, employees of the Bangkok Municipality, employees of the Port Authority etc. These flats are of a better quality than the low-income flats provided by the National Housing Authority and their location tends to be closer to the site of work and roads.

In response to the increasing demand for middle-income housing, private developers shifted from the production of expensive housing into this segment of the market to capture new opportunities. In 1986, a survey of recent purchasers of land and housing projects was conducted by the Bangkok Land Management study team. One leading question was how much of the household budget is spent on housing in the form of down payments or rent.

Of the 650 households, more than half resided in housing schemes, owning land and house and 14 % used housing provided by the National Housing Authority. The size of the average house was about 80 square meters, with those in private housing schemes being larger than those of the National Housing Authority. The survey found that on the average half of the price is spent in the form of down payments, and between 27 to 30 % of the income is used for the payment of mortgages. This pattern is consistent across all income categories, including the lower end of the middle-income groups. The study concludes, "The implications of the assessment of housing demand and affordability suggest that the private housing market is working well to meet the broad-based housing demand of most of the market" (cited in Business Review 1. August 1989:19).

Extension into the periphery

As land within Bangkok proper is already very expensive, and because density of population and pollution make life within the city less attractive, housing schemes catering for the middle-income groups are established at the periphery. Due to the "ribbon" development of Bangkok alongside the major roads, the periphery might be within the city in areas away from the main roads. Furthermore, the rapid extension of Bangkok (the area of Bangkok increased thirty times during the last thirty years), places which were at the urban fringe ten or twenty years ago, might now be part of the inner city area. Several of the older housing schemes are in fact now within the inner city, or created themselves new sub-centres of Bangkok like the area around Ramkamhaeng University, Ladprao, Bang Kapi, Nonthaburi etc. While in the area close to Bangkok a process of transformation from slum to middle and upper-class housing, that is from unprofitable land use to profitable land use, took place, or as in the case of Khingphetch, areas with fragmented land-ownership remained as middle-income living areas, the establishment of housing schemes induces a transformation of the periphery from village to suburb and finally city quarter (Thiravet 1979). More important than housing estates in the transformation of the urban fringe are, however, industries and enterprises, which tend to be located at the urban fringe. Industries surrounding Bangkok are no longer limited to the direct vicinity of the city but are already entering the provinces of Chachaengsao and Ayudhya.

In the development plan of the Greater Bangkok Metropolitan Region, as outlined by the NESDB and the Department for Town and City Planning, several industrial estates in the surroundings of Bangkok have been classified, for which infrastructure should be provided. The older industrial areas, namely at Samut Prakan, Prapradaeng and Bang Phli are still growing, and there infrastructure shortage is alread leading to severe problems. The development of the industrial estates is left primarily to the initiative of the enterprises themselves, which set up factories at a location regarded as convenient, or by private industrial estate developers, which are by and large free to set up these estates where they find it appropriate, as no general city plan has been promulgated yet. The Sixth National Economic and Social Development Plan proposes to "encourage factories that are starting up or expanding their activities to locate in industrial estates and industrial locations recommended in the general town plans" (Thiravet 1979:300). Thus, the legal possibilities for defining the locations for industrial estates are at present limited.

The enterprises developing industrial estates are often the same as the big real estate developers. The "International Resources Development Ltd." for example, has built the Charn Issara Tower (an office tower and shopping centre) in Bangkok, and is developing the Ladkrabang Industrial Estate, about 30 km east of Bangkok. An infrastructure is set up by the developers at the location, consisting of roads, power supply lines, telecommunication systems, flood protection, water treatment etc. The land is subdivided into parcels used for specific purposes like export processing, general industrial activities, warehouses, and in some cases customs offices, and sold to those interested.

Condominium: Extension into the sky

Within the inner city, the extension of Bangkok is primarily the building of high-rises, either as office tower, apartment house or condominium. The condominium market is split into those catering predominantly for a middle-income clientele and for the upper-income groups. The cheaper apartments are usually of a lower standard, but are, particularly for younger people, a possibility to find conveniently located housing in Bangkok. Bangkok experienced a first construction boom, especially of so-called town houses, that is four-storey houses with a shop or garage as the ground floor, in the early seventies. At that time, most of the already settled areas around the inner city proper were rebuilt in form of these town houses, which are still lining most of the roads and lanes of Bangkok. In the early eighties, a first so-called "condo-boom" (Manop Bongsadet) took place. On average once a week a new high-rise condominium or apartment house was built. The apartments for the higher income groups, like the Thai Ping Towers, were priced between 1,5 to 2 million Baht (or sometimes even higher). Those for the middle-income groups were priced between 250,000 to 400,000 Baht, a price comparable to the town houses, which, however, at that time were built already at locations further away from the city centre.

The condominium boom of the early eighties went into a crisis in 1983, when the Bank of Thailand recommended to all commercial banks to stop providing financial support for real estate projects under the categories of hotel, residential - and office condominium and commercial complexes, due to unpayable debts. Obviously, the mushrooming of real estate projects and the speculation in land and apartments led to a severe oversupply of the market. An example is the Emerald Tower at Wireless Road, catering for a rich clientele with prices per square meter of more than 25,000 Baht. The developer was unable to pay the interests on the debts, and in consequence, those who had already bought units did not receive the requisite property titles. The case was brought to the court by the Bangkok Bank, the main creditor of the developer of the Emerald Tower. Although the buyers do have valid agreements, it was not clear at all whether these could be transformed into property rights. This case made clear to the people in Bangkok that they have to be very careful when buying an apartment in a condominium.

The downswing of the business following 1983 was turned around in the second half of the eighties. Again each week an announcement for the construction of a new condominium was to be found in the newspapers. In 1988, the economic crisis which Thailand had faced was resolved, and rapid economic growth took place. Thai and foreign capital was available and searching for investment opportunities which might generate high and secure returns. The strategy seemed to work. Already at an initial stage up to 70 % of the planned units were sold. The rapid sale of the units prior to finishing the project is due to a steady increase in the prices. Initially, a unit might cost between 22,000 to 25,000 Baht per square meter. The developer themselves increase the prices on a monthly basis, to induce customers to purchase the units at an early stage. This, however, brings in the speculators, who purchase a title for the unit, and sell it when the price has increased. Speculation of this kind is perceived as a danger by the developers. "If the number of speculators is higher than the genuine buyers, it can become a threat to investment: that is when the speculators cannot finance the purchases after they find out that their units are not easily marketable". Estimates are that the fake demand created by "land sharks" might already outnumber the real demand.

If the real estate projects currently under construction and those planned at present are finished, the number of high-rises forming the skyline of Bangkok will have increased to more than two hundred. While for a long time the Chokchai building at Sukhumvit used to be the tallest building in Thailand, now the Bayoke tower with 43 storeys is the pivot of Bangkok. This position is challenged already by the World Trade Centre Bangkok with 60 storeys. The answer to this is the Bayoke Tower II with more than 80 storeys.

In the first half of 1989 construction in Bangkok expanded rapidly. In total permission for construction of more than 9 mio. square meters has been issued and the sale of cement increased during the first six months of 1989 by more than 30 % to 7,5 mio tons, and credits for real estate development increased to 140 billion Baht in June 1989 (Preyaluk 1989:418). One consequence of this boom is the shortage of construction material and qualified labour power for the establishment of needed infrastructure, particularly in Bangkok itself.

The success of real estate development in the form of condominiums depends on their location within Bangkok, which, following the advertisements, is in all cases a central location in the "heart of the city" to "avoid the hassle and frustration of Bangkok's interminable traffic". In a similar vein, "Century Heights" is supposed to be located "at a residential location in the heart of the city", at Sukhumvit, Soi 23. A central location has one drawback though, it is usually congested and polluted. The "Sathorn Park Place" found the proper answer to this problem: "Imagine living in a quiet area of refreshing greenery while the whole of Bangkok lies before you. Few luxury residential properties anywhere in the city centre can offer such pleasant surroundings and commanding views." A different idea was initiated by the "Tridhos City Marina", a high-rise condominium at the Chao Phya River. As the business centre of Bangkok is quite far away from the river, it is not the central location which is important, but the Tridhos City Marina as "the latest innovative real estate development to hit Bangkok. ... Tridhos City Marina offers a distinct contrast between old and new. A trip down the shimmering waters of the Chao Phya River is like a trip back in time."

Location within Bangkok is only one issue for condominiums. The production of locality can be regarded as the more important aspect. A condominium is not envisaged as residential space, but as a complete locality in itself. Thus, besides apartments, the condominium consists of a swimming pool, shops, and even offices. At "Kiarti Thanee City Mansion", the residents have the following facilities: Personalized parking space on the ground, with additional parking for visitors, landscaped gardens, playground plaza and games room, club and exercise room, men's and women's sauna, a huge swimming pool with separate children's pool, a Jacuzzi and waterfall cascades, and security services like closed circuit television, video intercom etc. At the "Bangkok Yacht Club", the building will include a large residential condominium, an arcade with a wide variety of facilities such as a mini-supermarket, restaurants, function rooms, a sport complex housing a modern health club, tennis court, swimming pool, badminton court and putting green.

In the area of Soi Soon Vijai, which so far has been developed primarily into middle-class housing estates, a gigantic project is planned by a joint venture of Thai and Singaporean capital. The project is located on a 86 rai plot, leased from the State Railway of Thailand. It consists of a residential complex and commercial areas, linked by a 1.8 km road. The shopping arcade will include a food park, a discotheque, a supermarket and boutiques. Probably a department store will be established close by as well. At a later stage, a hotel with 500 to 1,000 rooms is going to be built.

The services offered by the condominium are aiming predominantly at highly paid itinerant executives, expatriates and rich Thais, using the apartment as a second or third residence. As the demand from Thais is expected to be too small, foreigners, who are not allowed to purchase land in Thailand, are allowed to own up to 25 % of the units in a condominium. If the government wants to provide the foreigners with a larger percentage of ownership, it might consider the issue of a special decree to increase ownership to 30 to 40 %. As the itinerant experts and executives stay at the place for a limited period only, in most cases the apartments are rented out by the owners.

Condominium projects are produced localities at specified locations. As most of the services demanded by the inhabitants are provided by the condominium itself, the facilities available in the locality are less important. They are supposed to be central anyway. The inhabitants do not need to use the shops existing in the locality but either purchase the goods needed directly within the compound of the condominium or use the car to go to the supermarket and the department store. Everyday life is organized around the condominium and other locations in Bangkok in total, like the department store, the entertainment plaza etc. and finds no focus in the locality. The condominium is a produced locality, a unit of itself rather independent of the services offered in the vicinity. For the condominium, it is important that it is accessible by private transportation through quiet streets (Soi) and that it is connected with other "central" locations by major roads.

Real estate development in the form of high-rise buildings or housing estates at the periphery is done by private enterprises, who try to make a profit with these endeavours. To the development agencies and construction firms, the banks have to be added, as only the banks are able to provide the necessary credits for these projects. Furthermore, speculators who expect fast returns through increases of land prices are involved in the development of housing in Bangkok. The reason why the constructions are built where they are is profitability and access to bigger plots of land. Thus condominiums emerge particularly where a high demand for that kind of housing exists or is expected to exist by the developers, and where land-ownership is concentrated. The overall development of Bangkok, the congestion of the streets and the impacts on the environment are of limited concern.

The Real Estate Market Structure of Bangkok.

The most obvious trend of urban change in relation to the structure of urban land is a depopulation of the inner city area and the increase of population at the urban fringe and the periphery. This movement results predominantly from three linked processes: slum eviction through which the people either receive plots from the National Housing Authority in housing schemes at the urban fringe, the availability of decent housing for an appropriate price in estates for middle-income groups, the increase of employment opportunities at the urban fringe and periphery through the settlement of industries there, and the resettling of industries and offices from the inner city to the periphery.

The core districts of Bangkok like Phranakorn (the old city with the Royal Palace and important temples), Sampanthawong (the old commercial heart of Bangkok in which "Chinatown" and the big markets are located) and Phomprap are losing inhabitants. With densities of up to forty-thousand inhabitants per square kilometers, these are the most densely settled districts of Bangkok. Outmigration is due to new possibilities of finding accommodation and, as the example of Yaowarat indicated, business opportunities at other locations. Outmigration from Phathumwan, Phya Thai and Bang Rak, as districts which do not belong to the old core, is due to changes in land use. These districts are in the process of transformation into the centre of commerce and business of Bangkok. Real estate projects in these districts are primarily the building of big office towers and huge shopping centres which require big plots of land, thus making a mixed land use, so common in other parts of Bangkok, impossible. The strongest increase in population is found in the intermediate areas of Bangkok, those in between the periphery and the inner city proper, like Phrakhanong, Huay Kwang, Bang Khen, and the districts in Thonburi. In contrast to the city core, these are very large districts, which consist of areas clearly belonging to the inner city, and areas which still have a rural character. Phrakhanong in particular is a special case, as it incorporates the urban fringe and parts of the commercial centre of Bangkok.

What used to be the urban fringe during the sixties and seventies, the districts of Phrakhanong, Bang Rak, Phya Thai and Phathumwan, are now integrated into the inner city proper, and the former periphery like the districts of Bang Kapi, Bang Khen etc. are transformed into the urban fringe.

If the distribution of high-rise building projects and housing estates in relation to the districts of Bangkok is compared, a trend to create middle-income housing at the urban fringe and to fill the districts in between city core and fringe with high-rises to be used for commercial and housing purposes is indicated.

Phrakhanong, Phya Thai and Bang Rak are extending into the sky through the high-rises, while Bang Kapi and Bang Khen are being built up by housing estates. The special case of Phrakhanong is indicated by the table, as in Phrakhanong we find a concentration of high-rises and of housing estates.

Considering both processes together, the pattern of extension of Bangkok is on one hand the extension into the periphery through housing estates catering primarily for middle-income groups, housing schemes for the urban poor, the emergence of new slums at the fringe, and the location of employment opportunities for middle- and lower-income groups through the movement of industries and public institutions from the city core to the periphery. On the other hand, it is the extension of Bangkok into the sky through high-rise buildings catering for a solvent demand, be it for housing or for offices and commerce.

The two patterns of extension (into the sky and into the vicinity) are related to the development of land prices, patterns of land-ownership and possibilities of land use in Bangkok. Where land-ownership is fragmented and land prices low, localities emerge through the activity and social creativity of those residing there. These localities tend to extend on the ground. Where land prices are high and land-ownership concentrated, localities are produced by real estate developers. These localities tend to extend into the sky. A special case is land owned by public agencies and temples. Public agencies own huge plots of land, often in areas where the land prices are high, but do not have to use it and partly cannot use it in the most profitable way. The land has to be used for the construction of buildings serving the needs of the agency, to satisfy demands for decent housing by their employees, and as many slum areas are located on public land, the agencies have to devise land-sharing schemes for political reasons. Thus usage of land owned by public agencies does not unequivocally follow the real estate market. Nevertheless, public agencies are involved in the real estate market through leasing out land to real estate developers to produce localities in form of shopping centres, office towers and condominiums, which provides an additional source of income for the agency and decision makers within the agency.

Similar to the commercial areas, where centrality is based on the resources of the big business in producing centrality through the establishment of large shopping centres and department stores, in relation to the real estate market there are the localities created by the people and those produced by the real estate developers. The market economy, including the real estate market, integrates localities and the city through common prices and interdependencies. It allows as well that those who have the resources can produce what they need in terms of localities and in terms of centrality. The market emerges as the main mechanism for the structuration of Bangkok. Thereby, the meaning of the city and of the different parts of the city is dissolved into the rationality of profitability.

The only force limiting the market is the administration as large landowner, rather than as institution for the control and planning of urban development, and the people in demanding that the administration to provide housing or lease agreements for them. In addition, there still remain certain "sacred" symbols in Bangkok which cannot be ignored even by the real estate developers and which play a role particularly for the public landowners. It is impossible to demolish the temple in favour of an apartment house, or to set up a high-rise building overlooking a ministry or the Royal Palace. These limitations of the real estate market based on symbols find, however, a connection to the market. The temples own land, and are themselves influential in the real estate market. A developer of a high-rise overlooking the palace or the ministry first has to purchase the land, which belongs to the public agencies or the Bureau of the Crown Property. Due to this, the old centre of Bangkok where the buildings and squares arranged following a ritual order of the city are located, is somehow excluded from the market. The commercial centres and the produced localities are at different locations.

Bangkok is not developing from a city core, or city centre, but from several different cores and centres serving different functions. The socio-cultural and political centre of Bangkok still is the royal palace, squares used for state ceremonies (and demonstrations) and the important temples, located in the old city in the district of Phranakorn. These are however increasingly overshadowed by the thirty- and forty-storey high-rise office buildings at Phya Thai, Phathumwan, Phrakhanong and Bang Rak. While the centrality of the palaces, the temples and the ceremonial grounds was based on an intrinsic sacredness of the locality, and their constellation was based on cosmological principles, the centrality of the modern buildings, the temples in which the economy is celebrated, is based on the sacrality of the modern economy: the profitability of a locality produced through real estate development.

Social Relations and Local Organizations

For Sassen (1994), one implication of globalization is the over- and de-valorization of forms of labour, groups of people and cultures. Thereby globalization is directly linked to eviction. This is nowhere more clearly expressed than in the primate cities, the discourses about how to beautify and modernize them and urban reconstruction in form of Kampung demolition, slum eviction etc. "The state and Jakarta municipal administration have a clear interest in 'modernizing' the city. For the central state and the local government modernizing the city is commonly understood as programmes and projects to transform the 'traditional features of Jakarta' into 'modern' urban structures and infrastructures" (Somantri 1995:173). Similarly, Berner argues "Imelda Marcos' ideas about a more beautiful and modern Manila did not include widespread slums. ... In a beautification campaign of the Potemkin type, shanty towns were hidden from the eyes of foreigners and wealthy Filipinos behind white fences, large billboards or concrete wall. ... As the 1974 Miss Universe Pageant was approaching ten thousands of people lost their homes when areas along the parade route were bulldozed" (Berner 1995:46f.). But it is not only the state or local administration for whom the "blighted areas" are defined as eyesores of under-development. With the rapid extension of business centres land becomes an even scarcer and thus more valuable commodity which should be used for highly valorized labour and attempts to evict the inhabitants a common feature in Southeast Asian cities. Thus one line of conflict commonly found is resistance to these projects.

The actors in these conflicts identified by Somantri (1995) for Jakarta, namely the state, the municipal government, state-owned enterprises, private national and transnational companies, NGOs and the people on the land, are the same in Manila and Bangkok. However, responses by the people, possibilities for organizing resistance and success of the movements differ quite strongly between these cities. In this regard, the analysis of conflicts related to eviction provides an insight into one important aspect of urban change and the specifics of the primate cities in Southeast Asia. Before engaging in conflicts, certain resources for acting have to be developed. For the people in slum and *Kampung* areas, the only possibility is, following Elias, in creating a high degree of social cohesion. This in turn depends on the ability to and the possibilities for establishing local organizations based on the social relations existing in the localities..

The Social Organization of Slums and Kampung

In the discussion of slum and squatter areas or Kampung it is not clarified what is understood by it. The term *Kampung* bears at least an association to "villages" and communities; however, it cannot really be defined as a corporate community because social ties exist mainly between neighbours. The community aspect is pointed out by Sullivan, "*Kampung* community is about neighbourship and there are strong pressures on *Kampung* people to be good neighbours. Good neighbourship or 'neighbourliness' is quite precisely defined in the *Kampung* and powerful sanctions function to make community members behave in conformity with the conventions" (Sullivan 1992:71) or, "amidst its more frequently stated objectives the *Kampung* acknowledges a paramount goal: communal harmony, a situation in which people live together peacefully and compatibly, commonly designated by the word *rukun*" (Sullivan 1992:106,

Murray 1991), in contrast, has doubts about describing a *Kampung* as a community. "The *Kampung* is not an entity capable of devising a 'strategy' but a community of individuals adapting to their urban situation and the arrival of more and more people with a balance of co-operation and competition" (Murray 1991:61).

The more detailed analysis shows that communality, as far as it exists, is limited to small clusters of neighbours who co-operate with each other. "The whole *Kampung* was too large for any formal organization or sense of unity. The inhabitants identified less with the *Kampung* than with clusters of houses along the several paths" (Jellinek 1991:26). "In the *Kampung* ties of residential proximity seemed to be of greater importance than ties of kin" (Jellinek 1991:35). In her analysis of networks of reciprocity in a *Kampung* in Yogyakarta, Bremm found out that these networks are clearly localized among those whose doors face onto the same walkway, and thus have regular face-to-face contacts (Bremm 1988:52).

In constrast to Indonesian *Kampung*, slum areas are usually not administrative units in Bangkok. Only during the seventies, in connection with slum upgrading projects, were so-called development committees set up in the slums to act as linkage between the administration and the population within the slum. The pattern were similar to those used in rural community development projects. While formerly no specific Thai term was in use to describe these areas, in the context of upgrading projects slums became defined as "*Chumchon ae ad*", or blighted communities.

Certainly, slums in Bangkok bear features of communality, partly based on existing social networks among neighbours, friends and informal sector activities. The term community, however, implies a degree of segregation from the surroundings. For smaller pockets of blighted areas within high income residential or commercial spaces this might be the case; it cannot be taken for granted though but has to be shown empirically. For larger slum areas of several thousand inhabitants we do regard it as impossible that the whole area is one community.

Instead of starting with the view of a slum area as an integrated community, it is more sensible to look at the social relations that exist. Here we find several interesting differences between Jakarta, Manila and Bangkok.

From a study of Manila slum areas (Berner and Korff 1995) we conclude that one pre-condition for the existence of denser social networks is time. Thus in older established squatter and slum areas social relations tend to be more dense and local associations do exist. The development of social relations within a slum and the integration of migrants into an area follows a pattern in which initially close social relations emerge linked to spatial proximity, and are partly replaced in the course of time by relations covering a larger space.

For the choice of location of rural migrants or internal migrants in Manila kinship plays an important role, because knowledge of where to go is derived primarily through information from relatives, who provide initial access to land, assistance in constructing the house and help to find a job. "In short: during the first years, kinship is the only support and security network available" (Berner and Korff 1995). In settling down, relations to neighbours are established. Partly because this cannot be avoided due to congestion, partly due to the need for mutual help and co-operation. "It is proximity - physical, territorial, and social - that structures neighbourhood ties and establishes bonds of common interest among the people" (Jocano 1975:169). In his study of a Yogyakarta *Kampung* Sullivan shows the co-operation existing among neighbours, who borrow and lend household necessities among each other and help in the case of ceremonies or festivities. Thus Somantri's finding that intra-city migrants in Jakarta first of all develop ties with their neighbours through regular visits and mutual help is not astonishing. For Somantri, as well as Sullivan, this focus on neighbour-relations is based on traditional Javanese values. "According to Javanese values, the opinions and feelings of one's neighbours must be considered. When they conduct *slametan* or *kenduri* they have to invite the nearest neighbours first. When a neighbour is ill, he should be visited. When neighbours suffer a calamity a good Javanese should make a visit of condolence" (Somantri 1995:159).

Following the studies of Jellinek and Murray for Jakarta and Berner (1995) on Manila, neighbourhood is predominantly a female domain. For the men friendship relations beyond and outside neighbourhood and kinship play an important role. It is mainly through friendship relations that access to employment and help for larger activities like building a house etc. is provided. Although friendship has an instrumental aspect, it goes beyond this. Friendship ties have to be maintained and demonstrated through joint activities like eating together, having fun together and especially in Manila and Bangkok, drinking together, in short being seen together.

While kinship, neighbourhood and friendship are relations of social reciprocity, in the *Kampung* and slums, economic relations form a network of interdependencies. In all *Kampung* and Slum areas numerous small scale traders and peddlers can be found. Many inhabitants buy at least parts of their daily necessities at the shops and stalls within the living area. These shops and stalls are important for the supply of the residents of the *Kampung* and slums, and in turn, the inhabitants are important as customers.

While these networks and manifold relations among people indicate a degree of social cohesion, this does not by any means imply communality. *Kampung* and slum areas are not at all homogenous but socially differentiated and stratified.

One obvious differentiation in Indonesian *Kampung* is among those households living inside the *Kampung* and those living at the edge, alongside the street. But even the families within the *Kampung* are not all "equal". Here two different interpretations exist. Jellinek and Murray argue that "the better-off regarded themselves and were regarded by the rest of the neighbourhood as outsiders" (Murray 1991:41). These did not rely on their *Kampung* neighbours for services. This economic independence included a social independence. "They tended to associate more with people beyond the *Kampung* from their place of work, school or village of origin and were not inhibited by the cost of transport which limited their neighbours' mobility and access to the outside world" (Murray 1991:41f.). In contrast: "The *Kampung* as much as the (neighbourhood) cells are strongly structured in regard to status and status adequate behaviour and usage of the proper language. ... this hierarchy, this insistence on the meticulous recognition of differences in rank and status is itself an indispensable part of *Kampung* community structuring. This implies that the reality of inequality - the existence of a rather broad social mix - is just as essential to *Kampung* order as the *Kampung's* subtle ideologically shaped conception of equality (*podo podo*)" (Sullivan 1992:75).

The social differentiation in the *Kampung* of Jakarta is furthermore linked to formalized positions of political influence and power. Following Somantri, at least two sets of local leaders exist in Jakarta *Kampungs*: formal and informal. Among the formal leaders, the lurah is installed by the municipal administration as a government employee to supervise the area. Information and requests from the administration are channeled from the lurah to the elected heads of the neighbourhood cells and the community units. As informal leaders Somantri mentions the religious leaders and the old and influential residents who are usually rich (Somantri 1995:99). In this regard, we find an obvious hierarchical structure within the *Kampung* in which social stratification is linked to economic and political stratification.

For Manila's squatter areas Berner shows that a dividing line exists between the house owners[113] and the renters. The reason is that renters have entered the area only recently and usually regard their current residence as temporary, thus they integrate to a lesser degree into the social networks and are less integrated by the residents. Using *compradrazgo* relations as indicator for integration into social relations, Berner shows through a multivariate analysis that income and status as renter or landowner have an obvious importance; however, this does not explain everything. "Friendship, whether institutionalized (in *compradrazgo* relations,

---

[113]Even in squatter areas it is possible to find houseowners (although not owning the land) and renters.

H.D.E./R. K.) or not, is a fluid, highly individualistic concept and depends on personal traits more than on anything else. Even if it becomes a strategic instrument of alliance building it does not mean that it is consciously used that way. On the contrary: No one would talk openly about any favours or advantages he seeks for when entering *compradrazgo"* (Berner 1995:129).

Through the existing social relations in the form of friendship and *compradrazgo* ties organizations developed which can achieve three major ends. Firstly, they define a specific territory as their locality. Secondly, with the definition of a territory, a collectivity of all those residing on the territory is defined as belonging to the place. Thirdly, interests of this so-defined collectivity are articulated and the improvement of communal infrastructure is demanded.

In the analysis of a slum area in Bangkok in the early seventies, Akin points out that social networks beyond the household consisted primarily of patron-client relations, which imply stratification and hierarchy. The patrons were able to establish themselves through the control of resources needed by others. One of the leaders was a tile layer working as a foreman and providing employment for his clients. The other was a catfish trader who distributed catfish to peddlers. Both acted as well as moneylenders. Due to their position as patrons at least for some of the people, they were able to enforce social control in the area (Akin 1975:247). As Akin makes clear, the slum in total was not strongly integrated, but rather different groups, clients around some patrons, formed the basic networks.[114] In Klong Thoey a similar pattern existed until the mid-seventies. The informal slum leaders were people able to provide jobs, credit or other support to a clientele from whom allegiance was demanded. When in the context of slum-upgrading projects community leaders were selected to act as intermediaries between the administration and the people, these were the obvious choices.

From a study of Klong Thoey slum during the early eighties, a different picture can be drawn. While friendship certainly has an instrumental aspect, which implies firstly that especially the better off, as those able to provide support to others have many social relations and can apply these in order to a position of communal leadership, among the younger people equality and "communication" was much more pronounced. It is important in friendship relations to be seen together; in this way persons are identified with a group. Reciprocity is generalized among those in group and not within dyadic relations. Thus the

---

[114]Akin mentions the case of what happened after fire blankets were distributed by the leaders. A conflict arose, because one of these did not favour his clients but distributed the materials according to need.

instrumental aspect is secondary and rather indirect. "Persons defining each other as friends help each other because they are friends and not because this relation would demand it. In this way it makes sense that friends are important to find a job, to get help etc., but that friendship would never be defined by these aspects" (Evers and Korff 1986). This had implications for leadership within the slum. An initial change in the organization of communal leadership took place during the seventies, partly connected to slum upgrading projects, partly connected to political changes like the student movement in Thailand, and what We regard as most crucial, to the fact that some younger people had received a better education and started to engage in forms of social work within the slum. Through the initiative of some a school was set up and a youth club established to fight against drug abuse among the young.[115] Through these activities, groups emerged and became influential within the area. Later some of these formalized and transformed into NGOs. Although some members of these groups could be defined as "leaders", firstly, their position was not too far removed from those of the others, secondly, leadership was linked to achievement in the sense that these were the most active persons and thirdly, it was not connected to social differentiation.

Another important factor in Bangkok was that the persons were involved simultaneously in several different groups through multiple friendship relations. This had two main effects: Information from very diverse sources could spread rapidly within and in between different groups and the leaders were scrutinized and controlled. The slum committee emerging after later elections soon represented the different groups within the slum area and could develop into something like a "core" of the locality able to organize communal interests quite successfully and to act as "the voice" of the people of the slum vis-à-vis the administration and the Bangkok public.

From the above descriptions, some conclusions can be drawn. In Jakarta *Kampung* we find dense and close social relations within the neighbourhoods. Relations beyond the neighbourhood are mainly hierarchical and formalized by the administration or link social and economic stratification with leadership. This organizational pattern resembles a pyramid in which vertical links are pronounced while horizontal ties remain limited to the direct vicinity, i. e. the family and the neighbourhood. This limits the possibilities for organized communal activities outside of the formalized channels. Although most studies of *Kampung* in Indonesia mention communal projects, it is not clear at all

---

[115]These resembled features that would now be defined as NGO. However, these "clubs" were not initiated from outside but from within. One of the leading persons later received the Magsaysay award.

whether these emerge out of social integration and co-operation or from administrative orders. Murray argues in this regard, "The *Kampung* has been idealized in terms of social harmony (*rukun*) and supposedly traditional mutual help. The ideology of *rukun* and the patron-client model of society is institutionalized in the urban administrative structure as a means of imposing order, and the meaning of *rukun* - social harmony as a state of being - is interpreted as a desirable attitude of fatalism... *Gotong royong* has been taken up as a national political symbol and is formally imposed on the *Kampung* to achieve development goals" (Murray 1991:64).

For Bangkok neighbourhood does play a role but the internal social structure used to be formed through hierarchical patron-client relations. In this pyramid the vertical links are even more strongly pronounced than in Jakarta. This pattern changed during the last decade with the rise in importance of groups organized along the lines of equality and based on friendship. Hereby a pattern is emerging in which overlapping horizontal ties are prominent. On the basis of such a pattern communal activities are easier to initiate and organize. Furthermore, the organization of such activities becomes a requirement for the legitimacy of local leadership. For Klong Thoey several examples can be provided. For several years activities against drug dealing and abuse have been organized like a regular patrol on the alleys chasing away of dealers in thinner. Other activities are connected to communal "upgrading" like the "clean Muban" campaign, etc.

In Manila the comparatively open and democratic political system does not exercise much control of local organizations or limit their rise. In addition the *compradrazgo* concept provides a cultural framework based on which such organizations can develop. This leads to the emergence of rather dense, overlapping networks within the squatter areas and allows the rapid flow of information and potentially the mobilization of the people.

The most important communal activity in slum and *Kampung* areas is certainly the organization of resistance in the face of demolition threats. Here large differences between the three cities exist.

Localization as Resistance to Eviction
Kampung Demolition in Jakarta

Eviction does not necessarily start with *Kampung* demolition. Murray points at a close relationship between sanctions against informal sector activities, on which the income of many inhabitants of *Kampung* are based, and which is one means for the integration of the *Kampung*, and *Kampung* demolition. One reaction to these sanctions in the inner-city areas of Jakarta was migration to other places, where other employment possibilities exist. Thus Mangrai, an inner-city

Kampung of Jakarta, has lost population since the early eighties (Murray 1991:93). Jellinek describes how the people were afraid when rumors of demolition spread around their *Kampung* in the early eighties. Although meetings were arranged by the government and planning agencies, the information was spread primarily through informal channels, which often led to misunderstandings. A form of organization beyond some neighbourhoods and unrelated clusters of individuals did not emerge. A broader organization developed only through the three prayer houses in the area, in which the district headmen chaired meetings of the people, who were chosen as representatives of the community vis-à-vis the government. During one mass meeting, one of these started to openly criticize the government's policy in regard to the*Kampung*, and he demanded a higher compensation so that the people would be able to find new housing elsewhere. After this incident, some of the better-educated dwellers of the *Kampung* initiated a press campaign, making the issue a "public" one, and openly started a critique of the headman of the whole district. In addition they petitioned the Ministry of Interior and contacted the legal rights organization, an NGO. After the plans were re-designed and assurances were given that all people, even the poorest, would be provided with a flat, the spokesmen disagreed among themselves whether to accept this plan or not. The result was that the fragile unity was destroyed (Jellinek 1991:138). Some people took the compensation offered or signed for resettlement in the flats. Little by little, the organization of the *Kampung* as a whole collapsed. "The *Kampung* dwellers seemed increasingly suspicious of one another, their headmen and the government" (Jellinek 1991:139). The remnants of unity disappeared, when the headmen started to link up with low level officials to gain a share of the compensation. "The official figures were simply crossed out in government documents and new figures written in. Households with strong headmen who had contacts in the right places, money and powers of persuasion managed to have their compensation altered. Jealousy and friction intensified as some households were promised three to four times more than others because of their headman's ability to manipulate the system" (Jellinek 1991:140). Finally the whole area was demolished and the remaining families either resettled or moved to flats.

In this case, three phases can be differentiated. Initially the people were simply scared and relied entirely on their close networks of neighbours. In the second phase, when through the meeting at the prayer houses a base beyond the neighbourhood had been established, leaders emerged and established themselves as spokesmen. Apart from being headmen of cells of the *Kampung*, they had no closer relation. During this phase, an organized core emerged which was able to follow strategic actions in using resources and possibilities like petitioning the Minister of the Interior, the legal aid organization, contacting the press etc. for their ends. The third phase started when unity within this core broke up. Instead of a group of spokesmen for a mass of people, several different groups under different spokesmen emerged, following their particular interests and later even working against each other. Interestingly, the close neighbourhood ties weakened in this process and, as Jellinek showed, kinship relations became important again, especially in the search for a new place to stay.

The case indicates several problems facing the setting up of organizations articulating interests of the people in the *Kampung*. The internal organization of the *Kampung* is connected to income-generating opportunities, especially in informal forms of employment; a disruption of these already leads to difficulties within the *Kampung* and a weakening of the internal interdependencies. Other interdependencies are based on the administration (the neighbourhood and *Kampung* leaders) which can hardly be used for organizations struggling with the administration. Only the prayer houses provide a base for meetings beyond the neighbourhood. However, the interdependencies are too weak for a continuous effort, although they make it possible to find outside support.[116]

After comparing five recent cases of *Kampung* demolition Somantri (1995) shows that in all cases the people were evicted and differences concerned the sum of compensation paid to them. Success in the sense of increased compensation was, according to Somantri, based on bringing the issue into the public and making it a national political issue. This was, however, not achieved by the affected squatters and *Kampung* dwellers but by outsiders such as student groups and NGOs. Although they certainly provide help for the people, "often we observe that political parties of the Indonesian 'opposition' groups and faction groups of high ranking government officials as well as military groups often expose the problem for their proposes" (Somantri 1995:195). Thus it seems that the urban poor do not organize themselves, but that they are organized by outsiders. The lack of independent organization of resistance of the *Kampung* dwellers themselves is due to two main facts. Firstly the strong and repressive Indonesian state limits and even prohibits the chances for local organization outside of formalized and administratively controlled channels. Secondly, the willingness to develop local organization and to engage in prolonged and intensive struggles with the administration is limited. "For *Kampung* dwellers, to get a fair amount of compensation money and move elsewhere is more attractive than to continue to suffer severe repression by security officers in the urban arenas to preserve their communities. In this sense the worldview of many Jakarta's rural-urban migrants is still influenced by rural Javanese cosmology

---

[116]An important issue is of course the form of government in Indonesia, which makes the formation of organizations with a larger scope outside of the administration difficult.

and a moral economy of peasant life, which leads to their individualistic and dispersed style of urban social protest" (Somantri 1995:221).

Legalizing Squatters: The case of Manila

In Manila local squatter organizations exist in most slums. One of the main efforts of these organizations is to struggle against eviction and to organize land-sharing schemes. One important finding is that trust of the officers of the organization by the people in the area and identification with the area is crucial for success. Accordingly, most residents regard themselves as members of the local organization and are regarded as members by these organizations. To reach such a degree of integration time is crucial. "In all five research areas, the primary local organization was formed on the initiative of these key persons and is led by some of them. The role of the local association as core of the community is confirmed by a quantitative analysis: The officers have lived in the locality for a longer time than others, command a higher family income, and have more intensive personal relations" (Berner 1995:212).

The power of local organizations has an impact on the land price. Although the price of land is defined through the market, this is in many cases rather fictious. If the inhabitants resist eviction, a price has to be paid for compensation, legal consultations and demolition squads, which reduces the price that can be realized for the land. Whether or not resistance takes place is, according to Berner, related to the strength to organize resistance and the social value of the land, i. e. in how far people regard their place of life important enough to join in the struggle. Land-sharing schemes are a compromise between the social and the market value of the land. If the landowner cannot make the profits based on the market, as resistance can be expected, and if for the people the social value is high enough to pay regular fees, for the landowner the compensation paid by the people might be high enough. "The 'actual value' of squatter land is, thus, a double compromise: Firstly, the residents have to come to terms among themselves about what they are willing to pay for their land, and they can do so only if there is a functioning organization. Secondly, the association has to negotiate the actual selling price with the landowner who, of course, has the market values as his point of reference. An agreement can only be reached if both prices are not too far away from each other" (Berner 1995:217). Thus eviction from prime urban land can hardly be avoided, whereas in other locations compromises can be reached.

The associations Berner describes usually lack information about legal possibilities. Here external NGOs play an important role in publicizing issues and in informing about legal means. Although the NGOs can use the local urban poor organizations for their own purposes, Berner points out important differences to Indonesian NGOs. NGO activities in Indonesia are rather limited, focused on activities "complementary" to government programmes and lack an independent ideological system of concepts and values. Kastorius argues that Indonesian NGOs aim mainly at the lower ranks of the state bureaucracy and run the danger of becoming a sub-department of the bureaucracy. In the Philippines the NGOs are independent of the state and can define themselves as "movements". Their main political power derives from their occupation of the concept of development. Thus they describe themselves as the voice of the people and as those advocating development for the people. The occupation of development and the movement characteristic demand legitimacy from the "urban poor". In this respect the possibilities to instrumentalize the "poor" for their own ends are limited.

Slum upgrading in Bangkok

Slum demolition is an old issue in Bangkok. In contrast to Jakarta, where a high percentage of the inhabitants of the *Kampung* still own land or houses, Bangkok slumdwellers, similarly to their Manila counterparts, either occupy public land or pay a minimal rent to private landowners. The slums located in the inner city area, most of them located on private land, were demolished already during the sixties and seventies. In the early eighties, with economic development and internationalization of the economy of Bangkok, the demand for land increased. New apartment houses, offices and shopping centres were built and as one result, slum areas demolished.

Taking Klong Thoey as an example, a polarization between high-rise and slum is evident. Currently Klong Thoey is either space for the extension of the business centre or developing as a sub-centre. In 1990, 20 % of all new constructions in Bangkok were located in Klong Thoey. Of these fewer than 40 % were used for housing and the rest for commerce and office high-rise buildings. An indicator of the international scope of these projects is their size. Of a total of 105 buildings under construction, 87 have 6 or more storeys and 23 more than 30 (Bangkok Municipality, Statistical Report 1990:152ff.). But Klong Thoey is also the district with the highest number of slumdwellers in Bangkok. Thus a conflict between slumdwellers and land developers is unavoidable.

Eviction is not a new issue in Klong Thoey. The largest slum area is located on land of the Port Authority, and any extension of the harbour implies eviction of squatters. In the mid eighties, one large area was earmarked for extension of the container terminal. The existing groups, including the Klong Thoey NGO, started to organize resistance against the eviction plans. This implied the spreading of information within the slum and the publication of the issue among the Bangkok public. Through the existing groups and their linkages information spread rapidly. In addition public hearings were arranged and, using the amplifiers of the "Music-Club", broadcast over the whole slum area. Although outside groups got involved in the conflict, the issue was not instrumentalized but still under the control of the local groups. Finally an arrangement was found and the people resettled to an adjacent plot with the option of legal tenure for 25 years.

The efficiency of the existing organizations was demonstrated in 1992, when one part of the larger slum was burnt down. Although this area was earmarked for eviction during the next years[117], those affected by the fire were given compensation and material to rebuild their houses. During the night of the fire, a new NGO was established, which asked for support from other NGOs, the Bangkok Municipality and the National Housing Authority. When in the morning a general agreement had been reached, but the material was delayed, they themselves ordered building material and organized its distribution, quite a large task, as 250 houses had been burnt down.[118] In this case, those affected were not members of the organizations; however, the leaders of these took up the issue and provide support for them. Clearly, the scope of activities is beyond the level of close neighbour, but is concerned with the area, the locality, in total.

Conclusions

Globalization is certainly not the only factor behind eviction and slum demolition projects. However, globalization and modernization increase the pressure on urban land, which in turn leads to eviction and demolition. The *Kampung* is replaced by the office high-rise and shopping centre with McDonald's and/or Pizza Hut outlets. The state is always involved in these conflicts either directly as "evictor" or indirectly through the police, military, legal system etc. Further actors are NGOs, other groups and organizations like political parties, which integrate the eviction issue into their own respective programmemes. Finally there are the people who usually lack resources. Their only chance is to develop local associations and organizations through which information is spread internationally, resistance organized and the local interests articulated vis-à-vis all the other actors (including the NGOs). Thus globalization, national integration as associated with the state and with NGOs trying to gain political influence, and localization in the form of local organizations, are directly linked in the eviction issue. Taking this as starting point the diverse processes, groups and interdependencies through which the metropolises are structured can be looked at in a comparative way.

---

[117]For the inhabitants, new plots had been reserved already and compensation was fixed. The fire was not started to facilitate eviction.

[118]These groups and organizations form a core. That the whole slum is not fully integrated is indicated for example by the selling of the rent contracts after eviction had taken place. From those who were resettled at least 20 to 30 % had sold their contract during the following years.

While the impact of globalization is quite similar in the three cities under discussion, the role of the state and the cultural values which facilitate or hinder the emergence of local organizations differ. In Indonesia it is complicated to disentangle Javanese traditional values and state ideologies. Values such as integration into intimate relations in which consensus and harmony are supreme, neighbourhood and *Kampung* co-operation etc. do certainly have a background in Javaneseness, but are used as state ideologies as well. Thus it is complicated to analyze why organizations beyond the neighbourhood tend to be absent. This may be due, as Somantri argues, to traditional worldviews and cosmologies, but also to state repression and control by which the rise of organizations, be it *Kampung* associations or NGOs outside and parallel to administrative channels, is prohibited.

In Thailand and the Philippines the state and the administration is much less concerned with control down to the neighbourhood level. According to the findings of studies of Thai culture and personality, individualism is regarded as an important cultural value. Due to individualism, social relation and alliances tend to be fluid and shifting, with patron-client relations as the exception. Individualism and dyadic patron-client relations hinder the development of local organizations. In this regard the case of Klong Thoey indicates important changes in the urban context. Obviously the people in Klong Thoey, especially the youth during the seventies and eighties, created new forms of social organization and social relations on the basis of which local organizations later could develop. The state and the administration is not concerned with these organizations or tries to suppress them. It is interesting, and in this respect Klong Thoey is probably an exceptional case, that some people were able to establish their own NGOs and thereby reduce their dependency on external supporters. The people in Klong Thoey are able to express their interests by themselves.

In the Philippines the political system and even the administration depend on regular elections. As squatter areas are spread all over the city, hardly any district exists without a population of squatters. These often outnumber the rest of the electorate, so that a politician following an "anti-urban-poor" strategy will hardly gain a majority. This certainly does not prevent demolition, but leads to a form of populism in which especially the NGO can gain some success. As Berner shows, the NGOs are however bound to the urban poor and thus use political channels for the changing of laws in regard to access to urban land for the poorer population.

The political system is an important variable not only for the success or failure of local organizations, but indeed for the possibilities of the creation of such associations at all. Globalization has a double impact in this context. Through a diversification of the élites liberalization and democratization is increasing, thereby providing more opportunities for the rise of local movements. These, in turn, are able to articulate demands and requests. In consequence, conflicts become public and necessitate bargaining processes between the parties involved, thereby pushing towards more liberalization and less state control. The people in the Kampung and slums can play a political role and actively have an influence on the development of the city. In Bangkok and Manila, we can already discern developments in this direction while in Jakarta the Kampung dwellers are still mainly objects instrumentalized by different groups.

References

Abdullah, T., 1966: Adat and Islam: An Examination of Conflict in Manangkabau, in: *Indonesia*, Vol. 2, pp. 1-24

Abdullah, T., 1971: *Schools and Politics: The Kaum Muda Movement in West Sumatra (1927-1933)*. Ithaca, N. Y.: Cornell University Press

Abraham, C.E.R., 1997: *Divide and Rule. The Roots of Race Relations in Malaysia*, Kuala Lumpur: Insan

Abu-Lughod, Janet 1961: Migrant Adjustment to City Life: The Egyptian Case, in: *American Journal of Sociology*, Vol. 67, pp. 22-32

Akin Rabibhadana, 1975: *Bangkok Slum: Aspects of Social Organization*, Ph.D. Thesis, Cornell University Press

Akin Rabibhadana, 1978: Rise and Fall of a Bangkok Slum, in: *Social Science Review*, Bangkok

Ali, S. H., 1983: *Poverty and Landlessness in Kelantan, Malaysia. Bielefeld Studies in the Sociology of Development Vol. 19*, Saarbrücken and Fort Lauderdale: Breitenbach

Ames, M. M., 1964: Magical Animism and Buddhism, in: *Journal of Asian Studies*, Vol. 23, pp. 21-52

Amran, R., 1986: *Padang, Riwayatmu Dulu*. Jakarta: Mutiara Sumber Widya

Anderson, B., 1983: *Imagined Communities: Reflections on the Origin and Spread of Nationalism*. London: Verso

Anderson, B.R.O.'G., 1990: *Language and Power*. Ithaca, N. Y.: Cornell University Press

Arbeitsgruppe Bielefelder Entwicklungssoziologen, 1978: *Forschungsprojekt Land: Städtische Landbesitzstrukturen und Stadtentwicklung*. Abschliessender Sachbericht, Universität Bielefeld

Arbeitsgruppe Bielefelder Entwicklungssoziologen, 1979: *Subsistenzproduktion und Akkumulation. Bielefeld Studies on Development Sociology Vol. 5*, Saarbrücken and Fort Lauderdale: Breitenbach

Arbeitsgruppe Bielefelder Entwicklungssoziologen, 1981: *Forschungskonzeption: Unterentwicklung und Subsistenzproduktion. Working Paper No. 1*, Sociology of Development Research Centre, University of Bielefeld

244

Armstrong, W. and T. G. McGee, 1980: A Theory of Urban Involution, in: H. -
D. Evers (ed.), *Sociology of Southeast Asia: Readings on Social Change and
Development*. Kuala Lumpur: Oxford University Press, pp. 200-208

Armstrong, W. and T. G. McGee, 1985: *Theatres of Accumulation: Studies in
Asian and Latin American Urbanization*. London and New York: Methuen

Augel, J. (ed.), 1985: *Leben in Armut: Überlebensstrategien in brasilianischen
Elendsvierteln*. Mettingen: Brasilienkunde-Verlag

Aung-Thwin, M., 1987: Heaven, Earth and the Supernatural World: Dimensions
of the Exemplary Centre in Burmese History, in: B. Smith and H. B.
Reynolds (eds.), *The City as a Sacred Centre: Essays on Six Asian Contexts*.
Leiden and New York: E. J. Brill

Bachtiar, H. W., 1967: Negeri Taram: A Minangkabau Village, in:
Koentjaraningrat (ed.), *Villages in Indonesia*. Ithaca, N.Y.: Cornell University
Press, pp. 348-385

Bador, A. K., 1973: Social Rank, Status-Honour and Social Class Consciousness
amongst the Malays, in: H. - D (ed.), *Modernization in Southeast Asia*. Kuala
Lumpur: Oxford University Press, pp. 132-49

Bahrdt, H. P., 1971: *Die moderne Großstadt: Soziologische Überlegungen zum
Städtebau*. Hamburg: Wegener Verlag

Bairoch, P., 1988: *Cities and Economic Development: From the Dawn of
History to the Present*. Chicago: University of Chicago Press

Bangkok Municipality, 1990: *Statistical Report*, Bangkok

Barnes, T. and J. S. Duncan, 1991: *Writing Worlds: Discourse, Text and
Metaphor in the Representations of Landscape*. London: Routledge

Barras, R., Broadent, A. and D. Massey, 1973: Planning and the Public
Ownership of Land, in: *New Society* 21, pp. 676-679

Benjamin, G., 1976: The Cultural Logic of Singapore's Multiculturalism, in: R.
Hassan (ed.), Singapore: *Society in Transition*. Kuala Lumpur: Oxford
University Press

Bennholdt-Thomsen, V., 1982: *Bauern in Mexiko: Zwischen Subsistenz- und
Warenproduktion*. Frankfurt a. M.: Campus-Verlag

Berekoven, L., 1983: *Der Dienstleistungsmarkt in der Bundesrepublik
Deutschland: Theoretische Fundierung und empirische Analyse*, Göttingen:
Vandenhoeck & Ruprecht

Berger, J. and L. Weber-Voigt, 1982: *Informeller Sektor und alternative
Ökonomie. Forschungsschwerpunkt Zukunft der Arbeit*, University of
Bielefeld

Berger, J., 1985: *Alternativen zur Lohnarbeit? Selbstverwaltete Betriebe zwischen Anspruch und Realität.* Bielefeld: AJZ-Verlag

Berger, P., Berger, B. and H. Kellner, 1974: *The Homeless Mind.* Harmondsworth: Penguin Books

Berger, P. L and M. Novak, 1985: *Speaking to the Third World : Essays on Democracy and Development.* Washington: American Enterprise Institute for Public Policy Research

Berger, P. L. and T. Luckmann, 1966: *The Social Construction of Reality: A Treatise in the Sociology of Knowledge.* Garden City, N. Y.: Doubleday

Bergmann, N. J. et al., 1969: *Herrschaft, Klassenverhältnis und Schichtung, in: Adorno, Th. W. (ed.), Spätkapitalismus oder Industriegesellschaft: Verhandlungen des 16. Deutschen Soziologentages.* Stuttgart: F. Enke-Verlag

Berner, E., 1995: *A Place to Live in the City of Man: Localities and the Struggle for Urban Land in Metro Manila.* Ph.D. Dissertation, Faculty of Sociology, University of Bielefeld. Revisited as: Defending a Place in the City: Localities and the Struggle for Urban Land in Metro Manila. Manila: Ateno de Manila University Press, 1998

Berner, E. and R. Korff, 1995: Globalization and Local Resistance, in: *International Journal of Urban and Regional Research*, Vol. 18, No. 2, pp. 208-222

Berry, B.J.L. and H. Spodek, 1971: Comparative Ecologies of Large Indian Cities, in: *Economic Geography*, Vol. 47, No. 2, pp. 266-285

Betke, F., 1988: *Prospects of a Blue Revolution in Indonesian Fisheries: A Bureaucratic Dream or Grim Reality.* Unpublished doctoral thesis, University of Bielefeld

Betke, F., Weitekamper, J. and M. Grunewald, 1978: *Partner, Pläne und Projekte: Die personelle Hilfe der Bundesrepublik Deutschland in West Malaysia. Bielefeld Studies in the Sociology of Development Vol. 1.* Saarbrücken and Fort Lauderdale: Breitenbach

Biers, D. (ed.), 1998: *Crash of 97.* Hongkong: Far Eastern Economic Review

Boeke, J. H., 1980: Dualism in Colonial Societies, in H. - D. Evers (ed.), *Sociology of Southeast Asia: Readings on Social Change and Development.* Kuala Lumpur: Oxford University Press, pp. 26-37

Boerhan, B. and M. Salim (eds.), 1972: *Tanah ulayat dalam pembangunan: Padang: Penerbitan Fakultas Hukum dan Pengetahuan Masyarakat,* Universitas Andalas

Bohannan, P. (ed.), 1964: *Researches into the Early History of Mankind and the Development of Civilization*. Chicago: University of Chicago Press

Boonsanong Punyodyana, 1971: Chinese-Thai Differential Assimilation in Bangkok: An Exploratory Study. Data Paper No. 79, Southeast Asia Programme, Cornell University, Ithaca, N. Y.

Bourdieu, P., 1974: *Zur Soziologie der symbolischen Formen*. Frankfurt a. M.: Suhrkamp

Braudel, F., 1985: *Sozialgeschichte des 15. bis 18. Jahrhunderts: Der Alltag*. München: Kindler

Braudel, F., 1986a: *Sozialgeschichte des 15. - 18. Jahrhunderts: Der Handel*. Stuttgart: Kindler

Braudel, F., 1986b: *Sozialgeschichte des 15. - 18. Jahrhunderts: Aufbruch zur Weltwirtschaft*. Stuttgart: Kindler

Braudel, F., 1986c: *Die Dynamik des Kapitalismus*. Stuttgart: Klett-Cotta

Breese, G. (ed.), 1969: *The City in Newly Developing Countries: Readings on Urbanism and Urbanization*. Englewood Cliffs, N. J.: Prentice-Hall

Bremm, H., 1988: Nachbarschaftsbeziehungen in einem javanischen Kampung, in: T. Schweitzer, (ed.), *Netzwerkanalyse: Ethnologische Perspektiven*. Berlin: Reimer, pp. 47-62

Bruner, E. M., 1963: Medan: The Role of Kinship in an Indonesian City, in: S. Alexander (ed.), *Pacific Ports and Cities - A Symposium*. Honolulu: Bishop Museum Press, pp. 1-12

Castells, M., 1997a: *The Information Age: Economy, Society and Culture. Volume II: The Power of Identity*. Malden, Oxford: Blackwell

Castells, M., 1997b: *The Information Age: Economy, Society and Culture. Volume III: The End of the Millennium*. Malden, Oxford: Blackwell

Chakrabongse, C., 1960: *Lord of Life: The Paternal Monarchy of Bangkok 1782-1932*. London: Alvin Redman

Castells, M., 1979: *The Urban Question: A Marxist Approach*. London: Edward Arnold

Castells, M., 1983: *The City and the Grassroots: A Cross-cultural Theory of Urban Social Movements*. London: Edward Arnold

Castells, M., 1989: *The Informational City: Information Technology, Economic Restructuring and the Urban-Regional Process*. Oxford: Basil Blackwell

Castells, M. and P. Hall, 1994: *Technopoles of the World*, London: Routledge

Central Statistical Bureau's Statistik Pertanian, 1976: *Luas Tanah Sawah di DKI Jakarta dan Jawa Barat*, Jakarta

Chander, R., 1971: *Urban Conurbations-Population and Households in Ten Gazetted Towns and their Adjoining Build-Up Areas*. Kuala Lumpur: Jabatan Perangkaan Malaysia

Chander, R., 1970: *Socio-economic Sample Survey of Households 1967-68*. Kuala Lumpur: Deptartment of Statistics

Charnvit Kasetsiri, 1976: *The Rise of Ayudhya: A History of Siam in the 14th and 15th Centuries*. Bangkok: Duang Kamol

Chong, Y. L., 1976: *The Evolution of the Urban Pattern of Southeast Asia During the Nineteenth and Twentieth Centuries*, Ph.D. Thesis, School of Ortiental and African Studies, University of London

City Planning Office, 1989: *Bangkok Municipality*, Bangkok

Clammer, J., 1982/83: Symbolism and Legitimacy: "Urban Anthropology" and the Analysis of Singapore Society, in: Jurnal Antropologi dan Sosiologi, Vol. 10/11, pp. 3-14

Clarke, R. E., 1976: *Land and Neighbourhood as Features of Malaya Urbanism*. Vancouver, Ph.D. Thesis, University of British Columbia

Clauss, W., 1982: *Economic and Social Change among the Simalungun Batak of North Sumatra. Bielefeld Studies in the Sociology of Development Vol. 15*, Saarbrücken and Fort Lauderdale: Breitenbach

Clifford, H., 1897: *In Court and Kampong*. London

Clough, B., 1982 *Sinhalese-English Dictionary*, Colombo: Wesleyan Missions Press

Cobban, J. L., 1976: Geographic Notes on the First two Centuries of Djakarta, in: Y. M. Yeung and C. P. Lo (eds.), *Changing Southeast Asian Cities: Readings on Urbanization*. London: Oxford University Press, pp. 45-59

Cohen, E., 1976: Expatriate Communities, in: *Current Sociology*, Vol. 24, Pt. 3, pp. 1-133

Cohen, E., 1985: A Soi in Bangkok: The Dynamics of Lateral Urban Expansion, in: *Journal of the Siam Society*, Vol. 73, No. 1/2

Cohen, E., n.d.: *Social Ecology, A Multidimensional Approach*. Working Paper, Department of Sociology, University of Singapore (Forthcoming in Current Anthropology)

Colombijn, Freek, 1992: Dynamics and Dynamite: Minagkabau Urban Landownership in the 1990s, in: *Bijdragen tot de taal-, land- en volkenkunde* 148, pp. 428-464

Colombijn, Freek, 1994: Patches of Padang. The History of an Indonesian Town in the Twentieth Century and the Use of Urban Space. Leiden: CNWS Publications Vol. 19

Committee for the Rattanakosin Bicentennial Celebration, 1982: *History of Rattanakosin, Volume I-III*: Fine Arts Department, Bangkok (in Thai)

Cornelius, W. A., 1976: The Impact of Cityward Migration on Urban Land and Housing Markets, in: J. Walton and L. M. Masotti (eds.), *The City in Comparative Perspective*. New York: John Wiley, pp. 249-270

Damrong Vaivong, 1973: *Implementation of the Greater Bangkok Plan: A Critical Review*. Thesis, Institute of Social Studies, The Hague

Dewaraja, L. S., 1988: *The Kandyan Kingdom of Sri Lanka 1707-1782*, Colombo: Lake House Investments

Douglas, M., 1970: *Natural Symbols: Explorations in Cosmology*. New York: Pantheon Books

Douglas, M. and B. Isherwood, 1979: *The World of Goods. Towards an Anthropology of Consumption*. London: Allen Lane

Dumont, L., 1962: The Conception of Kingship in Ancient India, in: *Contributions to Indian Sociology* 4, pp. 48-77

Durand-Lasserve, A., 1980: *Speculation on Urban Land, Land Development and Housing Development in Bangkok: Historical Process and Social Function (1950-1980)*. Paper read at the 1st Thai-European Seminar on Social Change in contemporary Thailand, Amsterdam

Durand-Lasserve, A., 1982: *The Urban Land Issue and the Balance of Power between Public and Private Sectors: Some Characteristics of the Process of Land Appropriation in Bangkok during the Last Three Decades*. Paper read at the International Seminar "Land for Housing the Urban Poor: Towards a Positive Action in Asian Cities" at the AIT, Bangkok

Dutch Scholars, 1958: *The Indonesian Town: Studies in Urban Sociology*, The Hague, Bandung: W. van Hoeve

Eames, E. and J. G. Goode, 1973: *Urban Poverty in a Cross-Cultural* Context. New York: Free Press

Eco, U., 1988: *Einführung in die Semiotik*. München: Fink

Eisenstadt, S. N., 1979: *Tradition, Wandel und Modernität*. Frankfurt a. M.: Suhrkamp

Eisenstadt, S. N. and S. Rokkan (eds.), 1973: *Building States and Nations*, Berkeley, CA: Russell Sage

Eliade, M., 1986: *Kosmos und Geschichte: Der Mythos der ewigen Wiederkehr*. Frankfurt a. M.: Suhrkamp

Elias, N. and L. Scotson, 1965: *The Established and the Outsiders: A Sociological Enquiry into Community Problems*. London: Cass

Elwert, G., Evers, H. - D. and W. Wilkens, 1983: Die Suche nach Sicherheit: Kombinierte Produktionsformen im sogenannten informellen Sektor, in: *Zeitschrift für Soziologie*, Vol. 12, No. 4, pp. 281-296

Elwert, G. and D. Wong, 1979: *Thesen Zum Verhältnis Von Subsistenzproduktion und Warenproduktion in der Dritten Welt, in: Arbeitsgruppe Bielefelder Entwicklungssoziologen, Subsistenzproduktion und Akkumulation. Bielefeld Studies on Development Sociology Vol. 5*, Saarbrücken and Fort Lauderdale: Breitenbach, pp. 255-278

Elwert, G. and D. Wong, 1980: Subsistence Production and Commodity Production in the Third World, in: *Review*, Vol. 3, No. 3

Elwert, G., 1985: Märkte, Käuflichkeit und Moralökonomie, in: B. Lutz (ed.), *Soziologie und gesellschaftliche Entwicklung*. Frankfurt a. M.: Campus-Verlag, pp. 509-519

Evers, H. - D., 1966: The Formation of a Social Class Structure: Urbanization, Bureaucratization and Social Mobility in Thailand, in: *American Sociological Review*, Vol. 31, No. 4, pp. 480-488

Evers, H. - D., 1967a: Kinship and Property Rights in a Buddhist Monastery in Central Ceylon, *American Anthropologist* 67,1,1967:97-99

Evers, H. - D., 1967b: Monastic Landlordism in Ceylon: a Traditional System in a Modern Setting, *Journal of Asian Studies*, Vol. 28,3 (1969), 685-692

Evers, H. - D. (ed.), 1969: *Case Studies in Social Power*. Leiden: Brill

Evers, H. - D., 1972a: *Urban Involution: The Social Structure of Southeast Asian Towns*. Working Paper No. 2, Department of Sociology, University Singapore

Evers, H. - D., 1972b: Data tentang penduduk Kota Madya Padang tahun 1970, laporan sementara hasil sampel sensus (Data on the Population of Padang, 1970, Preliminary Report on the Results of a Sample Census), *Sumatra Research Bulletin*, I, 2, pp. 10-20

Evers, H. - D., 1972c: *Monks, Priests and Peasants: A Study of Buddhism and Social Structure in Central Ceylon*. Leiden: E. J. Brill

Evers, H. - D., 1973a: Group Conflict and Class Formation in Southeast Asia, in: H. - D. Evers (ed.), *Modernization in Southeast Asia*, London: Oxford University Press, pp. 108-131

Evers, H. - D., 1973b: Migration Patterns in a Sumatran Town. *Sumatra Research Bulletin*, Vol. II, No. 1

Evers, H. - D. 1974: Traditional Land Tenure in an Indonesia City. In: *LTC Newsletter*, Land Tenure Centre, University of Wisconsin, pp. 14-19

Evers, H. - D. 1975a: Changing Patterns of Minangkabau Land-ownership, in: Bijdragen tot de Taal, *Land- en Volkenkunde*, Vol. 131, No. 1, pp. 86-110

Evers, H. - D. 1975b: Urbanization and Urban Conflict in Southeast'Asia, in: *Asian Survey*, Vol. XV, No. 9, pp. 775-785

Evers, H. - D., 1976: Urban Expansion and Land-ownership in Underdeveloped Societies, in: J. Walton and L. H. Masotti (eds.), *The City in Comparative Perspective: Cross National Research and New Directions in Theory*. New York: Sage, pp. 67-80

Evers, H. - D., 1977: The Culture of Malaysian Urbanization: Malay and Chinese Conceptions of Space, in: *Urban Anthropology*, Vol. 6, No. 3, pp. 205-216

Evers, H. - D., 1978: Chettiar Moneylenders in Southeast Asia, in: *Asie du Sud, Traditions et changements, Colloques Internationaux du Centre National de la Recherche Scientifique*, No. 582, Paris, pp. 635-645

Evers, H. - D., 1980a: Group Conflict and Class Formation in Southeast Asia, in: H. - D. Evers (ed.), *Sociology of Southeast Asia: Readings on Social Change and Development*. Kuala Lumpur: Oxford University Press, pp. 247-261

Evers, H. - D., 1980b: Subsistence Production and the Jakarta "floating mass", in: *Prisma*, Vol. 17, pp. 27-35

Evers, H. - D., 1981a: The Contribution of Urban Subsistence Production to Incomes in Jakarta, in: *Bulletin of Indonesian Economic Studies*, Vol. XVII, No. 2, Canberra, Australian National University, pp. 89-96

Evers, H. - D., 1981b: Zur Theorie der urbanen Unterentwicklung, in: *Die Dritte Welt*, 9. Jahrgang, Nr. 1/2, pp. 61-68

Evers, H. - D., 1982: *Sosiologi Perkotaan. Urbanisasi dan Sengketa Tanah Indonesia dan Malaysia (Urban sociology: Urbanization and Land Disputes in Indonesia and Malaysia)*. Jakarta: LP3ES

Evers, H. - D., 1983a: *Bürokratisierung und Weltmarkt in Südostasien*. Working Paper No. 34, Sociology of Development Research Centre, University of Bielefeld

Evers, H. – D., 1983b: The Evolution of Urban Society in Malaysia, in: K.S. Sandhu and P. Wheatley (eds.), Melaka. The Transformation of a Malay Capital c. 1400-1980. Kuala Lumpur: Oxford University Press, pp. 324-350

Evers, H. – D., 1984a: Urban Landownership, Ethnicity and Class in Southeast Asian Cities, in: *International Journal of Urban and Regional Research* 8,4, pp. 481-496

Evers, H. – D., 1984b: Cities as a "Field of Anthropological Studies" in Southeast Asia, in: P. E. de Josselin de Jong (ed.): *Unity in Diversity - Indonesia as a Field of Anthropological Study*, Dordrecht-Holland/Cinnaminson-USA: Foris Publikcations, pp. 143-151

Evers, H. - D., 1989: Trends in Urban Poverty and Labour Supply Strategies in Jakarta, in: Gerry Rodgers (ed.), *Urban Poverty and the Labour Market,* Geneva: International Labour Office, pp. 145-172

Evers, H. - D., 1991: Religiöser Revivalismus und Modernität, in: W. Glatzer (ed.), *Die Modernisierung moderner Gesellschaften.* Opladen: Westdeutscher Verlag, pp. 97-100

Evers, H. - D., 1997, The Symbolic Universe of the UKM: A Semiotic Analysis of the National University of Malaysia, in: *SOJOURN, Journal of Social Issues in Southeast Asia* 12,1 pp. 46-63

Evers, H. - D. and S. Gerke, 1997: Global Market Cultures and the Construction of Modernity in Southeast Asia, *Thesis Eleven* 50, pp. 1-14

Evers, H. - D., Betke, F. and S. Pitomo, 1983: *Die Komplexität der Grundbedürfnisse: Eine Untersuchung über städtische Haushalte der untersten Einkommensschichten in Jakarta.* Working Paper No. 43, Sociology of Development Research Centre, University of Bielefeld

Evers, H. - D., Clauss, W. and D. Wong, 1984: Subsistence Production - a Framework for Analysis, in: J. Smith, I. Wallerstein and H. - D. Evers (eds.), *Households and the World Economy.* Beverly Hills: Sage Publications, pp. 23-36

Evers, H. - D. and S. Gerke, 1991: *A Dayak Lady Goes to Town: Cultural Dynamics in an Indonesian Province.* Working Paper No. 154, Sociology of Development Research Centre, University of Bielefeld

Evers, H. - D. and Goh Ban Lee, 1976: *Urban Land-ownership in Kota Bharu and Jeli, Kelantan.* Project Paper No. 5, Centre for Policy Research, Universiti Sains Malaysia, Penang

Evers, H. - D. and R. Korff, 1986: Urban Subsistence Production in Bangkok, in: *Development*, Vol. 4, pp. 50-56

252

Evers, H. - D. and T. Schiel, 1979: Expropiation der unmittelbaren Produzenten oder Ausdehnung der Subsistenzwirtschaft: Thesen zur bäuerlichen und städtischen Subsistenzproduktion, in: *Arbeitsgruppe Bielefelder Entwicklungssoziologen, Subsistenzproduktion und Akkumulation. Bielefeld Studies on Development Sociology* Vol. 5, Saarbrücken and Fort Lauderdale: Breitenbach, pp. 279-332

Evers, H. - D. and T. Schiel, 1988: *Strategische Gruppen*. Berlin: Reimer

Feher, F. and A. Heller, 1983: Class, Democracy, Modernity, in: *Theory and Society*, Vol. 12, pp. 211-244

Feige, E. 1987: The Anatomy of the Underground Economy, in: S. Allesandrini and B. Dallago (eds.), *The Unofficial Economy*. Aldershot: Gower Publishing Co., pp. 83-106

Fellmann, J. D., 1957: Pre-building Growth Patterns of Chicago, in: Annals, Association of *American Geographers*, Vol. 47, pp. 59-82

Fernandez, D. et al., 1975: *The Population of Malaysia*. Kuala Lumpur: C.I.C.R.E.D. Series

Fisk, E. K., 1975a: The Subsistence Component in National Income Accounts, in: The Developing Economies, Vol. 13, No. 3, pp. 252-279

Fisk, E. K., 1975b: The Response of Nonmonetary Production Units to Contact with the Exchange Economy, in L. G. Reynolds (ed.), *Agriculture in Development Theory*. New Haven and London: Yale University Press, pp. 53-83

Fox, R. G., 1977: *Urban Anthropology: Cities in their Cultural Settings*. Englewood Cliffs, New Jersey: Prentice Hall

Furnivall, J. S., 1948: *Colonial Policy and Practice: A Comparative Study of Burma and Netherlands India*. Cambridge: Cambridge University Press

Furnivall, J. S., 1960: *The Governance of Modern Burma*. New York: International Secretariat, Institute of Pacific Relations

Furnivall, J. S., 1980: Plural Societies, in H. - D. Evers (ed.), *Sociology of Southeast Asia: Readings on Social Change and Development*, Kuala Lumpur: Oxford University Press, pp. 86-96

Furst, H., 1956: *Einkommen, Nachfrage, Produktion und Konsum des privaten Haushalts in der Volkswirtschaft*. Stuttgart

Geertz, C. 1963: *Peddlers and Princes: Social Change and Economic Modernization in Two Indonesian Towns*. Chicago: University of Chicago Press

Geertz, C., 1965: *The Social History of an Indonesian Town*. Cambridge, Mass.: M.I.T

Gerke, S., 1999, Global Lifestyles under Local Conditions: The New Indonesian Middle Class, in: Chua Beng Huat (ed.): *Consuming Asians*. London: Routledge

Gibbons, D., 1977: *Public Policy towards Fisheries Development in Malaysia*. Paper read at a Seminar on the Development of the Fisheries Sector in Malaysia, Kuala Lumpur, Malaysia

Giddens, A., 1984: *The Constitution of Society: Outline of a Theory of Structuration*, Oxford: Polity Press

Giddens, A., 1994: Beyond Left and Right: The Future of Radical Politics. Cambridge: Polity Press

Ginsburg, N. S., 1976: The Great City in Southeast Asia, in: Y. M. Yeung and C. P. Lo (eds.), *Changing Southeast Asian Cities: Readings on Urbanization*. London: Oxford University Press, pp. 2-7

Gist, N. P., 1957: The Ecology of Bangalore, India: An East-West Comparison, in: *Social Forces*, Vol. 35

Goh Ban Lee, 1975: *The Pattern of Land-ownership in Central Georgetown*. Pulau Pinang, Centre for Policy Research, Universiti Sains Malaysia

Goh Ban Lee and H. - D. Evers, 1977: *Hakmilik Tanah di Enambelas Bandar di Semenanjung Malaysia. Project Paper*, Centre for Policy Research, Universiti Sains Malaysia, Penang

Goh Ban Lee and H. - D. Evers, 1978: Urban Development and Land-ownership in Butterworth, Malaysia, in: *Journal of Southeast Asian Studies*, Vol. IX, 1

Goh Cheng Teik, 1971: *The May thirteenth Incident and Democracy in Malaysia*. Kuala Lumpur: Oxford University Press

Goh Keng Swee, 1973: Economic Development and Modernization in Southeast Asia, in H. - D. Evers (ed.), *Modernization in Southeast Asia*. London: Oxford University Press, pp. 81-93

Goldschmidt-Clermont, L., 1982: *Unpaid Work in the Household : A Review of Economic Evaluation Methods*. Geneva: International Labour Office

Goldstein, S., 1976: Urbanization in Thailand, 1947-1967, in: Y. M. Yeung and C. P. Lo (eds.), *Changing Southeast Asian Cities: Readings on Urbanization*, London: Oxford University Press, pp. 100-115

Gould, P. and R. White, 1974: *Mental Maps*. Harmondsworth: Penguin Books

Government of Thailand, 1968: *Year Book*, Government Printing House, Bangkok

Government of Thailand, 1968: *Year Book*, Government Printing House, Bangkok

Gretschmann, K., Heinze R. G. and B. Mettelseifen, 1984: *Schattenwirtschaft, Wirtschafts- und sozialwissenschaftliche Aspekte, internationale Erfahrungen.* Göttingen: Vandenhoeck & Ruprecht

Guidoni, E., 1980: *Die europäische Stadt: Eine baugeschichtliche Studie über ihre Entstehung im Mittelalter.* Stuttgart and Mailand: Electa/Klett-Cotta

Gullick, J. M., 1955: Kuala Lumpur 1880-1895, in: *Journal of the Malayan Branch of the Royal Asiatic Society*, Vol. 28, Pt. 4, pp. 1-172

Guyot, J. F., 1969: Creeping Urbanism and Political Development in Malaysia, in: R. T. Daland (ed.), *Comparative Urban Research.* Beverly Hills: Sage Publications, pp. 124-161

Guyt, H., 1936: *Grondverpading in Minangkabau.* Bandoeng: A. C. Nix & Co

Habermas, J., 1981: *Theorie des kommunikativen Handelns.* Frankfurt a. M.: Suhrkamp

Hall, D.G.E., 1977: *A History of Southeast Asia.* London, Basingstoke: Macmillan

Hamka, 1967: *Ayahku; riwayat hidup Dr. H. Abd. Karim Amrullah dan perdjuangan kaum agama di Sumatera.* Djakarta: Djajamurni, 3rd ed.

Hamka, 1968: Adat Minangkabau dan Harta Pusakanya, in M. Naim (ed.), *Menggali hukum tanah dan hukum waris Minangkabau.* Centre for Minangkabau Studies, Padang, pp. 19-48

Hamm, B., 1982: *Einführung in die Siedlungssoziologie.* München: Beck

Harsono, B., 1971: *Undang-Undang Pokok Agraria: Sedjarah penyusunan ini dan pelaksanaannya.* Djakarta: Djambatan

Heinze, J., Schedl, H. and K. Vogler-Ludwig, 1986: *Wachstumsfelder am Rande der offiziellen Wirtschaft : Auswirkungen expandierender Produktions- und Beschäftigungsformen auf Produktivität und Strukturwandel.* München: Ifo-Institut für Wirtschaftsforschung

Hendry, J. B., 1964: *The Small World of Khanh Hau.* Chicago: Aldine

Hirschman, C., 1976: Recent Urbanization Trends in Peninsular Malaysia, in: *Demography*, Vol. 13, No. 4, pp. 445-461

Hofstee, E. W., 1972: Land-ownership in Densely Populated and Industrialized Countries, in: *Sociologia Ruralis*, Vol. 12, No. 1, pp. 6-26

Isaac, E., 1961: The Act and the Covenant: The Impact of Religion on the Landscape, in: *Landscape* Vol. 11, No. 2, pp. 12-17

Janssen, J. and M. Ratz, 1973: *Bodenpolitik und Bodenrechtsreform in der BRD.* Köln: Pahl-Rugenstein

Jellinek, L., 1991: *The Wheel of Furtune: The History of a Poor Community in Jakarta.* Sydney: Allen and Unwin

Jocano, F. L., 1975: *Slum as a Way of Life: A Study of Coping Behavior in an Urban Environment.* Quezon City: New Day

Jones, G. W., 1965: The Employment Characteristics of Small Towns in Malaya, in: Malayan *Economic Review*, Vol. 10, No. 1, pp. 44-72

Jones, G. W., 1975: *Some Information on Urban Employment in Palembang and Ujung Pandang, Bondan Supraptilah.* Lembaga Demografi, Fakultas Ekonomi, Universiti Indonesia, Jakarta

Joost, W. (ed.), 1983: *Die wundersamen Reisen des Caspar Schmalkalden nach West- und Ostindien 1642-1652.* Leipzig: VEB Brockhaus

Josselin de Jong, J.P.B. de, 1977: The Malay Archipelago as a Field of Ethnological Study, in: P. E. de Josselin de Jong (ed.), *Structural Anthropolgy in the Netherlands, A Reader.* The Hague: M. Nijhoff

Josselin de Jong, P. E. de, 1960: *Minangkabau and Negeri Sembilan, Socio-Political Structure in Indonesiaa.* Djakarta: Bhatara

Joustra, M., 1920: *Minangkabau, Overzicht van Land, Geschiedenis en Volk.* Leiden: Louis II, Becherer

Joustra, M., 1923: *Minangkabau's.* Gravenhage: M. Nijhoff

Kaempfer, E., 1727 (1987): *A Description of the Kingdom of Siam 1690, Itineraria Asiatica, Thailand Vol. IV.* Bangkok: White Lotus

Kahn, J. S., 1996: The Middle Class as a Field of Ethnological Study, in: Muhammad Imal Said, Zahid Emby (eds.), *Malaysia: Critical Perspectives. Essays in Honour of Syed Husin Ali.* Malaysia: Pandangan Kritis: Esei Penghargaan untuk Syed Husin Ali, Kuala Lumpur: Persatuan Sains Sosial Malaysia

Kasadra, J., Parnell, A. M. (eds.), 1993: *Third World Cities: Problems and Prospects.* Newbury Park, London, New Delhi: Sage

Kiat Chivakul (ed.), 1982: *Markets in Bangkok: Expansion and Development. Office of Research Affairs*, Chulalongkorn University, Bangkok (in Thai)

Kimani, S. M., 1972: The Structure of Land-ownership in Nairobi, in: *Journal of Eastern African Research and Development*, Vol. 2, No. 2, pp. 101-124

Korff, R., 1985: *Märkte in Bangkok.* Working Paper No. 70, Sociology of Development Research Centre, University of Bielefeld

Korff, R., 1986: *Bangkok: Urban System and Everyday Life*. Saarbrücken and Fort Lauderdale: Breitenbach

Korff, R., 1988: Informeller Sektor oder Marktwirtschaft? Märkte und Händler in Bangkok, in: *Zeitschrift für Soziologie*, Vol. 17, No. 4, pp. 196-307

Korff, R., 1989: *Political Change and Local Power in Thailand*. Working Paper No. 119, Sociology of Development Research Centre, University of Bielefeld

Korff, R., 1991: *Die Weltstadt zwischen globaler Gesellschaft und Lokalitäten*. Working Paper No. 151, Sociology of Development Research Centre, University of Bielefeld

Korff, R., 1993: Bangkok as a Symbol? Ideological and Everyday Life Constructions of Bangkok, in: P.J.M. Nas (ed.), *Urban Symbolism*. Leiden: E. J. Brill

Krom, N. J., 1923: *Inleiding tot de Hindoe Javaansche Kunst (Vol. 2)*. Den Haag: M. Nijhoff

Kuchler, J., 1968: *Penang, Kulturlandschaftswandel und ethnisch-soziale Struktur einer Insel Malaysias*. Geographisches Institut der Justus-Leibig Universität, Giessen

Kuhne, D., 1971: Petaling Jaya, Groß-Kuala Lumpur: Ansatzpunkt einer ethno-pluralen, industriell-burokratisch orientierten Gesellschaftsentwicklung in Malaysia?, in: *Mitteilungen des Instituts fur Asienkunde* Nr. 42, Hamburg

Kuhne, D., 1976: Urbanisation in Malaysia: Analyse eines Prozesses, in: *Schriften des Instituts für Asienkunde* Nr. 42, Wiesbaden: Otto Harrassowitz

Langfeldt, E., 1984: Konsequenzen einer wachsenden Schattenwirtschaft fur die geld-politische Steuerung in der Bundesrepublik Deutschland, in: W. Schäfer (ed.), *Schattenökonomie: Theoretische Grundlagen und wirtschaftspolitische Konsequenzen*. Göttingen: Vandenhoeck & Ruprecht, pp. 184-203

Laquian, 1972: The Asian City and the Political Process, in: D. J. Dwyer (ed.), *The City as a Centre of Change in Asia*. Hong Kong: Hong Kong University Press, pp. 41-58

Lee Boon Thong, 1976a: Patterns of Urban Residential Segregation: The Case of Kuala Lumpur, in: *Journal of Tropical Geography*, Vol. 43, pp. 41-47

Lee Boon Thong, 1976b: *Changing Ethnic Patterns and the Residential Structure of Urban Areas in Peninsular Malaysia*. Paper presented to the Symposium on The City in the Third World, Lancaster Polytechnic

Lee Boon Thong, 1977: Malay Urbanization and the Ethnic Profile of Urban Centres in Peninsular Malaysia, in : *Journal of Southeast Asian Studies*, Vol. 8, No. 2, pp. 224-234

Lee Kuan Yew, 1998: *The Singapore Story. Memoirs of Lee Kuan Yew*. Singapore: Straits Times Press

Lefebvre, H., 1976: *Die Revolution der Städte*, Frankfurt a.M.: Syndikat

Leinbach, T. R., 1972: The Spread of Modernization in Malaya: 1895-1969, in: *Tijdschrift voor Economische en Sociale Geografi*, Vol. 63, pp. 262-77. Reprinted in: Y. M. Yeung and C. P. Lo (eds.), Changing South East Asian Cities, Singapore: Oxford University Press, 1976, pp. 208-23

Leinbach, T. R., 1974: The Spread of Transportation and its Impact upon the Modernization of Malaya, 1887 - 1911, in: *Journal of Tropical Geography*, Vol. 39, pp. 54-62

Lerner, D., 1958: *The Passing of Traditional Society*. New York: Free Press

Lieberman, V. B., 1984: *Burmese Administrative Cycles: Anarchy and Conquest c. 1580 - 1760*. Princeton: Princeton University Press

Lieberson, S., 1969: Measuring Population Diversity, in: *American Sociological Review*, Vol. 34, No. 6, pp. 850-862

Lim, A. W. G., 1972: *Changing Patterns of Land-ownership and Social Stratification in Singapore: A Case Study of Upper Orchard Road*. Academic Exercise, Department of Sociology, University of Singapore

Lipietz, A., 1974: *Le Tribut Foncier urbain: Circulation du Capital et Propriété foncière dans la Production du cadre bâti*. Paris: Maspero

Lombard, D., 1976: Sumbangan kepada sejarah kota-kota di Asia Tenggara, in: *Masyarakat Indonesia*, Vol. 3, Pt. 1, pp. 51-69

Luther, H. U., 1970a: *Asien im Wandel*. Berlin: Colloquium-Verlag

Luther, H. U., 1970b: Reformer gegen Rebellen: Zur Situation der Bauern in Thailand. *Mitteilungen des Instituts für Asienkunde* Nr. 32, Hamburg

Lynch, K., 1960: *The Image of the City*, Cambridge, Mass: M.I.T. Press

Lyotard, J. F., 1986: *Das postmoderne Wissen: Ein Bericht*. Wien: Edition Passagen

Mabogunje, A. L., 1968: *Urbanization in Nigeria*. London: University of London Press

Mahajani, U., 1960: *The Role of Indian Minorities in Burma and Malaya*. Bombay: Vora

Mak Lau Fong, 1977: *The Emergence and Persistence of Chinese Secret Societies in Singapore and Peninsular Malaysia*. Ph.D. Thesis, University of Waterloo, Ontario, Canada

Manich Jumsai, 1977: *Popular History of Thailand*. Bangkok: Chalermit

Marx, K., 1955: Zur Kritik der Nationalökonomie: Ökonomisch-philosophische Manuskripte, in: K. Marx und F. Engels, *Kleine ökonomische Schriften*. Berlin: Dietz Verlag

McGee, T. G., 1963: The Cultural Role of Cities: A Case Study of Kuala Lumpur, in: *Journal of Tropical Geography*, Vol. 17, pp. 178-196

McGee, T. G., 1967: *The Southeast Asian City: A Social Geography of the Primate Cities of Southeast Asia*. London: G. Bell

McGee, T. G, 1976: Beach-Heads and Enclaves: The Urban Debate and the Urbanization Process in Southeast Asia since 1945, in: Y. M. Yeung and C. P. Lo (eds.), *Changing Southeast Asian Cities: Readings on Urbanization*, London: Oxford University Press, pp. 60-75

McGee, T. G., 1979: The Poverty Syndrome: Making out in the Southeast Asian City. In: R. Bromley and L. Gerry (eds.), *Casual Work and Poverty in Third World Cities*. Chichester, N.Y.: Wiley, pp. 45-68

McGee, T. G. and W. D. Mc Taggart, 1967: Petaling Jaja: *A Socio-economic Survey of a New Town in Selangor, Malaysia*. Wellington, New Zealand: Victoria University, Department of Geography

McGee, T. S. and Y. - M. Yeung, 1978: *Hawkers in Southeast Asian Cities*. Ottawa: IDRC

McGranahan, D., 1979: *International Comparability of Statistics on Income Distribution*, in: *UNRISD*, Geneva

McTaggart, W. D.: 1966: Private Land-ownership in a Colonial Town: The Case of Noumea, New Caledonia, in: *Economic Geography*, Vol. 42, No. 3, pp. 189-204

McTaggart, W. D. and Teoh Chin Eng, 1972: *Urban Property in Underdeveloped Countries as a Repository for Capital: Influences in the Development of Segamat*, West Malaysia. Paper presented at the International Geographical Union Meeting, Toronto

McTaggert, W. D. and R. McEachern, 1972: Kampong Pandan: A Study of a Malay Kampong in Kuala Lumpur, in: D. J. Dwyer (ed.), *The City as a Centre of Change in Asia*. Hong Kong: Hong Kong University Press, pp. 125-138

Meesok, O. A., 1978: *Income Distribution in Thailand*. Research Report Series, Faculty of Economics, Thammasat University, Bangkok

Meinkoth, M. R., 1962: Migration in Thailand with Particular Reference to the Northeast, in: *Economic and Business Research Bulletin* Vol. 14, No. 4

Mertens, M. and S. Alatas, 1978: Rural Urban Definitions and Urban Agriculture in Indonesia, in: *Majalah Demografi Indonesia*, Vol. 10, Dec. 1978, pp. 40-70

Mulder, N., 1975: *Mysticism and Daily Life in Contemporary Java*. Ph.D. Thesis, University of Amsterdam, Netherlands

Mumford, L., 1979: *Die Stadt: Geschichte und Ausblick*, München: DTV

Murray, A. J., 1991: *No Money, No Honey: A Study of Street Traders and Prostitutes in Jakarta*. Singapore: Oxford University Press

Nagata, J. A., 1974a: Who is a Malay? Situational Selection of Ethnic Identity in a Rural Society, in: *American Ethnologist*, Vol. 1, No. 2, pp. 331-350

Nagata, J. A., 1974b: Urban Interlude: Some Aspects of Internal Malay Migration in West Malaysia, in: *International Migration Review*, Vol. 8, Pt. 2, pp. 301-324

Nagata, J. A., 1975: Perceptions of Social Inequality in Malaysia, in: *Contributions to Asian Studies*, Vol. 7, pp. 113-136

Nagata, J. A., 1979: *Malaysian Mosaic: Perspectives from a Poly-Ethnic Society*. Vancouver: University of British Columbia Press

Naim, M. (ed.), 1968: *Menggali hukum tanah dan hukum waris Minangkabau*. Centre for Minangkabau Studies, Padang

Naim, M., 1971: *Merantau: Causes and Effect of Minangkabau Voluntary Migration*. Occasional Papers No. 5, Institute of Southeast Asian Studies, Singapore

Naim, M., 1972: *Merantau dan pengaruhnya terhadap pembangunan daerah di Sumatera Barat*. Centre for Minangkabau Studies, Padang

Naim, M., 1973: *"Merantau" Minangkabau Voluntary Migration*. Ph.D. Thesis, Departement of Sociology, University of Singapore

Narayanan, S., 1975: Patterns and Implications of Urban Change in Peninsular Malaysia, in: *Malayan Economic Review*, Vol. 20, No. 2, pp. 55-71

Nas, P. J. M., 1984: Settlements as Symbols: The Indonesian Town as a Field of Anthropological Studies, in: P. E. de Josselin de Jong (ed.), *Unity in Diversity*, Dordrecht: Foris, pp. 127-143

Nas, P. J. M., 1992: Jakarta, City full of Symbols: An Essay in Symbolic Ecology, in: *Sojourn* Vol. 7, No. 2, pp. 175-207

Nas, P. J. M. (ed.), 1993: *Urban Symbolism*. Leiden: E. J. Brill

National Economic and Social Development Board, 1987: The Sixth National Economic and Social Development Plan 1987 - 1991. Office of the Prime Minister, Bangkok

National Statistical Office, *Report of the Labour Force Survey, 1986: Round 2, May*, Office of the Prime Minister, Bangkok

Neubert, D., 1986: *Sozialpolitik in Kenya*. Münster: Lit Verlag

Obeyesekere, G., 1967: *Land Tenure in Village Ceylon: A Sociological and Historical Study*. Cambridge, UK: Cambridge University Press

O'Connor, J., 1983: *A Theory of Indigenous Southeast Asian Urbanism*. Research Notes and Discussion Paper No. 38, Singapore: Institute of Southeast Asian Studies

Oesterich, J., 1978: Chendana and Limao: Beobachtungen in zwei Spontansiedlungen in Kuala Lumpur, in: *Internationales Asien Forum* 14.1

Oevermann, U., Allert, T., Konau, E. and J. Krambeck, 1979: Die Methologie einer "objektiven Hermeneutik" und ihre allgemeine forschungslogische Bedeutung in den Sozialwissenschaften, in: H. - G. Soeffner (ed.), *Interpretative Verfahren in den Sozial- und Textwissenschaften*. Stuttgart: Metzler, pp. 352-434

Offe, C. (ed.), 1984: *Arbeitsgesellschaft*. Frankfurt: Campus

Ooi, J. - B., 1975: Urbanization and the Urban Population in Peninsular Malaysia, in: *Journal of Tropical Geography*, Vol. 40, pp. 40-47

Ooi, J. - B., 1963: *Land, People and Economy in Malaya*. London: Longman

Osborn, J., 1974: *Area, Development Policy and the Middle City in Malaysia*. Research Paper No. 153, Department of Geography, University of Chicago

Parson, J. J., 1972: Slicing up the Open Space: Subdivision without Homes in N. California, in: *Erdkunde*, Vol. 26, No. 1, pp. 1-8

Petersen, H. - G., 1984: *Ursachen und Konsequenzen einer wachsenden Schattenzwirtschaft, in: Staat, Steuern und Finanzausgleich*, Memorial Volume for Heinz Kolms, Berlin

Phisit Phakkasem, 1987: Problems of Development of Bangkok and the Vicinity, in: Society and Economy, *Journal of the NESDB*, Vol. 24, No. 5, pp. 5-10 (in Thai)

Pickvance, C. G. (ed.), 1976: *Urban Sociology*: Critical Essays. London: Tavistock

Pieters. J. M, 1951: *Land policy in the Netherlands East Indies before the Second World War*, in: Land Tenure Symposium Amsterdam 1950, organized by the Africa Institute Leiden. Leiden: Universitaire Pers Leiden, pp. 116-139

Pigeaud, Th. G., 1962: *Java in the Fourteenth Century*. The The Hague: Martinus Nijhoff

Polanyi, K., 1978: The *Great Transformation: Politische und ökonomische Ursprünge von Gesellschaften und Wirtschaftssystemen*. Frankfurt a. M.: Suhrkamp

Portes, A., Castells, M., Benton, L., 1989: *The Informal Economy: Studies on Advanced and Less Developed Countries*, Baltimore: John Hopkins University Press

Preyaluk Donavanik, 1989: Infrastructure Shortage, in: *Bangkok Bank Monthly Review*, April 1989

Prins, J., 1953/54: Rondom de oude strijdvraag van Minangkabau, in: *Indonesie*, Vol. VII, pp. 320-339

Provencher, R., 1971: *Two Malay Worlds: Interaction in Urban and Rural Settings*. Research Monograph No. 4, Centre for South and Southeast Asia Studies, University of California

Provencher, R., 1977: *National Culture and Ethnicity in Kuala Lumpur*. Paper read at the AAS Annual Meetings, New York

Pryor, R. J., 1974: An Analysis of the "Streams" of Interstate Migrants in Peninsular Malaya, in: *Southeast Asian Journal of Social Science*, Vol. 2, pp. 63-74

Pryor, R. J., 1975: *Movers and Stayers in Peninsular Malaysia: A Social and Economic Study*. Department of Geography, Occasional Paper No. 1, University of Malaya, Kuala Lumpur

Purcell, V., 1956: The *Chinese in Malays*. Oxford: Oxford University Press

Quaritch-Wales, H. G., 1931: *Siamese State Ceremonies: Their History and Function*. London: Bernard Quaritch

Quinn, J. A., 1971: *Human Ecology*. Hamden, Conn.: Archon Books

Ray, A., 1964: *Villages, Towns and Secular Buildings in Ancient India*. Calcutta

Redick, R. W., 1964: A Demographic and Ecological Study of Rangoon, Burma. in: E. W. Burgess and D. J. Bogue (eds.), Contribution to Urban Sociology. Chicago: Chicago University Press

Reid, A., 1980: The Structure of Cities in Southeast Asia, 15th to 17th Centuries, in: *Journal of Southeast Asian Studies*, Vol. 11, pp. 235-250

Resnahadi, 1980: *Migrasi Intern di Jakarta. Sarjana Dissertation*, University of Indonesia

Robinson, R., 1978: Toward a Class Analysis of the Indonesian Military Bureaucratic State, in: *Indonesia*, Vol. 25, pp. 17-35

Rokkan, S., 1973: Centre-Formation, Nation-Building, and Cultural Diversity: Report on a UNESCO Programme, in: S. N. Eisenstadt and S. Rokkan (eds.), *Building States and Nations: Models and Data Resources, Volume I*. Beverly Hills and London: Sage

Rüland, J. (ed.), 1996: *The Dynamics of Metropolitan Management in Southeast Asia*. Singapore: ISEAS

Sa'danoer, A., 1971: *Pola-pola kewarisan di Sumatera Barat dewasa ini. LPHN Fakultas Hukum dan Pengetahuan Masyarakat*, Universitas Andalas, Padang

Saleh, M., 1972: *Status Tanah, in B. Boerhan and M. Salim (eds.): Tanah ulajat dalam pembangunan. Fakultas Hukum dan Pengetahuan Masjarakat*, Universitas Andalas, Padang, pp. 9-18

Sandhu, K. S., 1969: *Indians in Malaya*. Cambridge: Cambridge University Press

Sandhu, K. S., 1964: The Saga of the "Squatters" in Malaya: A Preliminary Survey of the Causes, Characteristics and Consequences of the Resettlement of Rural Dwellers during the Emergency between 1984 and 1960, in: *Journal of Southeast Asian History*, Vol. 5, No. 1, pp. 143-177

Santos, M., 1975: *L'espace partage: Les deux circuits de l'économie urbaine en pays sous-développés et leurs répercussions spatiales*. Paris: M. Th. Genin, Librairies Techniques

Santos, M., 1979: *The Shared Space: The Two Circuits of the Urban Economy Underdevelopment Concept*. London: Methuen

Sargent, C. S., 1972: Land Speculation in Buenos Aires, in: *Economic Geography* 28: pp. 358-374

Sarkisyanz, E., 1965: *Buddhist Backgrounds of the Burmese Revolution*. The Hague: Martinus Nijhoff

Sassen, S., 1991: *The Global City*. New York, London, Tokyo, Princeton: Princeton University Press

Sassen, S., 1994: Cities in a World Economy. London and New Delhi: Thousand Oaks

Sassen, S., 1998: *Globalization and its Discontents*. New York: Free Press

Saw Swee Hock, 1972: Patterns of Urbanization in West Malaysia, 1911-1970, in: *Malayan Economic Review*, Vol. 17, Pt. 2, pp. 114-120

Schiel, T., 1985: *Despotism and Capitalism: A Historical Comparison of Europe and Indonesia*. Bielefeld Studies of Sociology of Development Vol. 30, Saarbrücken and Fort Lauderdale: Breitenbach

Schiel, T., 1987: Suche nach Sicherheit und Sehnsucht nach Geborgenheit: "Dualwirtschaft" und "informeller Sektor" als Phänomen und Fiktion, in: *Zeitschrift für Soziologie*, Vol. 16, No. 2, pp. 92-105

Schouten, J., 1671 (1969): *A True Description of the Mighty Kingdoms of Japan and Siam.*, Historical Archives Series, Bangkok: Chalermit

Schrage, H., 1984: Schattenwirtschaft: Abgrenzung, Definition, Methoden der quantitativen Erfassung, in: W. Schäfer (ed.), *Schattenökonomie: Theoretische Grundlagen und wirtschaftspolitische Konsequenzen*. Göttingen: Vandenhoeck & Ruprecht, pp. 11-37

Schrieke, B., 1928: *Rapport van de Commissie van Onderzoek (Westkust Rapport)*. Weltevreden: Landsdrukkerij

Schrieke, B., 1960: *Indonesian Sociological Studies*. Bandung: Sumur Bandung

Schütz, A., 1981: *Der sinnhafte Aufbau der sozialen Welt*. Frankfurt a. M.: Suhrkamp

Scott, J. C., 1968: *Political Ideology in Malaysia: Reality and the Beliefs of an Élite*. New Haven: Yale University Press

Scott, A. J., 1988: *From the Division of Labour to Urban Form*. Berkeley: University of California Press

Semsek, H. - G., 1986: Alltagspraxis und in formelles Wirtschaften: Die "dichte Beschreibung" eines Kairoer Stadtviertels, in: *Zeitschrift fur Soziologie*, Vol. 15, No. 6, pp. 438-456

Sethuraman, S. V., 1974: *Towards a Definition of the Informal Sector. Working Paper, World Employment Programme*, Geneva: ILO

Sethuraman, S. V. (ed.), 1981: *The Urban Informal Sector in Developing Countries: Employment and Environment*. Geneva: ILO

Shamsul A. B., 1998, Ethnicity, Class, Culture or Identity? Competing Paradigms of Malaysian Study, in: Akademika, Jurnal Sains Kemasyarakatan dan Kemanusiaan 53, pp. 33-60

Siddique, S., 1977: *Relics of the Past? A Sociological Study of the Sultanates of Cirebon, West Java*. Ph.D. Dissertation, Faculty of Sociology, University of Bielefeld

Sihombing, H., 1972: Penguasaan/Pemakaian Tanah, in: B. Boerhan and M. Salim (eds.): *Tanah ulayat dalam pembangunan. Fakultas Hukum dan Pengetahuan Masjarakat*, Universitas Andalas, Padang, pp.71-84

Singapore Trade and Industry, 1973: *Special Report on the Real Estate Market*, July, pp. 5-25

Skinner, G. W., 1958: *Leadership and Power in the Chinese Community of Thailand*, Itaca, N. Y.: Cornell University Press

Skinner, G. W., 1964: Marketing and Social Structure in Rural China, in: *Journal of Asian Studies*, Vol. 24, pp. 3-43, pp. 195-228 and Vol. 36, pp. 3-99

Soja, E. W., 1971: *The Political Organization of Space*. Resource Paper No. 8, Commission on College Geography, Association of American Geographers, Washington, D. C.

Somantri, G., 1995: *Migration within Cities: A Study of Socio-Economic Processes, Intra-City Migration and Grassroots Politics in Jakarta*. Ph.D. Dissertation, Faculty of Sociology, University of Bielefeld

Somchit Pongpangan, 1978: Land Policy and Feasibility for Public Housing, in: Wadanyu Nathalang (ed.), *Housing in Thailand, Southeast Asian Low Cost Housing Study*, Bangkok

Sovani, N. V.: 1969: The Analysis of "Over-urbanization", in: G. Breese (ed.), *The City in Newly Developing Countries*. Englewood Cliffs, N. J.: Prentice-Hall, pp. 322-331

Spengler, O., 1923: *Der Untergang des Abendlandes: Umrisse einer Morphologie der Weltgeschichte*. München: Beck

Spiegel, E., 1986: Die Wiederentdeckung der traditionellen Gesellschaft in der Subsistenzökonomie: Zu einer neueren Richtung in der "Entwicklungssoziologie" in der BRD, in: *Asien, Afrika, Lateinamerika (Berlin)* 14, 4, pp. 592-600

Städtebauliche Forschung, 1972: *Innenstadt und Erneuerung: Eine soziologische Analye historicher Zentren mittelgroßer Städte*. Bundesminister für Raumordnung, Bauwesen und Städtebau, Bonn

Stauth, G., 1982: *Konfliktpotentiale lokaler Gemeinschaften in peripheren Gesellschaften: Alltagserfahrung und Protestverhalten in Kairoer Slums*. Working Paper No. 29, Sociology of Development Research Centre, University of Bielefeld

Sternstein, L., 1972: Planning the Future of Bangkok, in: D. J. Dwyer (ed.), *The City as a Centre of Change in Asia*. Hong Kong: Hong Kong University Press, pp. 243-254

Sulak Sivaraksa, 1985: *Siamese Resurgence. Asian Cultural Forum for Development*. Bangkok: Sukhsit Siam

Sullivan, J., 1992: *Local Government and Community in Java. An Urban Case Study*. Singapore: Oxford University Press

Sumardi, M. and H. - D. Evers (eds.), 1979: *Golongan Miskin di Jakarta*. Jakarta: PPSM, Yayasan Tenaga Kerja Indonsia

Sumardi, M. and H. - D. Evers, 1980: *Urbanisasi: Masalah Kota Jakarta*. Jakarta: PPSM, Yayasan Tenaga Kerja Indonesia

Sumardi, M. and H. - D. Evers (eds.), n.d. (1982, 2nd edition 1985): *Kemiskinan dan Kebutuhan Pokok di DKI Jakarta*. Jakarta: C.V. Rajawali

Sundrum, R. M., 1977: Changes in Consumption Patterns in Urban Java, 1970-76, in: *BIES*, Vol. XIII, No. 2, pp. 102-116

Sundrum, R. M., 1990: *Income Distribution in Less Developed Countries*. London: Routledge

Suntaree Komin, 1985: The World View through Thai Value System, in: CUSRI (eds.), *Traditional and Changing Thai World View*. Bangkok: CUSRI, Chulalongkorn University

Sutcliffe, A., (ed.), 1984: *Metropolis 1890-1940*. London: Mansell

Swift, M. G., 1972: Minangkabau and Modernization, in: *Oceania*, pp. 225-267

Tanner, N., 1969: Disputing and Dispute Settlement Among the Minangkabau of Indonesia, in: *Indonesia*, Vol. 8, pp. 21-67

Taylor, J. G. and A. Turton (ed.), 1988: *Southeast Asia*. New York: Monthly Review Press

Textor, R. B., 1961: *From Peasant to Pedicab Driver*. Cultural Report Series No. 9, Yale University, Southeast Asia Studies, New Haven

Thailand, Ministry of National Development, 1964: *Relationship between Land Tenure and Rice Production in Five Central Provinces*. Ministry of National Development, Bangkok

Than, M. and A. Rajah, 1997: Urban Management in Myanmar: Yangon, in: J. Rüland (ed.), 1996: *The Dynamics of Metropolitan Management in Southeast Asia*. Singapore: ISEAS

Thiravet Pramuanratkarn, 1979: *Impact of Urbanization on a Peripheral Area of Bangkok, Thailand*. Ph.D. Thesis, University of Seattle

Third Malaysia Plan, 1976: *Prime Minister's Department*, Malaysia

Tilman, R. O., 1964: *Bureaucratic Transition in Malaya*. Durham, NC: Duke University Press

United Nations, 1968: Urban-Rural Population Distribution and Settlement Patterns in Asia. *International Social Development Review*, No. 1

Urry, John, 1995: *Consuming Places*. London: Routledge

US Congress, 1980: *Committee on Ways and Means, Underground Economy: Hearings before the Subcommittee on Oversigh*t, Serial 96-70. Washington, D. C.: US Government Printing Office

US Department of Agriculture, 1972: *The Agricultural Economy of Thailand*. United States Department of Agriculture, Washington, D. C.

Vance, J. E., Jr., 1971: Land Assignment in the Precapitalist, Capitalist, and Postcapitalist City, in: *Economic Geography*, Vol. 47, No. 2, pp. 101-120

Vichit-Vadakan, V. (ed.), 1975: *Urbanization in the Bangkok Central Region*. Bangkok: TURA

Vollenhoven, C. van, 1925: De *Indonesier en zijn Ground, in: Een Adatwetboekje voor heel Indie*. Leiden: E. J. Brill

Wallerstein, I., 1982: *Household Structures and Labour-Force Formation in the Capitalist World-Economy*. Paper read at the Seminar "Households and the World Economy", Sociology of Development Research Centre, University of Bielefeld

Weber, M., 1958: *The City*. New York: Free Press

Werlhof, C. von, 1985: *Wenn die Bauern Wiederkommen: Frauen-Arbeit und Agrobusiness in Venezuela*. Bremen: EP-Con

Werlhof, C. von, Mies, M. and V. Bennholdt-Thomsen, 1983: *Frauen, die letzte Kolonie*. Hamburg: Rowohlt

Wertheim, W. F. (ed.), 1958: *The Indonesian Town: Studies in Urban Sociology*. The Hague / Bandung: W. van Hoeve

Wertheim, W. F. 1969: From Aliran towards Class Struggle in the Countryside of Java, in: *Pacific Viewpoint*, Vol. 10, pp. 1-17

Wertheim, W. F., 1980: Changing Southeast Asian Societies: An Overview, in: Evers, H. - D (ed.), *Sociology of Southeast Asia: Readings on Social Change and Development*. Kuala Lumpur: Oxford University Press, pp. 8-24

Wheatley, P., 1959: *A City that was made for Merchandise the Geography of Fifteenth Century Malacca*. Bulletin 1, Institute of Southeast Asia, Nanyang University, Singapore

Wheatley, P., 1967: *The City as Symbol*. London: University College London

Wheatley, P., 1972: *The Pivot of the four Corners: A Preliminary Enquiry into the Origins and Character of the Ancient Chinese City*. Edinburgh: Edinburgh University Press

Wheatley, P., 1983: *Nagara and Commandery: Origins of the Southeast Asian Urban Tradition*. Research Paper Nos. 207-208, Department of Geography, University of Chicago

Wheelwright, E. L. and B. McFarlane, 1970: *The Chinese Road to Socialism: Economics of the Cultural Revolution*. New York: Monthly Review Press

Wickremeratne, A., 1987: Shifting Metaphors of Sacrality: The Mythic Dimensions of Anuradhapura, in: B. Smith and H. Baker-Reynolds (eds.), *The City as a Sacred Centre: Essays on Six Asian Contexts*. Leiden: E.J. Brill, pp. 45-591

Willinck, G. D., 1909: *Het Rechtsleven bij de Minangkabause Maleiers*. Leiden: E. J. Brill

Winstedt, R. O. and R. J. Wilkinson, 1974: *A History of Perak*. Kuala Lumpur: Malaysian Branch of the Royal Asiatic Society

Wolfe, H. R., 1967: A Chronology of Land Tenure, Influences on Suburban Development Patterns, in: *Town Planning Rev*. 37, Vol. 4, pp. 271-290

Wolters, O. W. (ed.), 1976: *Southeast Asian History and Historiography: Essays Presented to D.G.E. Hall*. Ithaca, N.Y.: Cornell University Press

Wong, G. S., 1963: *A Gallery of Chinese Kapitans*. Singapore: Dewan Bahasa dan Kebudayaan Kebangsaan

World Bank, 1979: *Staff Working Paper No. 364*, Washington, D. C.

Wuthnow, R., 1987: *Meaning and Moral Order: Explorations in Cultural Analysis*. Berkeley: University of California Press

Yamin, M., 1952: Repolusi adat Minangkabau, in: *Member Indonesia*, Vol. 19, No. 5

Yomo, K. S. (ed.), 1997: *Southeast Asia's Misunderstood Miracle. Industrial Policy and Economic Development in Thailand, Malaysia and Indonesia*, Boulder: Westview

Zukin, S. W., 1991: *Landscapes of Power. From Detroit to Disney World, Berkeley, Los Angeles*, Oxford: University of California Press

Hans-Dieter Evers is Professor of Development Studies and Chairman, Sociology of Development Research Centre, University of Bielefeld. He was formerly Lecturer of Sociology, Monash University; Associate Professor of Sociology and Director of Graduate Southeast Asian Studies, Yale University, Professor and Head, Department of Sociology, University of Singapore and Visiting Professor of Sociology at the University of Indonesia, Gadjah Mada University, the National University of Malaysia and the Science University of Malaysia.

Rüdiger Korff is Associate Professor of Development Science, National University of Malaysia. He was formerly Reader of Urban Studies at the Sociology of Development Research Centre, University of Bielefeld and Visiting Lecturer of Sociology at Chulalongkorn University.